Langford L. Price

Economic science and practice:

Or, Essays on various aspects of the relations of economic science to practical

affairs

Langford L. Price

Economic science and practice:
Or, Essays on various aspects of the relations of economic science to practical affairs

ISBN/EAN: 9783337717339

Printed in Europe, USA, Canada, Australia, Japan

Cover: Foto ©ninafisch / pixelio.de

More available books at **www.hansebooks.com**

ECONOMIC SCIENCE AND PRACTICE;

OR

ESSAYS ON VARIOUS ASPECTS OF THE RELATIONS OF
ECONOMIC SCIENCE TO PRACTICAL AFFAIRS.

L. L. PRICE
FELLOW OF ORIEL COLLEGE, OXFORD

METHUEN & CO.
ESSEX STREET, W.C.
LONDON
1896

PREFACE

THE following papers, which have been written at various times, and for different occasions, during the last eight years, on economic subjects—in which the author has been specially interested—are connected by certain common characteristics. They deal generally with the relations of economic theory to proposals of practical economic reform. In the first, an attempt is made to set forth the moral, if it may be so called, of the present position. In the six succeeding Essays, different aspects of various methods of industrial reform, which have lately engaged a large measure of popular attention, are brought under review. In the eighth, the general relations of economic theory to practical affairs are considered; and in the three, which immediately follow, the application of these general relations to three particular questions of the day, briefly treated in the eighth as illustrative examples, is more fully developed. In the two concluding Essays, the nature of the changes, which have recently passed over economic theory, and have resulted generally in the incorporation of the older traditional teaching, exemplified by Adam Smith, with the newer presentation, and connection with later facts and practice, supplied by contemporary writers such as Professor Marshall, is examined. The Essays have been revised, with a view to the elimination of the more fugitive portions of the reasoning; and it is hoped that, as in their original composition an attempt was made to bring passing events into connection with abiding truths, and to investigate particular details in the light of general principles, they may be considered not entirely unworthy of the more permanent shape in which they now appear. An excuse for some repetition, and perhaps inconsistency, of argument, may be found in the fact that they are the result of continued reflection on cognate topics, with the consequence, sometimes of modifying, and more often of strengthening, earlier convictions. Some have been published before in various journals, and others, such as Nos. I., V., and XI., appear in print for the first time. Nos. II., III., and VIII. have already been published in the *Journal of the Royal Statistical Society;* Nos. IV., VII., X., XII., and XIII., are reproduced from the *Economic Journal;* Nos. VIII. and IX. have been previously printed *in extenso* in the *Reports of the British Association for the Advancement of Science;* and No. VI. has been retranslated from *La Riforma Sociale*.

The author desires to express his thanks to the editors of the various journals, to whom he applied, for their kind permission to publish the Essays in their present form. L. L. P.

ORIEL COLLEGE, OXFORD,
July, 1896.

CONTENTS

	PAGE
I. SOME TYPICAL FALLACIES OF SOCIAL REFORMERS	1

Read before the British Association, 1890.

II. THE RELATIONS BETWEEN INDUSTRIAL CONCILIATION AND SOCIAL REFORM . . . 18

Read before the British Association, 1889.

III. THE POSITION AND PROSPECTS OF INDUSTRIAL CONCILIATION 38

Read before the Royal Statistical Society, 1890.

IV. PROFIT-SHARING AND CO-OPERATIVE PRODUCTION 66

Contributed to the *Economic Journal*, 1892.

V. CO-OPERATION IN ITS RELATIONS TO TRADE UNIONISM AND SOCIALISM . . . 97

Delivered to the Oxford Co-operative Society, 1896.

VI. METHODS OF INDUSTRIAL REFORM . . . 118

Delivered to the London Branch of the Christian Social Union, 1893.

VII. THE REPORT OF THE LABOUR COMMISSION . 143

Read before the British Association, 1894.

CONTENTS

	PAGE
VIII. THE RELATIONS OF ECONOMIC SCIENCE TO PRACTICAL AFFAIRS	161

Delivered to the British Association, 1895.

IX. THE RELATIONS BETWEEN INDUSTRIAL CONCILIATION AND ECONOMIC THEORY . . 190

Read before the British Association, 1888.

X. SOME ASPECTS OF THE THEORY OF RENT . 211

Contributed to the *Economic Journal*, 1891.

XI. INTERNATIONAL BI-METALLISM . . . 245

Delivered to the Economic Society of Newcastle-upon-Tyne, 1895.

XII. ADAM SMITH AND HIS RELATIONS TO RECENT ECONOMICS 273

Read before the British Association, 1892.

XIII. A RECENT ECONOMIC TREATISE . . 296

Contributed to the *Economic Journal*, 1892.

I.

SOME TYPICAL FALLACIES OF SOCIAL REFORMERS.[1]

THERE is a characteristic passage in Bagehot's *Physics and Politics*,[2] in which he attributes the success of England to the possession of the quality of "animated moderation." "If you ask," he proceeds to remark, "for a description of a great practical Englishman, you will be sure to have this, or something like it: 'Oh, he has plenty of go in him; but he knows when to pull up.'" Among the many happy expressions to be found on almost every page of Bagehot's writings there are perhaps few, which are more felicitous than this phrase of "animated moderation." There are few, if any, more full of suggestion, more pregnant with meaning. There are few which abide more continuously in the memory when once they have obtained a lodging, for the phrase seems to comprise in two appropriate words characteristics, of which the developed analysis would require several sentences.

An epithet is sometimes applied to Englishmen by unfavourable critics, which might be described as the uncomplimentary synonym of this quality of "animated

[1] A Paper read before Section F of the British Association, at Leeds, 1890.
[2] Page 200.

moderation." We are sometimes accused of being "illogical," because we are willing to proceed to a certain length on a path of reform or action, and refuse to advance further. It may be that this apparent want of logic is really and strictly logical; or it may be that he was an acute observer, who declared that the "salvation" of Englishmen had been their want of logic. Of this, at any rate, there can be no doubt, that the accusation rests on the possession of the very quality which Bagehot described as "animated moderation." "This great union," he declared, "of spur and bridle, of energy and moderation, will remain" to the Englishman. "Probably he will hardly be able to explain why he stops when he does stop, or why he continued to move as long as he, in fact, moved; but still, as by a rough instinct, he pulls up pretty much where he should, though he was going at such a pace before."

In the light of these remarks of Bagehot we may, perhaps, with advantage consider some incidents of contemporary discussion and action in the matter of social reform. For there can be little doubt at the present moment of the realisation of the first half of Bagehot's phrase in connection with this matter. We may not be, as a leading politician has declared, "all Socialists now"; but most of us are social reformers, and the question of social reform is undeniably in a state of "animation." On the other hand, some fear may be entertained that the second part of Bagehot's phrase is less likely to be realised than the first. We are "animated" indeed; but do we exhibit "animated moderation"? We apply the "spur" to social reform; but do we employ the "bridle"? We are full of "energy"; but do we combine this with "moderation"?

TYPICAL FALLACIES OF SOCIAL REFORMERS 3

The objection may, it is true, be raised at the outset that, according to Bagehot's own language, the quality of "animated moderation" manifests its presence in obedience to a kind of "rough instinct"; and that it is unconscious rather than conscious. That may be so; and we may repose sufficient confidence in the sanity and sobriety of Englishmen to believe that in social reform, as in other departments of action, the quality will ultimately appear. But it is not on that account idle or misleading to attempt to set forth some of the consequences which might be expected to follow its fuller realisation; and to endeavour to indicate some of the points in contemporary discussion, where error may have arisen from a failure to recognise those consequences.

Again, it may be objected that it is difficult to obtain from Bagehot's remarks any solid basis for a philosophical theory of social reform, or any easy or ready test of practical action. The Englishman, he observes, will "probably" "hardly be able to explain why he stops when he does stop, or why he continued to move as long as he, in fact, moved." This might seem to furnish but a sorry foundation for a theory, and to be but a lame conclusion for practical guidance. And yet it does suggest the reflection that true logic may consist, not in pushing a theory to its furthest conclusions, but in recognising the limiting conditions of its application to practice; and that the genius of the English character may be more adapted to moderate and gradual social reform, based on past experience of fact, than to extreme proposals, however logical and complete may seem to be their theoretical foundation. And, if it be urged that this is nothing more than the exposition of a truism, it is at least a truism which seems in danger of neglect at the present time.

Let us, then, turn our attention to one or two instances of the apparent lack of this quality of "animated moderation" in contemporary discussion and action on matters of social reform. The limits of time will only allow us to offer a few typical illustrations, and to accord to these what may, after all, prove an inadequate treatment; but we may select for consideration three examples of tendencies which, in one form or another, appear to be now diffused in many different quarters.

I. One of the most obvious is found in a failure to recognise the differences between theory and practice. There is a tendency to believe that nice distinctions of economic theory are applicable in the same degree to practice.[1] We have heard much lately of the "unearned increment"; and the agitation for the nationalisation of land finds its theoretical basis in this conception, however different in detail may be the practical schemes to be erected on the common foundation. But the question may immediately be raised whether a crucial distinction between theory and practice does not exist in this matter of the "unearned increment." There can be no doubt that, in the economic theory of rent, a clear and definite distinction can be established between that part of the rent of land, be it agricultural, or be it urban, which is due to what may be called the "natural advantages" of the land itself, as compared with other land —to its natural fertility of soil, or to the favourableness of its situation—and which may be regarded, strictly and literally, as "economic rent," and that part, which may perhaps more fittingly be treated as interest, and considered to be due to the expenditure of capital, or, it may be, to the effort of labour, by landlords and tenants in the past. In theory it is possible to draw a line between that part of the rent of

[1] Cf. Essays viii. and x. below.

TYPICAL FALLACIES OF SOCIAL REFORMERS

land, which is due to nature or society, and is, therefore, "unearned" by the individual, and that part, which is due to individual effort or expenditure, and is therefore "earned." And, so long as we remain in the region of theory, it would seem to be a fair and proper conclusion that that, which is due to nature or society, should belong to society, and that the claim of the individual should be confined to that which is due to his own effort or expenditure. The theory of the "unearned increment," as a theory, can hardly be impeached.

But, when we consider it as a guide to practical action, we must, if we are not to go astray, keep firmly in mind the limiting conditions of the application of theory to practice. We are not arguing at present against the possibility of successfully introducing in practical affairs the broad outlines of the conception of the "unearned increment"; and it might be contended that some, at least, of the proposed applications of the so-called principle of "betterment" were free from the special difficulties we are now considering. What we do maintain is this—that we cannot expect to discover in practice the nice distinctions which can be established in theory, and that, so far as our conclusions are based on the nicety of these distinctions, so far they are, *ipso facto*, inapplicable to practical affairs. The separation between the earned and the unearned increment, so clear and definite and precise in theory, is blurred and uncertain in practice. We cannot distinguish with exactness that part of the rent of agricultural land, which is due to the effort or expenditure of the individual, from that part which is due to nature or to society. We cannot tell in many—perhaps in most—cases what is the natural fertility of the soil, apart from the results of the capital and labour bestowed on its cultivation and improvement. We cannot estimate, in the majority of instances, how much of the rent paid by the farmer for the use of the land represents the improvements in communication, which are due to the expenditure or effort of an individual landlord or landlords, and how much is due to the expenditure or effort in this respect of society at large. Nor can we often tell, in the case of urban land, how far the rent of a central site is due to the accidental growth of business, or influx of population, and how far it is due to the deliberate purpose and exertion of a landlord or landlords. All these are distinctions which are clear in theory, but obscured in practice, and we should therefore be cautious in applying to practical affairs conclusions based on the nicety of such distinctions.

The exception, which we previously made in favour of some applications of the principle of "betterment," serves to strengthen the argument; for the justification of that principle, in English theory, and in American practice, seems to rest on the fact that a *definite* improvement is contemplated, the *definite* benefits of which will accrue to the owners of *definite* property. The nature of the improvement, the general identity of the property which will mainly benefit by it, and the expenditure which it necessitates, are, or should be, *ex hypothesi*, known with perfect or approximate exactitude; and the practice may fairly lay claim to almost, if not quite, as much precision as the theory. There seem, therefore, to be weighty reasons — though some may be urged on the other side—for charging some part, at least, of the cost of the improvement expressly on those who will reap the chief benefit of it.

But a closer examination throws into relief differences between the cases of "betterment" and of "unearned increment," and lends additional force to the conclusions at which we previously arrived. The theory of rent implies, it must be remembered, the possibility of an "unearned decrement," even as respects the very property which yields the unearned increment; and no such possibility seems to be contemplated in the ideas which underly the principle of betterment. There is, *ex hypothesi*, no doubt that the improvement proposed will add to the value of the property, at the partial expense of the owners of which it is to be carried out. But recent agricultural experience in England and other old countries has shown unmistakably that the possibility of an "unearned decrement" may become an unpleasant reality; and it certainly appears to be a strange illustration of the bondage, which a theory may exercise over unpractical minds, that at a time of severe and protracted agricultural depression, when landlords of agricultural land are known to be a distressed rather than a prosperous class, an agitation should be started, and should meet with a favourable reception over a wide area, the theoretical basis of which is the continuous acquisition by the owners of land of a large unearned increment. This, however, is by the way; and the point we are now urging, is that, the longer the theory of the unearned increment is examined, the nicer appear the distinctions on which it is founded, and the more unlikely it is that those same distinctions can be either discovered, or established, in practice. Some of the writers, who have laid the greatest stress on the theory, such as John Stuart Mill,[1] declare that some agricultural improvements, which are admittedly due to the expenditure and effort of individual landlords, become incorporated to such a degree with the land itself, that the income arising from them must be treated as rent, or, to use the phrase employed more recently by Professor Marshall, as "quasi-rent"; for it

[1] *Principles*, book ii. chap. xvi. 5; book v. chap. ii. 5.

cannot be distinguished from that part of the rent paid by the farmer, which is due to the "natural" fertility of the soil itself.

Again, we perhaps realise more vividly the nicety of the distinctions on which the conception of the unearned increment rests, when we consider the extension of it to other forms of wealth implied in the theory of business profits, to which prominent notice has recently been given by the American economist, General Walker.[1] General Walker's exposition of the theory may be open to assault for pushing the conception too far; but it is generally admitted by economists that natural ability of all kinds, whether it be found in aptitude for business enterprise, or in capacity for professional or handicraft labour, does secure a reward, which is, to some extent, of the nature of rent; and there is also no doubt that most, if not all, forms of wealth are susceptible of increase, due to causes apart from those connected simply and solely with the exertion and expenditure of the individual possessor. Opportunity, and chance, and social influences, play no inconsiderable part in the creation of fortunes in business, and the determination of professional and other earnings; and, from the standpoint of theoretical completeness, it can hardly be disputed that other forms of wealth besides land may yield an "unearned increment"—an increment, that is, due to something else than the act of the individual possessor. But in the case of these other forms of wealth the nicety of the distinctions, on which the conception rests, is more evident than it is in that of land; and from the consideration

---

[1] *Political Economy*, part iv. chap. iv. General Walker regards profits as analogous to rent, the advantages of exceptional ability in the one case corresponding to those of natural fertility in the other, and the advantages of exceptional opportunity to those of situation.

TYPICAL FALLACIES OF SOCIAL REFORMERS 9

of them we may accordingly gain a more vivid realisation of the difficulty of carrying the conception into practice. Is there not, then, a want of true logic in the failure to appreciate this difficulty? Or, rather, might we not expect the English quality of "animated moderation," and that apparent want of logic, which has been the "salvation" of Englishmen, to manifest themselves, not in endeavouring to push to its furthest conclusions in practical affairs the conception of the unearned increment, but in realising and enforcing the conditions, which necessarily attend its application to practice?

II. The second example, to which we may direct our attention, is, perhaps, best illustrated by that utterance of a leading politician, which was previously quoted. "We are all Socialists now," Sir William Harcourt is reported to have said; and, although this remark might, perhaps, be dismissed with scant notice as a hasty assertion made in the heat of debate for a controversial purpose, yet it deserves more attention if we regard it, as we fairly may, as illustrative of assumptions underlying more elaborate and reasoned argument in other quarters. At the meeting of the British Association at Bath in 1888, the philosophical calm, which generally characterises the proceedings of the Economic Science and Statistics section, was rudely disturbed by the reading of a paper on the "Transition to Social Democracy," by Mr. Bernard Shaw. In the discussion, which followed, Mr. Shaw accused those economists, who were in favour of some extension of State interference, and some further limitation of individual liberty, of being "illogical," because they did not proceed to embrace the whole programme of Social Democracy. Mr. Shaw's paper was afterwards republished in the *Fabian Essays in Socialism*,[1] and

[1] Pages 174, etc.

among the ablest of the contributors to that volume was Mr. Sidney Webb. Some while ago Mr. Webb wrote a pamphlet for the American Economic Association, entitled *Socialism in England*, and the pamphlet has been republished in the form of a book. In this book Mr. Webb, it is true, characterises such utterances as those of Sir William Harcourt as "vague"; but he nevertheless seems, in some passages, to include among the signs of the times, illustrating the development of socialism in England, tendencies and incidents fully as vague as Sir William Harcourt's declaration, and he numbers amongst these such reasonings of economists as those to which Mr. Shaw referred at Bath.

But, we may ask, Is there not, in all this, evidence of some failure to appreciate the virtue and consequences of that quality of "animated moderation," to which Bagehot attributed the success of England? The facts, which Mr. Webb adduces, must be admitted to show that there is some tendency in modern philosophical thought, and modern practical action, to extend the area of governmental interference; and so far the tendency may be called "socialistic." But does this necessarily warrant the conclusions, which Mr. Webb, and, in a more extravagant degree, other writers and speakers, have based upon it? It should be remembered that it is only in the most extreme forms of theoretical opinion that the functions of the State have been regarded as purely negative—as merely the repression of violence and the prevention of fraud. It should be remembered that economists like Adam Smith, who are popularly regarded as advocates of "natural liberty," also admitted, in some cases explicitly, in others implicitly, the advantage, if not the necessity, of State interference.[1] It should be remembered that the legislation of the Free

[1] Cf. Essay xii.

Trade era, though it undoubtedly tended in the direction of increasing individual liberty, did not extinguish the positive action of government. Mr. John Rae, some few years ago, in the first of two instructive articles on "State Socialism" in the *Contemporary Review*,[1] pointed out how easy it was to find in the writings of so "orthodox" an economist as McCulloch—using the term "orthodox" in a narrow sense—instances of the advocacy of State Socialism, if by that were meant the interference of government.

The question would, therefore, seem to be essentially one of degree. Few, if any, persons think that the State or the individual is to be so paramount that no room is left for the action or authority of the other; and it may, therefore, be held to be strictly "logical" to advocate the extension of the area of governmental authority to a certain point, and to protest against its further extension. If it be "socialism" to urge *any* limitation of the freedom of the individual, and *any* increase of the power and duties of the State, then it is true that most of our economic writers, and practical legislators, are "socialists"; and if those, who advocate any such limitation, or any such increase, are "illogical," unless they are prepared to adopt the entire socialist programme of the State as the one landlord and the one capitalist, then most of our economic writers and practical legislators are unquestionably "illogical." But, unless a qualifying or explanatory parenthesis is added, to show the sense in which the term is employed, it is, to say the least, misleading to describe these writers and legislators as "socialists"; and it would appear to be really "illogical" to regard their attitude or action as indicative of the development of the more extreme forms

[1] For August, 1888.

of socialism. The term is undoubtedly vague, and it is difficult to make it precise; but if it be used indifferently to include Professor Sidgwick and Mr. Hyndman, or even John Stuart Mill and Karl Marx, then the attempt at any precision is wholly abandoned, and the term is employed to comprehend men opposed to one another almost as much as, perhaps more than, professed individualists like Mr. Herbert Spencer, and advanced socialists like Mr. Belfort Bax.

A difference of degree, it may be urged, is here as important as a difference of kind; and the question is essentially one of more or less. It may be possible in the future—the task has not yet been achieved in the present—to construct an adequate and complete theory of the proper limits of individual liberty, and the true province of governmental authority. But it might be argued, with no little cogency, that the formal construction of such a theory was of no very great importance; and that Mill's confession,[1] that the "admitted functions of government embrace a much wider field than can easily be included within the ring-fence of any restrictive definition, and that it is hardly possible to find any ground of justification common to them all, except the comprehensive one of general expediency: nor to limit the interference of government by any universal rule, save the simple and vague one that it should never be admitted but when the case of expediency is strong"—it might be argued that this confession, however illogical and incomplete it might appear to a Frenchman or other foreigner, yet reflected the characteristic quality of "animated moderation," which Bagehot ascribed to the Englishman; and, if there were, in a popular sense, a "want of logic" in our theory and our

[1] *Principles of Political Economy*, book v. chap. i. 2.

practice in the matter of individual liberty and State interference, that "want of logic" had proved our "salvation." May we not, then, take our stand on this apparent "want of logic," and refuse to be branded as "socialists," unless a qualifying expression be added, if we urge the extension of the interference of the State in quarters where it seems to be warranted by examination of past experience, or consideration of present expediency, and consent to be termed "illogical," if by this be meant our insistence on the importance of differences of degree in the matter of the proper limits of individual liberty?

III. A third illustration of the point we are examining will suffice. The question of social reform is, as we saw, in a state of "animation"; and the air is full of the schemes of social reformers. But in many, perhaps in most, cases each of these eager advocates puts forward his own pet scheme as the sole "panacea," and refuses to give a place in the society of the future to the successful adoption of the proposals of others.

This is a failing characteristic of some advocates of *Co-operation*.[1] The co-operative movement in this country might now be described as passing through a critical stage in its history. A prominent feature at recent Co-operative Congresses has been a sharp division of opinion on the subject of co-operative production; and the utterances, which have proceeded from the mouths of some leading advocates of co-operation, appear to rest on the assumption that the movement must be pronounced a failure, if an immediate and extensive advance is not made in the direction of co-operative production. Such declarations might, perhaps, be said to be vitiated by the failure, implicit in them, to appreciate the distinctions between

[1] Cf. Essays iv. v. and vi. below.

co-operation in the consumption or distribution of wealth, and co-operation as applied to its production; and few greater services could be rendered to the co-operative cause than to examine carefully into the conditions, which have conduced to the unmistakable and extensive success of the first branch of co-operation in England, to show that these conditions have been such that the triumphant progress of retail and wholesale co-operative distribution, gratifying as it is, and advantageous as it has proved, is not, on the whole, so remarkable as it has sometimes been represented to be, and to point out that the problems of co-operative production present indeed certain features of resemblance to those of co-operative distribution, but that they are also characterised by differences, which go far to explain its comparative want of success till the present time. The failure to accord adequate recognition to these differences would, then, seem to be a weak point in the argument of many zealous advocates of co-operation; and in this lack of discrimination they would appear to resemble those writers and speakers on the "unearned increment," and on socialism, who previously engaged our attention. But the point, on which we are now insisting, is rather that these advocates seem to regard co-operation as the panacea for all social ills, and to look forward to a future society organised on that basis alone.

And, again, the system of industrial partnership, or *profit-sharing*, has been put forward by some advocates in a similar spirit. That system has unquestionable merits; and we may expect in the future, as we are witnessing in the present, the origination of instructive experiments on this basis. We may expect this, as we may hope to see some successful experiments in co-operative production. Perhaps we may look with even greater confidence to the

TYPICAL FALLACIES OF SOCIAL REFORMERS 15

successful extension of the principle of industrial partnership than to that of co-operative production, for the former seems to avoid certain difficulties which attach to the latter.

A valuable and exhaustive record of the different trials, which have been made of the system of industrial partnership in various countries, has been published by an American writer, Mr. Gilman.[1] The Preface to the book is marked by a tone of balanced moderation, to which no exception can be taken; and the author there expresses the hope that the "only rhetoric to be discovered in his pages" is that "rhetoric of understatement of which Dr. Holmes somewhere speaks." In the same spirit he declares, in the body of the book,[2] that "any attempt at a panacea" for social ills is "plainly irrational," and that "relief must be sought in very many ways," and the "labour question" be "attacked from all sides, if it is to yield to the wit and the philanthropy of mankind." From these passages we might have hoped that Mr. Gilman would have given a place in the future economy of society to some other scheme, or schemes, but his own; and, were it not for occasional remarks, this hope might be said to be fulfilled. But, on some occasions, at least, his enthusiasm is too much for his endeavour to be judicial and impartial. He will, so it seems, allow very little, if any, room for co-operative production; for, he declares,[3] "co-operation is too revolutionary a substitute" for the present wages system. The sliding scale, again, he dismisses[4] on the ground that "as a general remedy for the rigidity of the wages system it has shown itself, thus far, quite ineffective"; and arbitra-

---

[1] *Profit-sharing between Employer and Employee*, by N. P. Gilman.
[2] Page 3.   [3] Page 7.   [4] Page 58.

tion is, he states,[1] "essentially a makeshift," to "rest" upon which, "as a final solution" of the labour problem, "would be a confession of impotence which modern civilisation could scarcely make, and retain its self-respect." While, therefore, declining [2] to endorse the "unqualified" declaration of Von Thünen, that profit-sharing is the "only salvation of the labouring class," he maintains that it is the "most equitable and generally satisfactory method of remunerating the three industrial agents."

We have selected Mr. Gilman's book as an illustration of the point we wish to urge because in many respects it tells against us. It is the momentary departures from his ideal standpoint, it is the few occasional remarks and the little traits, which reveal his inclination, despite of his better self, to regard his own scheme as the one complete remedy, and the schemes of all others as partial and inadequate, which enable us to realise the extent of the error and mischief of more extravagant writers, and to appreciate the subtle and dangerous nature of the failing to which they, with him, are liable. For in the mind of a sober thinker, who sits down, in a calm hour, to meditate on the future, there can be little doubt that society, if it is not to run counter to all the experience of the past, will continue to be characterised by diversity, and not uniformity; and that, therefore, there may be room for the trial and adoption of many varieties of many schemes of social reform. Is it not a pedantic adherence to a false logic to suppose that any scheme need be pushed to its furthest conclusions until it embraces the whole of society? And is not the English quality of "animated moderation" rather to be found in the ungrudging recognition of the merits of different proposals adapted to varying conditions? The social reformer may,

[1] Page 61. [2] Page 412.

and, if he is to accomplish work which will stand the test of experience, he must, be critical; but his criticism should be permeated by a catholic spirit. There is so much work to be done, and such serious and persistent evil to be combated, that he should welcome rather than repel, and encourage rather than envy, his fellow-workers in the same or adjoining fields.

II.

THE RELATIONS BETWEEN INDUSTRIAL CONCILIATION AND SOCIAL REFORM.[1]

IT is a pleasant privilege to be allowed to discuss in Newcastle the important question of the peaceful settlement of industrial disputes. Those of us, who live in the south of England, are accustomed—some with envy, others, perhaps, with misgiving—to look upon the towns of the north as the typical representatives of advanced opinion; and the industrial district, of which Newcastle is the centre, may not inappropriately be regarded as leading the way in the special department of reform we are now about to consider. It is indeed true that during the last few years the peaceful settlement of industrial quarrels has been subjected to a very severe strain on Tyne-side;[2] and it may be that it has not passed through that strain entirely unharmed. But nevertheless it is by no means extravagant to assert that in the north of England more than anywhere else the methods of avoiding strikes and lock-outs—the wars of the industrial world—

---

[1] A Paper read before Section F of the British Association at Newcastle-upon-Tyne, 1889, and printed in the *Royal Statistical Journal* for June, 1890.

[2] In the Northumberland coal trade the sliding scale, previously in existence, was terminated in the winter of 1886-87, and a protracted strike followed.

by means of conciliation, by mutual discussion and agreement, that is, between representative masters and men—by arbitration, or the reference of the quarrel to the decision of some third and neutral party—by sliding scales, or the selection of a "standard wage" and a "standard price," and the determination of the manner in which variations in the former are to depend "automatically," if we may say so, on variations in the latter—these different methods have been exemplified in greater variety within the limits of a defined industrial area, have been carried out with more completeness, and have had, perhaps, more serious and manifold difficulties to confront, in the north of England than anywhere else. If their failings have been revealed by the pitiless logic of facts, their virtues have also been brought into prominence; and it is not certain, although this may indeed seem a paradox, that the peaceful settlement of industrial disputes does not owe as much real and permanent advance to the former process as to the latter. In no subject, at any rate, are the lessons of experience—both bitter and pleasant—likely to be more important and helpful.

We do not propose now to examine into the details of conciliation, or arbitration, or the sliding scale. We purpose rather to confine our attention to some considerations of a general—and, perhaps, academic and theoretical—nature on the character of the relations existing between industrial conciliation—using the term in a wide and comprehensive sense—and general social reform.

There is a conclusion, to which the study of social and industrial questions—on its theoretic no less than on its practical side—must lead in the long run, if it be pursued with sufficient thoroughness and open-mindedness; and that conclusion is that social and industrial reform is, in the last analysis, dependent on moral reform. In a London newspaper, some months ago, a quotation appeared from a speech delivered by a Norwegian thinker,[1] whose fame has obtained recognition in other countries besides his own. He says: "Mere democracy cannot solve the social question. An element of aristocracy must come into our life. Of course I am not thinking of the aristocracy of birth, or of the purse, or even of intellect. I am thinking of the aristocracy of character, of mind, of will. That alone can make us free." In other words, to put this language into prosaic shape, social and industrial reform is inseparably connected with moral reform. It has often been said — so often that it is sometimes impatiently dismissed as a threadbare truism—that you cannot make a people moral by Act of Parliament. But, while such an assertion fails to afford any adequate excuse for a policy, which it is often employed to shield — a policy of unadulterated *laissez-faire*—and, while it is well-nigh as unreasonable to attribute nothing, as it is to attribute everything, to the influence of governmental machinery and legislative regulation, there is a measure of truth in the assertion, which in these days we are sometimes inclined to neglect. The high-pressure speed, at which our railway engines carry us on the "race" from one part of the country to another, at which the machinery in our factories is worked, and the business in our markets and on our exchanges transacted, has infected our hopes for the future, our verdict on the experience of the past, our opinions and ideas of the present. We are inclined to be impatient with slow results. We are prone to have recourse to plans which promise immediate and gigantic consequences, and the natural outcome is that we are

[1] Henrik Ibsen.

disposed to pay more attention to the "machinery" of social and industrial reform than to the "material" of human nature with which reform has to deal. All experience teaches that human nature changes slowly—bit by bit—and yet in our impatience we are either inclined to believe that it may be changed with rapidity and completeness; or, if we find this impossible, we throw up our hands in despair, and exclaim that it is futile to attempt to change it at all. And yet more sober and continued reflection might show us—in the words of a political thinker fresh from the observation of men and manners in that "American Commonwealth,"[1] which has seemed to some to hold out the highest hopes of human improvement, and to others to furnish material for not a little despondent pessimism—that, "though the ascent of man may be slow, it is also sure"; and that, while sudden and complete change in human nature is really as impossible as it would be dangerous, gradual and partial change is not only possible, but can hardly be avoided.

Let us apply these general considerations to the subject immediately before us. In connection with the narrower, as with the wider question, we find persons who have held the extravagant belief that, once the machinery for the peaceful settlement of industrial disputes has been provided, industrial strife will become unknown; and we also find persons, who, confronted with the failure of this machinery, perhaps in one, perhaps in more than one instance, have abandoned their belief with the same absoluteness and precipitancy as they manifested when first they adopted it. They tell us despondently—not to say dogmatically—that all these methods of securing the peaceful settlement of industrial disputes are mere makeshifts; that conciliation has not

[1] Cf. BRYCE's *American Commonwealth*, vol. iii. p. 685 (1st edit.).

made much way, and is confined to a comparatively narrow industrial area; that arbitrators' awards have proved ineffectual to prevent in some cases the continuance, in others the early renewal, of strife; and that the sliding scale is complicated in detail, and limited in application. They first ignore the material of human nature to be dealt with by the machinery, in which they have reposed such implicit confidence; and then—by a not unnatural reaction—they attach such exclusive importance to the material of human nature that they believe that it cannot be brought at all under the influence of the machinery. In reality, the one attitude is as unreasoning and as truly illogical as the other. If it is wrong to neglect the material of human nature, it is equally wrong to nullify the power of the machinery supplied in conciliation, in arbitration, and in the sliding scale, to handle and to modify that material. Human nature being such as it is, we must be prepared to discover occasions when the machinery works with difficulty, and sometimes stops altogether; but we may still retain our belief in the possibility of bringing that human nature into greater accord with the machinery, and of improving the machinery itself so as to make it fulfil its purpose better; and we may hold that familiarity with the machinery tends to expedite these results.

And so we must not attach too much importance to the efficacy of conciliation, or arbitration, or the sliding scale. It is possible that differences may arise between masters and men meeting round a table, and engaged in frank and friendly discussion, which do not admit of peaceful adjustment. It is possible that the temper or claims of the representatives of masters and men before an arbitrator, or of their constituents, may on occasions be such that the arbitrator's award fails to secure a lengthy, or even a brief, respite from industrial contention. It is possible that times may come, or circumstances arise, when a sliding scale appears to the one party or to the other to work with an excess or deficiency of automatic regularity. It is nothing more or less than a truism—though it is a truism which, like many others, is often forgotten—to observe that the tone and temper, with which the two parties meet one another, are likely to be the tone and temper with which any agreement they arrive at is accepted or observed. The machinery depends in a large measure on the material for its easy and effective working; and the general attitude of men and masters towards one another is beyond comparison far more important than the establishment, or the detailed arrangement, of conciliation, or arbitration, or the sliding scale.

But if, on the one hand, these considerations of human nature supply the corrective to excessive confidence, they are equally incompatible with extravagant pessimism. Human nature may not admit of sudden and complete change, but it does seem to allow of partial and gradual modification. And, again, if the material may sometimes arrest the orderly working of too advanced machinery, it may also be possible to deal with it by means of machinery which may in some parts be defective; for successful results depend on the material even more than on the machinery. It may, then, be the case that it is difficult to obtain accurate data for an arbitrator, or to determine by theoretical considerations[1] what should be the exact nature of the principle on which his award should be based, or an

[1] Cf. a Paper by the present writer on "The Relations between Sliding Scales and Economic Theory," read before the British Association, at Bath, and printed *in extenso* in the "Report" for 1888, p. 523, etc. (Essay ix. below.)

agreement arrived at by a board of conciliation, or a sliding scale established. But these difficulties may really become less formidable than they appear, if only there be a favourable tone and temper evinced on either side. And, once more, it may be that the matter in dispute can be determined, and determined alone, by the "higgling of the market"; but a frank, if not friendly, buyer and seller will come to terms with a rapidity and ease, which admit of no comparison with those possible when buyer and seller are, and are determined to be, relentless foes. If the moral reform be accomplished, the social and industrial reform will easily follow.

And, if we look around us, we can hardly refuse to recognise that there are the elements of a moral reform: that there has taken place an improvement in human nature as between masters and men. In measuring this improvement the student enjoys an advantage over practical men. He can stand aside from the din and turmoil. He can take up a post from which he can quietly observe; and he may detect signs of progress, which are almost invisible to those who are actually engaged in the conflict. It is impossible to look into any recent economic treatise without discovering that it bears some testimony to the change, which has been effected in the relations of employers and employed. And it is certainly impossible to review the aspect of practical affairs from almost any standpoint without being conscious of influences tending in this direction. We must not, indeed, entertain extravagant expectations. We must not imagine that the industrial reform will do more, or much more, than keep pace with the moral reform, if it will even do as much as this. And, bearing in mind how comparatively recent is this improvement in the relations between masters and men, how bitterly their interests are opposed in some matters, however much they may be in accord in others, how suddenly changes of considerable magnitude take place in the conditions and prospects of particular industries, or of general trade, in modern times, how difficult, if not impossible, it is, on purely theoretical grounds, to establish any standard, by which industrial disputes can be adjusted, save some such standard as a relation between the wages of the workers and the selling prices of the commodities as has become traditional—bearing in mind all these circumstances, we should be quite prepared to find that conciliation has not made much way, and is confined to an area narrow by comparison with the whole field of industry; that arbitrators' awards have sometimes failed to prevent the continuance, or the early renewal, of strife; and that the sliding scale is comparatively limited in application. Its complexity, indeed, may, as we shall see hereafter, be as much an advantage as a drawback.

Let us notice, then, the signs of change and improvement in the relations between masters and men. We may select for exclusive consideration one of the most obvious and, perhaps, the most important and characteristic of those signs. No one, who reads his daily or weekly newspaper, or engages in conversation outside a very limited circle, can fail to observe a change—more marked in some places, less noticeable in others—in the tone and temper with which the objects and the action of trade unions and trade unionist leaders are now discussed. It cannot be denied that you may discover some quarters where the most bitter hostility is felt and displayed—and, perhaps, not without reason—towards those organisations. But any candid and intelligent observer will agree that a change has passed over the tone and temper of general conversation and general opinion with regard to the matter. And it has found, or is finding, its way into theoretical treatises. For it is impossible to establish such a divorce of theory from fact as the theorist, who looks with contempt on the practical man, or the practical man, who despises the theorist, would fain persuade us exists. Theory is acted upon by practice, and, in its turn, reacts on practice; and it is undoubtedly evidence of no little value of a change in practice when we find economists in various countries—Professor Marshall, for example, in our own, M. Leroy-Beaulieu in France, and, we may almost say, a whole school of thinkers here and in Germany and America—recognising, some in a fuller, some in a narrower, sense, that there is a legitimate and definite sphere for trade unions to occupy, even in the theoretical determination of market, if not normal, wages; that they may give to the workman the position of a strong and combined, instead of a weak and isolated, seller of labour, and may enable him to hold out for a reserve-price. We may take this change in the general tone and temper of society as admitted and irrefutable.

But what does this imply, interpreted in the most limited sense? It implies that employers are more disposed to meet on terms of equality representatives of working-men. It implies that public opinion—a force for good or for evil, the potency of which, if once thoroughly awakened, it is impossible to deny—will sanction, will encourage, and will exercise some moral compulsion to bring about, that meeting. And it also implies that trade unions, occupying a position of acknowledged importance and responsibility, will become more sensible of the duties of that position, will be more ready to abandon an attitude of determined hostility, more disposed to court publicity and to enlist public support and sympathy, more inclined to oppose argument to argument rather than force to force, and to convince public opinion that the strength of the argument, not merely of the force, lies on their side. And here, once again, public opinion cannot fail to exercise some moral compulsion. It may be weak, it may be strong, but it will, beyond a doubt, increase with succeeding years.

But not only does this change in the general tone and temper of conversation and opinion promote and indicate a moral reform, which is the essential condition of industrial reform, but it is also of immense practical importance in facilitating the smooth and effective working of the particular machinery of reform known as conciliation, or arbitration, or the sliding scale. It disposes masters and men to be conciliatory; it inclines them, if they cannot come to an agreement themselves, to be willing to refer the decision of the matter under dispute to a neutral arbitrator; it induces them to seek for some means by which occasions of quarrel may be avoided, for a time at least, through the automatic operation of a sliding scale. But it does more. It is impossible that negotiations, whatever form they take, and whatever the character of the arrangement in which they result, can be conducted with ease or success unless a few representative negotiators are selected on either side. But a trade union supplies a basis for the representation of the men, and imposes a binding force on the represented, which are difficult to secure by any other satisfactory means. And so a change in the tone and temper, with which trade unions are regarded, implies greater facility for effective representation.

But here, again, we must not neglect the material of human nature. We will not trespass upon the considerations suggested by recent events[1] in the Northumberland coal trade, more than to say that they afford a singular contradiction to that idea of trade unionist leaders as the promoters of strife, which is still current in some quarters; and that they show us that there may be cases where the opinion and advice of the leaders are unable to prevail against an impulse on the part of their followers, and that, even when we have secured representation, we have not done everything. Our anticipations may conceivably be upset by the incalculable elements of human nature. We ought not, on that account, to depreciate the importance and value of representation; but we must not expect too much from it, or be excessively discouraged if, on occasion, it fails.

And this leads us to notice another aspect of the general considerations we have been discussing. Although machinery is not everything, yet it is something; and it is not difficult to point out some of the ways in which methods of securing the peaceful settlement of industrial disputes may help to modify that human nature on which the possibility of that settlement ultimately depends. It is the merest folly not to recognise that, if you can once induce masters and men to meet round a table avowedly for informal, and, if possible, friendly and effective discussion, you have not merely afforded the machinery for that discussion, but you have helped to implant a habit of resorting to it in lieu of a struggle of force, you have affected—it may be in a greater, it may be in a less degree—the attitude of the one party to the other, you have established a presumption in favour of mutual arrangement, and you have contributed to influence human nature for good. Or again,

---

[1] During the strike in 1887, the relations between the unionist leaders and the men became strained. (*Vide* the following Essay.)

if the two parties refer the matter under dispute to the decision of a neutral arbitrator, they have, by the mere reference, taken a step which they can only retrace with some difficulty, they have, to some extent, committed themselves, and their constituents, to abide by the arbitrator's award, they have in some measure, though it be only in a slight measure, accustomed themselves to the possibility—though not, we may suppose, to the probability —of an adverse decision. And, though they may argue their case with copious, and indeed with contentious, insistence; though they may expect that the award will go in their favour, until they are undeceived; though they may accept the decision with sullen reluctance, if not with outspoken irritation : yet they have familiarised themselves with the machinery, they have incurred an obligation binding in honour, if it is not in legal force, they are conscious of the feeling that their reputation is at stake, if the award is disobeyed, they have contributed to produce some change —though it be small—in human nature. They are not quite the same men after the reference to arbitration as they were before. And, lastly, in the case of the institution of a sliding scale, results somewhat similar to these are achieved. A relation between the wages of the workers and the selling prices of the commodity, or between the former and a combination of the latter with other circumstances of production, has received the sanction, for a time at least, of a formal arrangement, and has so far been recognised as fair and traditional; an automatic adjustment of matters, which might otherwise have occasioned contention, has for some time at least been in operation, and has so far become familiar; a harmonious concord has for some time at least enjoyed the benefit of being the rule, to which a quarrel is the exception : and human nature cannot fail to have been to some extent modified. The machinery of industrial peace — whether it be provided in the form of conciliation, or arbitration, or the sliding scale, or of a mixture or development of any of these varieties — may effect but a little change in human nature, and afford the occasion for as much despondent pessimism over its failures, as it supplies by its successes the material for sanguine optimism; but it is nevertheless to be cordially welcomed if it effects any change at all; and there can be no possibility of doubt about the advantage, if not the necessity, of making the machinery as easy and effective in working, as perfect and complete in detailed arrangement, as we possibly can. It may be the case, as we saw before, that its deficiencies are, in the light of an improvement in human nature, not so important as we might imagine; but there can be no question that it is desirable to reduce their number, and diminish their magnitude.

This may be done by dint of patient investigation and lengthened and varied experience; but, preserving that attitude of general reflection, which we adopted at the outset, we may say that the one quality above all to be desired, if indeed it be not indispensable, in the machinery of industrial peace, is elasticity, or, to adhere more closely to the metaphor, adjustability. And this quality we may understand in more than one sense. The machinery must be capable of adjustment to the varying circumstances of trade generally; it must also admit of adjustment to the varying circumstances of each particular industry, and to those, which vary from one industry to another; and, fourthly and lastly, it must allow of adaptation to varying stages of improvement in the relations between masters and men.

If there is one fact more than another, which the comparatively brief history of sliding scales has brought into prominence, it is that friction and irritation are likely to arise when the arrangements of the scale produce, or seem to produce, a lengthy interval between changes in prices and consequent changes in wages.[1] From the nature of the case it is clear that some such interval there must be, for the prices can only be ascertained after they have been realised; and it would be a waste of time and expense for the accountants—appointed by one, or by both sides, to examine into the books of some or all of the masters—to make this examination, and declare the resulting average price, with too great frequency. But, on the other hand, the changes in wages should follow the changes in prices with as much celerity as is conveniently possible. There may be arrangements of the details of a scale, which may facilitate a more perfect and speedy adjustment of wages to the real circumstances of production—such as, for instance, a more rapid fall in wages when selling prices have fallen to, or below, the expenses of production—but it is not our purpose at present to enter on a discussion of detail. The principle alone it is on which we are concerned to insist—the principle true and important, on theoretic no less than practical grounds—that the provisions of a scale should permit of a correspondence, which can be effected with as much rapidity and completeness as is possible, between the wages of the workmen and the actual contemporaneous circumstances of production. It is for these reasons that conciliation—with free, informal, and speedy discussion and decision between masters and men—is to be preferred to the more elaborate, formal, and necessarily lengthy proceedings before an arbitrator; and that the intermittent awards of an arbitrator, or determinations of a board of conciliation, are to be placed on a lower level of advantage

[1] Cf. the following Essay.

than the automatic and sustained regularity of a sliding scale. Conciliation affords more opportunity for frequent discussion and rapid decision: a sliding scale, during the time of its continuance, obviates the necessity for discussion or decision at all on major points. It is from this point of view as superior logically to conciliation, as conciliation itself is to arbitration; for in this sense it is more elastic—more rapidly and easily adjustable.

But there is also another sense in which methods of securing the peaceful settlement of industrial disputes should be elastic and easily adjustable. They must admit of adaptation to the varied circumstances of different industries. And here we may conveniently divide our reflections under two heads. They must admit of being adjusted to circumstances varying within the limits of a single industry—not merely changing from one time to another, as we noticed before, but also existing contemporaneously in different quarters—and they must also allow of adaptation to circumstances varying from one industry to another. This is the point of view from which the complexity of a scale is to be deemed an advantage rather than considered a drawback. For the internal economy of an industry is often as complex in reality as it may seem in outward appearance to be simple and uniform; and it is therefore important to secure a principle, which shall be so simple in its main features that the least educated and intelligent man can understand it, and yet so complex in its detailed application that it can be adjusted to the varying requirements of minutely different circumstances. This has been the case with the sliding scales in the coal and iron industries of England. To an outsider the principle of wages varying with prices, or some other circumstances of production, may appear to be very simple; but, if he inquires into the detailed working of the scale, he is only too likely to be suddenly arrested by the complexity of the particular arrangements. And, similarly, the difficulties of an arbitrator sometimes commence only when he has to apply a general principle, allowed by both parties to be fair, to the particular details of the question before him; and the advantage of conciliation lies to some extent in the fact that masters and men, recognising the broad purpose for which they are met, and agreeing on some general principle, bring their knowledge of minutiæ to bear on the arrangement of complex details.

Similar observations might be made on the need of adaptation to the varying circumstances of different industries. There may be some to which the principle of a sliding scale is not easily applicable, at any rate according to the form which has prevailed in the coal and iron mining industries, where the selling price of the commodity affords a tolerably adequate index of the changes, which should be made in wages, if employers and employed are to reap jointly the benefit, and sustain jointly the injury, of increased or diminished prosperity. There may be industries, again, which are not sufficiently advanced, so far as the feeling between masters and men is concerned, to permit of an arrangement so comparatively permanent and automatic in character as a sliding scale, but nevertheless it is possible to establish with immediate success, and a fair prospect of permanence, a board of conciliation. And, once more, there may be industries where masters and men are not prepared to meet habitually with the object of settling their differences by free and friendly discussion, but will, on occasion, agree to submit their quarrels to the decision of a neutral arbitrator. Again, there may be varieties in the details of a scale, or of the constitution of a board of conciliation, or of the procedure of a court of arbitration, which may assume a different shape as we pass from one industry to another. Some may be suited to one, and ill adapted to another. Or, once more, there may be in some industries a combination of two or more of the different methods we have enumerated; for they are not of course mutually exclusive. The basis of a scale may be determined by conciliation or arbitration; and joint committees of masters and men may, during its continuance, themselves adjust, or refer for decision to an arbitrator, differences on minor matters. Or, again, the constitution of a board of conciliation may allow, if it does not actually provide, for the occasional intervention of an arbitrator; and the procedure of a court of arbitration does not necessarily exclude a resort to conciliation. There can be no doubt that methods of securing the peaceful settlement of industrial disputes must, if they are to succeed, be varied and capable of adaptation to varied and varying circumstances; and with equal assurance we may assert that they do admit of this variation.

And—and this is the last point we propose to consider—it may be the case that a method, which is suited to one period in the history of an industry, and of the relations prevailing in it between masters and men, may be unsuited to another. It may be, and apparently is, the fact that arbitration has in some cases paved the way for conciliation, and conciliation for the sliding scale; and the sliding scale may in its turn give place to a more advanced method of attaining and preserving industrial peace. In logical order of thought, and in reference to varying stages of improvement in the relations between masters and men, it would seem that the sliding scale is superior to conciliation, and conciliation to arbitration. But here, once again, we must not forget the character of that material of human nature with which the more, equally with the less, advanced machinery has to deal. We must remember that human nature changes not merely gradually, but also bit by bit; and we must therefore expect to find some persons, and classes, and industries, at a more advanced stage in this respect than others, and therefore more able to appreciate and practise the more advanced methods of industrial reform. All the many varieties—arbitration, conciliation, the sliding scale, and perhaps other means, yet undiscovered, of preserving industrial peace, and of promoting industrial reform—may have a sphere in which, without interfering with the contemporaneous adoption elsewhere of others, they may be profitably and successfully applied; for human nature is complex and varied, and changes gradually, bit by bit.

It is this consideration, which makes us distrust from the outset those who proclaim their own pet scheme of reform as a panacea, and condemn other schemes as partial and inadequate. We distrust them, because we are conscious of the immense variety of human kind, and we therefore believe in the catholicity of social reform. It may be easy to point out defects in the present wages system; it may not be difficult to show that conciliation, and arbitration, and the sliding scale, fail to administer a complete corrective to these defects; it may not be impossible to prove conclusively that systems, such as those of profit-sharing and co-operative production, furnish a more thorough solution of the difficulties of the wages question, and that there are tendencies in the methods we have been considering, which, fully developed, might issue in those more advanced systems. All this might be urged, and urged with reason; and yet we might reply that the present wages system is not only widely prevalent in fact, but is in a sense natural in theory; that the obstinacy, with which human nature makes its failings evident in the imperfections of conciliation, or arbitration, or the sliding scale, might conceivably occasion disappointment to the hopes which had been formed of profit-sharing or co-operative production; and that there are also tendencies in the former methods which, fully developed, would seem to be incompatible with the latter systems. We might reply in some such fashion: and yet the safer and more conclusive answer would be to point to the variety of human kind, to the capacity of human nature, for gradual and partial modification, to its aversion to sudden and complete change, to its liability to undergo a reaction in the contrary direction as sudden and complete as the original impulse it has first received. In the light of these considerations it seems more probable that future, as present and past, industrial society will present manifold diversities: that, although in some quarters, with an improvement in human nature, a place may be found for the more advanced systems of profit-sharing and co-operative production, yet in others the wages system will still prevail in its simplicity and variety, and in others again conciliation, arbitration, and the sliding scale, perhaps improved and developed, will be discovered.

The ideal attitude of the true social reformer may, we venture to hold, be described most appropriately as at once catholic and critical, ready to examine all promising schemes, and to listen to all reasonable proposals, prepared to make allowance for the enthusiasm, which, while it is necessary to carry any scheme successfully into effect, is calculated to make the proposer neglect its difficulties, and overrate its advantages, but resolved also to scrutinise severely the claims of these different plans in the dry light of past and present experience, and inclined to discredit the professions of proposals, which promise sudden and complete changes in human nature, and to repose more faith in plans which appear more excellent in their performance than they are ostentatious in promise, which hold out a fair prospect of effecting some gradual change in some parts of human nature, which neither ignore nor magnify the difficulties with which every scheme of social reform is confronted. We want, in short, in the department of social and industrial reform, more of that "animated moderation," which Bagehot[1] used to regard as desirable, and as the typical characteristic of the ideal English man of business — not content to remain still, and yet not afraid of being called illogical, if he has gone to a certain length on any path of reform or action, and has refused for the time to proceed further. By taking up such an attitude we may incur the hostility and contempt of extreme individualists and extreme socialists alike; by both our position may be termed illogical, and deemed halting; but it has yet to be shown that in social and industrial reform a *via media* is not as possible and advantageous as it is truly logical and characteristically English.[2]

[1] *Physics and Politics*, p. 200.   [2] Cf. Essay i. above.

III.

THE POSITION AND PROSPECTS OF INDUSTRIAL CONCILIATION.[1]

THREE years ago I had the privilege of submitting to the Royal Statistical Society a paper entitled "Sliding Scales and other Methods of Wage-Arrangement in the North of England,"[2] in which I attempted to give some account of the methods by which industrial disputes had been prevented, or adjusted, in the coal and iron industries. In returning on the present occasion to the subject of the peaceful settlement of industrial quarrels, I have the advantage, or, perhaps, I should more properly say the disadvantage, of dealing with a topic, which is engaging a considerable share of public attention. It is no new thing in the history of industry to hear of strikes, and rumours of strikes; and he would be a sanguine, if not a foolhardy, prophet who should predict with confidence their cessation in the near, or even distant, future. But at the time, when my former paper was read, the industry and commerce of the country were suffering from continued depression, or were at any rate slowly recovering from it;

---

[1] A paper read before the Royal Statistical Society in May, 1890, and published in the *Journal* for September, 1890.

[2] Cf. vol. l. pt. 1 of the *Journal*, afterwards published, with additions, as a book (*Industrial Peace: its Advantages, Methods, and Difficulties*).

and it is an attested fact of industrial experience that strikes occur in greater abundance, and are more frequently successful, at moments of rising than of falling prices, of improving than of declining trade. For this reason, were there no other, the question of the peaceful adjustment of industrial disputes would be more prominent in 1890 than it was in 1886.

But there are other reasons. Whatever verdict may be pronounced upon the justice or injustice, the reasonableness or the want of reason, the permanent success or the ultimate failure, of the strike among the dock labourers in the Port of London during the autumn of 1889, there can be no doubt that by its magnitude and peculiar incidents it riveted for a time the attention of the public; and it contributed to bring into prominence the methods and means by which such disputes might be prevented or adjusted. It had the additional consequence that it occasioned similar movements—some successful, some unsuccessful—among other classes of unskilled labourers; and it set in motion—whether for good or for evil—disturbance in the labour-market generally. The space devoted in the columns of the daily newspapers to "Labour and Wages" appreciably increased after the occurrence of the strike; and, although this fact did not necessarily imply that industrial quarrels were more abundant or serious than they had been at previous periods, it signified that the public was more fully and speedily acquainted with their occurrence, causes, incidents, and results.

And, again, the vast proportions of the strike, which recently threatened in the coal trade, and the large numbers embraced in the combination of miners on the one side, and colliery owners on the other, served the purpose of a conspicuous illustration in arousing the public to the desirability of seeking for some practicable means of effecting a peaceful adjustment of industrial quarrels.

One other reason may be given for the present prominence of the subject. It is not merely, or perhaps chiefly, in England that the "Labour Question," as it is sometimes called, is pressing for solution. The occurrence of prolonged and bitter contests in the mining industry of Germany may be considered to share with the electoral successes of the Social Democrats, and the traditional policy of protecting the poor of the Hohenzollern dynasty, the responsibility for the International Labour Conference at Berlin.[1] In Belgium and France, again, the existence of *conseils de prud'hommes* has not prevented industrial disputes. There is considerable misunderstanding on the precise function of these bodies. They are not concerned with the determination of the rates of wages for the future, but supply a convenient mechanism for the settlement of quarrels between employers and employed on the payment of wages in the past, and on questions of dismissal and apprenticeship.

In Belgium, a Commission was appointed in 1886 to inquire into the conditions of labour; and witness after witness advocated in some cases an extension of the authority of the *conseils de prud'hommes* to questions connected with the future rates of wages, in others the establishment by their side of councils of conciliation, or courts of arbitration, after the "English" pattern. It is a curious and instructive circumstance that these Continental *conseils* should undoubtedly have suggested the model for the councils of conciliation authorised in England by Lord St. Leonard's Act of 1867,[2] but never, so far as I am

[1] In 1890.   [2] 30 & 31 Vict. cap. 105.

aware, established in any district, and that the copy should follow the pattern so closely as to be expressly precluded from any determination of the future rate of wages; and that a witness before the recent Belgium Commission should be reported as explaining what is done in England by means of conciliation and arbitration to avoid the strikes, which have occasioned such injury and annoyance in his own country.

Nor is the state of affairs materially different in France. In the *Times* of the 20th March, 1890, a summary was given of a report on the French *conseils de prud'hommes*, sent from the British Embassy at Paris to the Foreign Office; and in that report it was stated expressly that the *conseils de prud'hommes* had no voice in the settlement of strikes, as they were not concerned with the fairness, or unfairness, of wages. M. Lockroy, it was stated, had recently submitted two Bills to the French Chamber of Deputies—not merely one for extending the jurisdiction of the hundred and thirty-six existing *conseils* from the trades, to which at present they alone applied—the trades engaged in the transformation of materials—to all trades and manual labour generally, and for simplifying their procedure, but also another Bill for the constitution of boards of arbitration on the English model. The latter Bill, the report affirmed, had been introduced expressly on the ground that it was not thought possible to make the *conseils de prud'hommes* deal with strikes. M. Victor Turquan, in a paper on "Strikes in France since 1874," published in the Journal of the Statistical Society of Paris in September, 1889, gave a total of 804 strikes reported during the years 1874-85 by the préfets to the Minister of Commerce and Industry. The Continental *conseils de prud' hommes*, then, do not as a matter of actual fact prevent, nor are they, it would seem, intended to prevent, the occurrence of disputes on that industrial question, which of all others is the most likely to occasion contention—the question of the settlement of wages for the future—and the Continental workman is undoubtedly ceasing to deserve in the matter of strikes the epithet of "inert" applied to some members of his class by an American consul in 1887.

This prominence, which attaches at the present time to the question of industrial disputes, has advantages and drawbacks. It has undoubtedly the great advantage of leading men to seek for some practicable means of preventing, or at least of adjusting, such disputes. At a time, when the gravity of the question is brought home to the public mind by some conspicuous example, the arguments in favour of the peaceful settlement of industrial quarrels acquire additional weight, and men are more inclined to accord an experimental trial to plans and proposals, which promise success. The scheme of the London Chamber of Commerce for the constitution of a "permanent body," under the name of the "London Conciliation Board," since carried into effect, might, it is true, have been propounded in the ordinary course of affairs, had no strike occurred among the dock labourers of the Port of London; but it is only prophesying after the event to say that the strike furnished the occasion for the scheme, if it did not suggest it. The dispute, again, between the colliers and colliery owners in the spring of the year,[1] which at one time threatened to issue in a general strike, and was only adjusted when work had been actually suspended, promised to leave behind an "arrangement" of some systematic and permanent character for the settlement of wages questions.[2]

[1] 1890.

[2] As the consequence of a later dispute, in 1893, this arrangement has, to some extent at least, been realised.

POSITION OF INDUSTRIAL CONCILIATION 43

And it is scarcely fanciful to say that such a desirable consequence might be ascribed in some measure to the very magnitude of the combinations of masters and men on either side, and in some measure also to the pressure of public opinion, seriously alarmed by the imminent prospect of a coal famine in London.

Once more, if we look abroad, we can hardly fail to recognise that the proposals to establish courts of arbitration after the English pattern in France and in Belgium would not have been urged so pressingly, had it not been for the outbreak of labour troubles in both countries;[1] and that the presence of such veterans in conciliation and arbitration as Mr. David Dale, of Darlington, and Mr. Thomas Burt, of Northumberland, at the International Labour Conference at Berlin—a conference which, as we saw, might be said in some measure to owe its origination to the miners' strike in Westphalia—must have resulted in acquainting Germans with the methods of wage-arrangement pursued in the iron and coal trades of the North of England.[2]

Indeed, it is only at times like this that the general public becomes aware of what has, as a matter of actual fact, been

[1] Especially in the coal mining industry of St. Étienne, in France, in August, 1888, and in Belgium in the latter months of the same year. With regard to Belgium, Mr. Burnett remarked (p. 103) in his report to the Board of Trade on the Strikes and Lock-outs of 1888, that "experience has shown that the practice of striking is highly contagious"; and described the disturbances in the coal field in 1888 as taking the form of a "strike epidemic." "Violence and bloodshed," he observed (p. 104), "seem concomitants of most Continental strikes."

[2] After the strikes in Westphalia tribunals of arbitration were established in the State mines in obedience to the commands of the Emperor, and the resolutions of the Labour Conference comprised a declaration in favour of conciliation and arbitration. Mr. Dale is reported to have given an account to the conference of the work accomplished in this direction in England.

done in the past to prevent or adjust industrial disputes. It is only at such a time that it is possible to awaken effective interest in the important chapter of industrial history, which contains the record of the Board of Conciliation and Arbitration in the Manufactured Iron Trade of the North of England. In my former paper I arranged, for purposes of convenience, the methods of adjusting industrial quarrels in three rough stages, the first of which I distinguished as irregular negotiations between employers and employed, the second as the establishment of a regular board of conciliation and arbitration, and the third as the institution of a sliding scale. As an illustration of the second of these stages I selected the Board of Conciliation and Arbitration in the Manufactured Iron Trade of the North of England, and attempted to give a history of the constitution and working of that board. Were I to endeavour to bring my history down to date, I do not know that I should have to add much to my former account beyond the fact that the board was still in existence, and still successful.[1] But I must enforce the contention that this board may fairly be regarded as a crucial instance of the feasibility of the peaceful adjustment of industrial disputes. I do not believe that it would be possible to discover any trade, in which the difficulties of establishing, and maintaining, such a board could be more serious than they appear to have been in the manufactured iron trade. Nor do I think that it would be easy to find any other industry,

[1] At the annual meeting of the board in 1888, when it was entering upon the twentieth year of its existence, the President declared that he "could not tell the blessing the board had conferred on the employers and operatives of the North of England."

The title of the board is now the Board of Conciliation and Arbitration for the Manufactured Iron *and Steel* Trade of the North of England.

in which a board of conciliation and arbitration had been attended by such indisputable success.

And so I venture to regard this board as supplying an example of what Bacon called an *instantia crucis*.[1] What has as a matter of fact been done here can be done elsewhere; and the solid results, which have been attained in this industry, are worth making an attempt to attain in others. In studying the record of this board we are not indulging in fanciful speculation, or *à priori* deduction, but we are endeavouring to gather the lessons of actual experience.

Let me then, referring to my previous paper for detailed evidence,[2] briefly review the difficulties, which have confronted the Board of Conciliation and Arbitration in the Manufactured Iron Trade of the North of England; and let me adduce as proof of the success, with which it has overcome those difficulties, the fact of its continuous existence for a period of more than twenty years.[3] What then, let me ask, are the chief conditions, which would be likely to conduce to the establishment and effective working of such a board? In the first place the trade itself must not be liable to sudden and frequent fluctuations; for, if prices rise, the men will want an advance of wages, and, if prices fall, the masters will insist on a reduction; and the more often these changes in prices occur, and the wider the range over which they extend during any one period, the more likely are the existence of irritation and friction, and the occurrence of actual conflict, between masters and men. The second condition of the peaceful settlement of industrial

---

[1] The metaphor seems to be derived from a sign-post, standing at the point where two or more roads diverge, and indicating the direction to be taken by the traveller.

[2] This is contained in chapter iii. of *Industrial Peace*.

[3] Now (1896) twenty-seven years.

disputes may be said to consist in a friendly disposition of employers and employed towards one another; and these amicable relations are, *cæteris paribus*, more likely to arise when masters and men are personally known to one another. The third and final condition is that the men should be educated and intelligent.

But of these three conditions not one was to be found in the manufactured iron trade of the North of England. The iron industry was especially subject to violent fluctuation; its development in the Cleveland district had been marked by a rapidity almost fabulous, and the population of the town of Middlesbrough had increased, in a brief period of time, to a surprising extent, owing to immigration of the most various classes of workers, including several Irishmen, from other districts; and, thirdly and lastly, the character of the work was such as to preclude the possibility of intellectual self-culture among the workmen. "Puddlers as a class," said one of their number, were "not very intelligent, and, if they were very intelligent, they would not be puddlers."

Such, then, are the adverse conditions—the effect of which was intensified by the occurrence of a bitter and prolonged dispute on the eve of the formation of the board—which have attended conciliation and arbitration in the manufactured iron trade of the North of England; and I ask whether the fact that the board of conciliation and arbitration established in that trade in 1869 is still in existence, and has during the interval successfully adjusted upwards of 900 disputes, is not sufficient to prove the feasibility, and to illustrate the advantage, of the systematic peaceful settlement of industrial quarrels. What has been accomplished here can be accomplished elsewhere; and the study of the particular mechanism adopted in this industry is likely to conduce to its successful application to other trades. One advantage, which attaches to the prominence of the question of industrial disputes, is that an opportunity is offered for drawing attention to such an instructive chapter of industrial history as that connected with the Board of Conciliation and Arbitration in the Manufactured Iron Trade of the North of England.

A third advantage may be said to follow from the prominence of the question. Not only are men more disposed to give a trial to plans, which promise to be successful; not only are they inclined to lend a more attentive hearing to the account of experiments, which have, as a matter of actual fact, been attended by success: but, by dint of the very abundance of discussion on the subject, and of the study of previous experiments, they are more likely at this than at other times to apprehend some elementary principles.

It has been remarked that the greatest discovery of modern politics is the system of representative government. It is scarcely an exaggeration to say that the cardinal condition of industrial conciliation consists in the application to industrial affairs of the principle of representation. It is obvious that successful negotiation between employers and employed can only be conducted, if there are a few representatives on either side; and it is obvious also that an agreement attained by such negotiation will only be observed, if the negotiators are considered by the general body of masters and men to be really representative. And thus the keystone of the matter is found in representation; and, if it be adequate, a guarantee is offered for the success of negotiation; but, if it be defective or non-existent, the chance of successful negotiation is certainly lessened, if it is not entirely removed.

It matters not what is the particular form of conciliation adopted. If there are irregular negotiations between masters and men, the negotiators should be true representatives. They should be regarded as such, and armed with full authority to act in that character. If there is a board or committee of conciliation, the masters and men sitting on this board, and engaged in full and frank discussion, must be limited in number, and enjoy the confidence of those whom they represent. If there is a reference of the matter to arbitration, the arbitrator's award is not likely to be observed, unless the masters and men feel that their case has been fully set before him by their chosen advocates. If there is a sliding scale regulating wages according to changes in prices, or some other factor, the basis of the scale must have been settled by conciliation or arbitration; and the decision of the committee of conciliation, equally with the award of the arbitrator, must find its ultimate sanction in the character of the representation of masters and men. If some fresh method, not yet perhaps discovered, be introduced for the peaceful settlement of industrial disputes, it is impossible to conceive that it will be able to dispense with the necessity for effective representation.

But then the question arises: How is effective representation to be secured? So far as the employers are concerned, they are comparatively few in number, and the difficulty may therefore be said to lie more on the side of the men. Even there, however, the answer to the question is not far to seek. A trade union supplies the readiest and most effective means of securing the representation of the men, and it is at present, at any rate, the only effective means readily available. The authority of the leaders of an union, although it rests in many cases on a more

POSITION OF INDUSTRIAL CONCILIATION 49

democratic foundation than is sometimes supposed, and although, as we shall see later, it is on occasions disputed, is yet more likely than any other authority to secure the adherence of the general body of the men to the decision of a board of conciliation, to the award of an arbitrator, to the basis of a sliding scale. Mr. Burnett, in his report to the Board of Trade on the Strikes and Lock-outs of 1888, after noticing[1] the "considerable" extension "during the last twenty years of the methods of settling disputes by arbitration and conciliation," proceeded to add that "these methods of arranging difficulties have only been made possible by organisation of the forces on both sides, and have, as it were, been gradually evolved from the general progress of the combination movement."[2] The organised representation, then, of the men by a trade union is an elementary condition of the problem, and it is gradually winning its way to general recognition.

There are few more striking changes than that which has passed over the tone and temper of public opinion on the position and action of trade unions; and the more favourable light, in which these bodies are now regarded by the general public, has been accompanied by an alteration in their own character. There are, of course, exceptions. There are still unions, generally perhaps of more recent formation and of smaller numbers, where violence of language is more conspicuous than moderation, and a desire for conflict is more often evinced than a wish for

[1] Page 17.
[2] In the *Newcastle Daily Chronicle* of the 1st January, 1887, it was stated, with reference to the manufactured iron trade of the North of England, that the fact that many of the iron workers were not unionmen made it more difficult to deal with them: and further organisation was urged on the ground that otherwise the board of conciliation and arbitration would become a "farce." Cf. *infra*, Essay vi.

peaceful negotiation. And there are still individuals and classes of men, who make no secret of their relentless, indiscriminating hostility to trade unions. But the general tone and temper of public opinion, and the general character of trade unions themselves, have undergone change. There is, on the whole, a greater belief in the capacity of legitimate organisation to ensure the peaceful and effective settlement of industrial disputes; and there is a stronger disposition on the part of the organisation itself to have recourse to negotiation, sometimes irregular and casual, sometimes of a regular and permanent character, in preference to engaging in actual conflict.

Mr. Burnett, in the report to which we have previously alluded, expressed an opinion[1] that "so far as any conclusion can be arrived at"—and, he added, "no absolutely definite judgment is possible"—"strikes are somewhat less frequent than they were from ten to twenty years ago, and are more readily brought to a conclusion"—a "result," which "has been largely due to the more general adoption of systems of reference to arbitration, of sliding scales," and of "mutual conciliation." "Within the last quarter of a century," he remarked,[2] "a strong body of opinion has been growing up that these trade battles are neither necessary nor inevitable"; and, summarising[3] the "suggestions," which had been made by employers in answer to an inquiry addressed to them with regard to the "best means of preventing or settling disputes," he said that the "general tendency of these suggestions is in the direction of peaceful modes of settlement, and a much less combative spirit is now manifested than used to prevail"; while the answers of the unions to the same question showed that on this point they "are much more in harmony

[1] Page 36.   [2] Page 3.   [3] Page 41.

with employers than might have been anticipated." "In fact, the executive committees of all the chief unions are to a very large extent hostile to strikes, and exercise a restraining influence," and "of recent years the control of the central executives over strike movements has been gradually becoming more rigorous." "Many" unions "make a rule that in all cases where the initiative is taken by the men, no strike can be entered upon except by a certain fixed proportionate vote of the whole organisation taken under the ballot."[1]

These quotations from Mr. Burnett's report supply a fair illustration of the change, which is passing over the character of trade unions, and the opinion of the general public. They show that while, on the one hand, trade unions undoubtedly furnish the most available means for effective representation of the men, on the other they are more disposed themselves, and are more likely to meet with the support of a friendly public opinion in giving practical effect to their inclination, to substitute peaceful negotiation for battle to the death. Mr. Bellamy, in his popular novel, *Looking Backward*, regarded[2] the formation of "great labour organisations" on the one side as necessarily issuing in strikes against the "big corporations" on the other; but it is possible to conceive that the greater organisation may really prove the condition for more systematic and effective peaceful negotiation.

If the strike of the dock labourers in London in 1889 be regarded from this point of view, it may assume a different guise from that which it seemed to some spectators to present. The strike undoubtedly showed that it was possible for unskilled labourers to form, and maintain, an organisation; and this was a result, which before the strike

[1] Page 7.   [2] Page 40.

had hardly seemed to be possible. But, if organisation prove to be feasible, not merely during the continuance of a struggle, but after the excitement is past, it is also possible that, even where unskilled labourers are concerned, permanent boards of conciliation may be successfully established. That appears to be the characteristic of the strike, which is most pregnant with consequence, and to distinguish it in an especial measure from previous disputes.

It was no new thing in industrial quarrels for public sympathy to be aroused; and there are few, if there are any, contests where public opinion is not a factor to be considered in favour of the one side or of the other.[1] Nor was it a new thing in industrial history that outsiders should intervene; and, when it is urged that in the dock strike this intervention assumed the shape of advocacy rather than impartial arbitration, it must in fairness be remembered that it is an elementary condition of negotiation that the representatives of the one side should be willing to meet the representatives of the other, and that the dock directors are reported[2] to have stated on one occasion that they declined to meet any leaders of the men but those in their own employment—a distinction which, if generally urged, would prevent that negotiation between employers and trade union officials, which is the basis of amicable arrangement in other industries.

But it was a new thing in the history of industry that unskilled labour should receive such support from skilled labour; and it was a new thing that it should be able so effectually to combine. So new a thing indeed was it that

---

[1] This is shown in more than one instance included in the list of historical English strikes contained in Mr. Burnett's report, pp. 21-9.

[2] See *The Story of the Dockers' Strike*, by H. Llewellyn Smith and Vaughan Nash, p. 126.

we might have expected much more violence of speech, if not of action, and much greater irritation on either side, than seem to have been the case. The injudicious language of the Chairman of the Dock Directors, and the Strike Committee's manifesto for a general suspension of work in London, might, I suspect, be easily paralleled by incidents in the early history of the organisation of skilled labourers.[1] The infancy of an union may be characterised by excesses, of which it may be ashamed when it reaches maturity; but, although this possibility should steadily be kept in mind when we are considering recent movements among unskilled labourers, it does not vitiate the conclusion that organisation is a necessary preliminary to the peaceful settlement of industrial disputes.

The prominence, then, which attaches to the subject of industrial disputes, involves the advantages we have noticed. It disposes men to seek for some practicable means of peaceful arrangement; it attracts attention to the successful experiments of the past; it impresses on the public mind some of the elementary conditions of the problem. For these reasons we might conclude—and the conclusion would undoubtedly be, in a large measure, correct—that the position of industrial conciliation was advantageous, and its prospects encouraging. But we must not neglect to notice considerations, which bear on the other side; for disadvantages, as well as advantages, attach to the prominence of the subject.

It is true that a general interest in the matter is aroused, and attention given to previous experiments; but that interest sometimes leads to hasty conclusions, and to a hurried examination of detail. The experiments of the past are studied indeed; but they are studied in their broad

---

[1] See the table in Mr. Burnett's report referred to above.

outlines, and men are too impatient for action to devote much time to preliminary reflection. They are inclined to think that what has been applied with success to one industry can be immediately adopted in another, without consideration of the differences of detail, which more prolonged and exhaustive examination might show that it was expedient to make. They are prone to rest content with the fact of success, without inquiring into the factors which have contributed to produce it. And thus they incur a risk of failure, which they might have avoided, had the times been less excited, and the interest in the subject less general—had they, in fact, been able to spend some hours in patient study and calm reflection.

It is true, again, that at such a time the tone and temper of employers and employed, and of the public generally, are, in some respects, such as to favour the trial of methods of industrial conciliation. There is undoubtedly a serious desire that the methods should meet with success, and that very fact conduces to the attainment of the result desired; for the tone and temper of masters and men in such matters are beyond all comparison more important than the particular character or details of the form of conciliation adopted. But, on the other hand, men are inclined to entertain extravagant expectations of the results to be achieved, and to exhibit corresponding disappointment, if their hopes are not fully realised. They forget that the success of all such arrangements depends, to a large extent, on the merits or demerits of the system adopted, but, to a far greater extent, on the changeable disposition of the human agents, who bring it into operation. There is a moral factor in the problem, which you cannot eliminate; there is the element of human nature, with which you must reckon. The most admirable mechanism that human ingenuity can devise for the settlement of industrial quarrels can never escape the liability to break down on occasions, under the strain put by the incalculable caprices of human nature.[1]

But the moral is, not to abandon the mechanism in despair, but to improve and amend it, and to keep within reasonable bounds the hopes based upon it. We must remember that there may be occasions when the tone and the temper of employers and employed are such that they will be too impatient to wait for the results, which would, in due time, follow the automatic operation of a sliding scale. They desire, as the case may be, an immediate advance or reduction of wages; and they know that, in the nature of things, an interval of time must elapse under the scale between the changes in prices and the consequent changes in wages. Or they hold that the basis of the scale is unfair, and the conditions of trade have altered so much, that an arrangement grounded on a previous state of affairs is inapplicable to the present; and here, once more, they know that, in the nature of things, a scale can be constructed with a capacity of adaptation only to changes of a limited extent, and the arrangement of a fresh basis cannot be effected without delay. Or, again, they are too impatient to wait for the reference of the matter in dispute to an arbitrator, or too convinced of the righteousness of their own cause, and the incurable defects of their opponents' contentions, to be ready to submit to the decision of a third and neutral person, or to believe in his neutrality, if he decides adversely. Or, once more, they may be too suspicious of one another to be willing to meet for full and frank discussion across a table, or, if they are ready to meet, on occasions too estranged to

[1] See the previous Essay.

arrive at any agreement. Or, lastly, it may not be possible to induce them to enter even into irregular negotiations. All these contingencies may arise to hinder the working of the most perfect mechanism of industrial conciliation, and the failure to recognise them leads at once to extravagant hope and irrational despair.

In my former paper I selected, as an illustration of what I ventured to distinguish as the third and most advanced stage of industrial conciliation, the sliding scales existing in the coal and iron mining industries, and I devoted special attention to those in operation in the coal trades of Durham and Northumberland. At the time it seemed as if the peaceful settlement of industrial quarrels had been finally substituted in the latter county for the barbarous antiquated methods of strikes and lock-outs. It appeared as if there, at any rate, industrial peace was established on a firm basis, and the third and most advanced stage [1] of conciliation had been permanently attained, and had approved itself to masters and men. For upwards of ten years there had been no general strike in the Northumberland coal trade, and since 1873 a joint committee of masters and men had successfully adjusted more than 3000 local disputes affecting particular mines.

During the interval, however, which elapsed between the preparation and the reading of my paper, the employers gave notice of an intention to terminate the sliding scale at the end of the year, and to claim a reduction of 15 per cent. in wages. With the close of the year, accordingly, the sliding scale, which had been originally established in

[1] With regard to this trade, Mr. Burnett remarks in his report (p. 18) that "organisation among the men has led on occasions of difference to negotiation, negotiation has led to conciliation, conciliation has led to arbitration, and arbitration to the formation of a sliding scale which has almost automatically adjusted wages."

1879, and revised in 1883, came to an end. The men at once held a meeting, and appointed a committee to negotiate with the employers. Their object, as they expressed it, was to secure the advantages of arbitration, and avoid the delay and expense usually entailed; but they did not entrust the committee with full, but only with limited, powers of negotiation. They might make certain concessions to the masters; but any arrangement, which exceeded that limit, was to be referred to the different lodges for confirmation or rejection. The conference between the representatives of the masters and men was held with little delay, and the question of dispute was brought within such a narrow compass that the masters asked for a reduction of $12\frac{1}{2}$ per cent., and the men proposed a reduction of 10; and the proceedings, according to a newspaper report, were characterised by an entire absence of "acerbity." The representatives of the men agreed to submit to their constituents the question of the acceptance or rejection of the masters' terms; but a meeting of delegates, which was immediately held, determined on a strike by a large majority; and, when ballot papers had been issued to the different lodges, the voting showed that the requisite majority of two-thirds were in favour of a strike. Accordingly it commenced, and continued until the end of May, 1887, when the masters' terms were accepted by the men.

More than once during the intervening period proposals of a conciliatory nature were submitted to the votes of the men, but without success. At the beginning of February, on the instance of Mr. John Morley, a proposal was made, the general aim of which was the resumption, on a more likely basis, of negotiations with the masters, but it was rejected by more than the necessary two-thirds majority. In the middle of March a proposal for submitting the question to arbitration, which seemed to the executive committee of the union, from the reports that had reached them from several collieries, to be likely to meet with a favourable response, was negatived by a large majority. In the middle of the following month a clear majority was still in favour of continuing the strike; and it was not until the beginning of May that the men were willing to submit the matter to arbitration—a course, which the masters declined to entertain—and only in the third week of the month did a committee receive full powers to re-open negotiations and effect a settlement.

The strike was closed by the acceptance of the masters' terms; a reduction of $12\frac{1}{2}$ per cent. in wages was made, and a new sliding scale established, with the standard price of 4s. 7d. instead of the old price of 4s. 8d. In November, however, at a meeting of the delegates of the men, a resolution was passed to terminate the new scale at the end of the year; and, between that date and the end of 1889, five advances of wages, amounting altogether to some 37 per cent., were obtained by means of negotiations between the representatives of the workmen and the general body of the owners; but no arrangement of a more permanent character, such as a sliding scale, was re-established.

The account given would at first sight appear very discouraging. Just as the history of the Board of Conciliation and Arbitration in the Manufactured Iron Trade of the North of England might seem to show the possibility of overcoming any difficulties that can well be conceived, so the history of the abandonment of the sliding scale in the Northumberland coal trade would appear to indicate the possibility of failure at the very moment when success seemed fully assured. If the one illustrated the manner in which progress may be made, the other might exemplify the ease with which the results of progress might be lost. And it is useless, or mischievous, to refuse to recognise the fact. There is much that is discouraging in the circumstances we have briefly reviewed.

They seem to show, in the first place, that a sliding scale may occasion dissatisfaction at periods of rapid and extensive fluctuations in prices. For, while the close of the strike was followed by the establishment of a new scale, that scale was terminated at the earliest opportunity; and in November, 1888, when the question of the re-introduction of the system was raised, the men objected to entertain the proposal for the present.[1] Mr. Ralph Young, of the Northumberland Miners' Mutual Confident Association, has furnished me with an account of the Northumberland coal trade from the determination of the 1887 scale until December, 1889. He expresses the opinion that, if the scale, which was terminated in 1886, had continued in force, it would "have been better for both employers and men"; but he thinks that the account, which he gives, indicates that the scale would not have "worked quickly enough." He supplies a list of the dates and amounts of the successive advances in wages since the termination of the 1887 scale, with the average prices realised at the time. The list runs as follows:—

Date.	Average Price.	Advance.
November, 1888	4s. 4·82d.	5 per cent.
February, 1889	4s. 9·67d.	7½ ,,
June, 1889	5s. 4·09d.	7 ,,
(2 per cent. not to be paid till a month after).		
September, 1889	5s. 7·34d.	3 per cent.
December, 1889	5s. 9d. to 5s. 10d.	10 ,,

[1] No scale has since been introduced, but a Conciliation Board was formed for the arrangement of general wages.

For the three months ending November, 1886, immediately previous to the abandonment of the 1883 scale, the average realised price was, he states, 4s. 6·73d. For the three months ending February, 1888, it was 4s. 3·40d.; for the three months ending May, 4s. 3·21d.; for the three months ending August, 4s. 4·60d.; for the three months ending November, 4s. 4·82d., as above. The fall in price thus indicated was, he thinks, very probably "caused by the attempt to regain the trade lost through the strike," and on that assumption the reduction in wages, which was effected, and did not exceed 3d. or 3½d. per ton, meant that the employers "lost just about as much in price as they gained from the reduction in wages." Had therefore "no change taken place in prices or wages," they "would have been in the same position from the end of 1886 to February, 1889, as they found themselves with the loss in price equal to what they gained from wages." "In February, 1889," he proceeds to observe, "the amount taken from wages in May, 1887, was restored to the workmen. The scale would have given the same. In June, 5 per cent. more was given when the price was 5s. 4d.; the scale would have given exactly the same amount. In July, 2 per cent. more was given, and in September another 3 per cent., when the price was 5s. 7·34d. Had the scale been in operation, only 1¼ per cent. of this last 3 per cent. would have been due; and, if the price at the end of December was, say, only 5s. 9½d., as I have no doubt it was, the further advance of 10 per cent. given, to commence on the 29th December, exceeds by 9½ per cent. the amount the scale would have given." This "excess" is, he argues, partly due to the fact that the "strike drove a large number of workmen out of the county into the neighbouring county, Durham, where the work is much easier, and the wages were 2*d.* a day higher than in Northumberland after the reduction," and the "employers were anxious to give whatever they fairly could to induce those men to return." But the excess was also due to the fact that the "scale would not have worked quickly enough." It is "almost certain," he believes, "that the average price realised at the moment when the last 10 per cent. given came into force, viz., the 29th December, would have been quite equal to what it would have been required to be under the late scale for it to give the same advance." But the "impatience of the men would not allow a scale to run for any length of time in a state of trade like that we are having just now, unless means are devised for obtaining as nearly as possible the average selling price up to date."

This quotation from Mr. Young's letter seems to indicate very forcibly the chief point in which a scale may be liable to fail. It shows not only that the disposition and expectation of masters and men may be such as to lead them to abandon an arrangement, from which they would ultimately have derived more benefit than that which they have secured at greater cost, but also that in seasons of rapid fluctuation of trade, even if the basis of a scale be acknowledged as fair, the interval between the changes in prices, and the consequent changes in wages, may seem too long for natural impatience to wait. In the end, no doubt, the scale would work equitably for both masters and men; but, for the present, it seems to favour unduly the one side or the other, and it requires a mental effort, and an act of imaginative foresight, to recognise the ultimate, and not merely the immediate, effects. The septennial average of the Tithe Commutation Act presents an instructive parallel. At a time of agricultural depression the tithe-payer finds it hard to believe that he is not unfairly treated, while the tithe-owner may experience the very same feelings at a time of reviving prosperity. The chief feature, in fact, of the brief history of sliding scales has been a desire to reduce the interval between the changes in prices and the consequent changes in wages to as small a compass as possible; but some such interval there must be, and in this necessity we may perhaps discover some explanation of the fact that in the coal trade, during the past few years,[1] when it is scarcely extravagant to say that prices advanced by leaps and by bounds, sliding scales fell into disrepute.

The recent history of the Northumberland coal trade is more discouraging on another account. It shows, in a significant manner, that when we have secured effective representation of the men, through the organisation of a trade union, it is possible that the counsel of the leaders may be rejected by their constituents. There can be little, if any, doubt that the leaders were averse to the strike of 1887; and there can also be little, if any, doubt that considerable irritation was felt, and evinced, regarding their attitude by many of the men themselves. On one occasion, in fact, during the strike the officials of the union offered to resign their position; and, although the offer was declined, indications of continued resentment were manifest. Not until the very close of the strike were the representatives of the men invested with full powers of negotiation; and some time after it was over the miners refused to grant a hearing, at their Gala Meeting, to one of their number, who was known to have advocated arbitration at an early stage of the dispute. The question of continuing the payment of the salaries

[1] Ending with 1890.

POSITION OF INDUSTRIAL CONCILIATION 63

of Messrs. Burt and Fenwick, as members of Parliament, was submitted, in August, 1887, to the votes of the different lodges, and decided in the negative; and, although the decision was rescinded at the annual meeting of delegates in the following December, the question was only determined in the affirmative by a majority of 300 votes in the April of the succeeding year.

Such, then, are the discouraging features of the recent history of the Northumberland coal trade. One or two considerations of importance should be stated on the other side. In the first place, at the conclusion of the strike, a local newspaper remarked[1] that no "extravagance" or "violence" had been manifest throughout it. There had even been no attempt on the side of the owners to evict the men from the houses, in some instances provided as part of their wages. In the second place, throughout the struggle the representatives of either side were ready to meet one another for purposes of negotiation; and the declaration of the strike itself was formally submitted, in an open and regular manner, to the decision of the general body of the men, and, according to the rules of the union, could only be determined by a two-thirds majority. In the third place, although the system of the sliding scale fell into disuse, yet the five successive advances in wages between 1887 and the end of 1889 were obtained as the result of open negotiation between masters and men, the Joint Committee continued in existence for the adjustment of local disputes, and the Northumberland miners abstained from taking part in recent coal strikes.[2] These considerations

[1] See *Newcastle Daily Chronicle*, 25th May, 1887.
[2] Subsequently more permanent provision was made in the trade for the peaceful decision of questions of a general advance or reduction of wages by the formation of a Conciliation Board.

seem to show that the work of previous years was not thrown away, and that the disuse of the advanced form of the sliding scale did not carry with it the entire rejection of the methods, and total abandonment of the spirit, of industrial conciliation.

Thus we are led to consider the real nature of the claim which may properly be advanced in its behalf. It cannot claim to be a panacea. It cannot pretend to remove occasion for strife. It cannot maintain that, by its adoption, a complete and radical change is effected in human nature. It can merely put itself forward as an advantageous and reasonable alternative to strikes and lockouts, which may commend itself to sensible men as a practicable means of adjusting disputed questions, with tolerable assurance of success under fairly ordinary circumstances. It must allow that it is liable to failure; it must admit that it has, on occasions, failed. But in that it may contend that it is only subject to conditions, which attach to all human schemes and proposals; and that a careful analysis might reveal liability to failure in the more advanced systems, as they seem, of profit-sharing or co-operative production.[1]

It can point to instances where it has succeeded in the face of serious difficulties, and to the undoubted advantages, which have followed its successful adoption. It can maintain that men are more likely to be conciliatory when they have met one another—in irregular negotiations, it may be—than when they have not; that the existence of a regular board of conciliation, or court of arbitration, establishes a presumption in favour of amicable arrangement; that at such a board either side may learn to recognise the merits, and appreciate the difficulties, of the

[1] Cf. the following Essay.

POSITION OF INDUSTRIAL CONCILIATION 65

other, and at such a court to furnish arguments, and not merely force, in support of its case, and to admit that it may itself be possibly biassed in judgment; and that the automatic mechanism of a sliding scale tends, where it is feasible, to lessen the frequency of occasions for dispute. These are considerable advantages, and it is worth running the risk of failure in an attempt to secure them.

Failure, it is true, disheartens; and progress sometimes seems to be terribly slow. But it is better to advance by gradual stages, than by a sudden and extensive change to incur the risk, if not to ensure the certainty, of reaction. Of recent years there has been progress in the matter of industrial conciliation; and, if I have laid stress on some discouraging circumstances, I have done so because I am sensible of the great importance of forming a clear idea of what we may, and of what we must not, expect. We may expect that industrial conciliation will effect an improvement in the relations of employers and employed; we must not expect that it will cause a radical change in human nature. The history of the manufactured iron trade of the North of England shows us what we may, the recent history of the Northumberland coal trade what we must not, expect. In the enthusiasm, which the former may arouse, we should not ignore the moderating reflections suggested by the latter; in the despondency, which the latter may awaken, we ought not to overlook the encouragement afforded by the former:—

> " For some cry 'Quick,' and some cry 'Slow,'
> But, while the hills remain,
> Up hill 'Too-slow' will need the whip,
> Down hill 'Too-quick' the chain."

IV.

PROFIT-SHARING AND CO-OPERATIVE PRODUCTION.[1]

THAT the gift of successful prophecy is rare, but the temptation to predict the future irresistible, has more than once been proved true in the history of economic study. In this, as in other departments of thought, it would be an easy and superfluous task to compile a lengthy catalogue of unfulfilled predictions. The changing circumstances of human life, and the continual enlargement of the boundaries of knowledge, render such a result inevitable; and it furnishes as much ground for encouragement as it may at first sight suggest reasons for disappointment.

In a chapter[2] of his *Political Economy* Mill discusses the "probable future of the labouring classes." "Hitherto," he writes, "there has been no alternative for those who lived by their labour, but that of labouring either each for himself alone, or for a master. But," he proceeds, "the civilising and improving influences of association, and the

---

[1] Published in the *Economic Journal* for September, 1892. Mr. Benjamin Jones, in a subsequent number of the *Journal*, criticised the interpretation here given to the term *Co-operative Production;* but it is submitted that the interpretation accords with common economic usage. (*Vide* the following Essay.)

[2] Book iv. chap. vii.

efficiency and economy of production on a large scale, may be obtained without dividing the producers into two parties with hostile interests and feelings, the many, who do the work, being mere servants under the command of the one who supplies the funds, and having no interest of their own in the enterprise except to earn their wages with as little labour as possible. The speculations and discussions of the last fifty years, and the events of the last twenty, are abundantly conclusive on this point. If the improvement, which even triumphant military despotism has only retarded, not stopped, shall continue its course, there can be little doubt that the *status* of hired labourers will gradually tend to confine itself to the description of workpeople, whose low moral qualities render them unfit for anything more independent; and that the relation of masters and work-people will be gradually superseded by partnership in one of two forms : in some cases, association of the labourers with the capitalist; in others, and perhaps finally in all, association of labourers among themselves."

And then, after narrating the history of various examples, which may almost be said to be "classical," of the first form of partnership, Mill adds these emphatic words : " The form of association, however, which, if mankind continue to improve, must be expected in the end to predominate, is not that which can exist between a capitalist as chief, and work-people without a voice in the management, but the association of labourers themselves on terms of equality, collectively owning the capital with which they carry on their operations, and working under managers elected and removable by themselves."

These confident anticipations represent the deliberate judgment of a philosophic thinker, who was unquestionably the most eminent economist of his time, and occupies a position second to few among English writers of all periods on economic subjects. Nor are they merely the emphatic expression of an individual belief: they are also a faithful reflection of opinions which were generally current. The support given by the Christian Socialists, among others, to the co-operative movement, undoubtedly proceeded on the belief that a complete regeneration of human society, or, at least, an entire transformation of the industrial system, might be accomplished by means of the movement, and was, as a matter of fact, intended. The murmurings of disappointment, which have made themselves heard in the utterances of such veteran co-operators as Judge Hughes, would furnish sufficient evidence of the larger aims of these early supporters of the movement, were not such evidence discoverable in the hopes and feelings recorded in contemporary literature. These zealous enthusiasts were by no means disposed to rest content with co-operative distribution, as the supply of articles of consumption through the agency of the co-operative retail stores and Wholesale Society is commonly termed; but they confidently looked forward to the successful and general establishment of the system usually distinguished as co-operative production — the system, which Mill intended by his second form of association. In his remarks he was giving formal expression to a feeling, which was in the air; and it is worth while to dwell on the point, because a hurried perusal of some portions of a recent essay on the co-operative movement might allow the reader to carry away an erroneous view. Mrs. Sidney Webb, in her remarkable and suggestive examination of the movement,[1] has succeeded in showing that the intention of Robert Owen, its founder, admits of a different interpretation from

[1] *The Co-operative Movement in Great Britain.*

that which has often been given to it; but, whatever may have been the intention of Owen himself and of his associates, the belief of the Christian Socialists, as Mrs. Webb allows, seems to have been such as we have attempted to indicate, and it is reflected in the passage we have quoted from Mill.

There were many grounds, on which such a creed would appeal to the sympathies of social reformers. Cairnes,[1] writing some years later, could discern no hope of economic salvation for the working classes, unless they could raise themselves from the position of wage-earners to that of owners of capital. Forming, no doubt, a narrow and unduly limited conception of the actual facts of the case, and content with an inadequate analysis of what was implied in co-operative production, he thought that, with a law of diminishing returns governing the production of the chief objects of the labourer's expenditure, and with little hope of any effectual check to the increase of population, he was doomed to see his condition deteriorate unless he could bring profits to reinforce wages. Co-operation, in the sense of co-operative production, offered a means of escape from this unhappy position, and as such he welcomed it. Other writers and thinkers, before and after Cairnes, without following the same chain of reasoning, so far acquiesced in his conclusion that they conceived of co-operative production as offering to the wage-earner secure independence in exchange for precarious and degrading dependence, and as substituting unbroken harmony for continued disturbance of the industrial peace. And these economic and moral considerations were assisted by the plausible logic of a development from the status of hired labourers through Mill's first form of association

[1] *Some Leading Principles.* Part ii. chap. v. sects. 6, etc.

to his second. The order of progress seemed to be so natural as to be almost inevitable; and profit-sharing was commonly regarded as the stepping-stone from the wages system to co-operative production.

Such, then, was the nature of the prophecy; and, whatever may be the case with instructed economic students, it retains its hold on the mind of the general public. The wages system is still very commonly regarded as a passing economic phenomenon, appropriate perhaps to the present stage of social progress, but destined to be supplanted by improved methods of organisation; and the most popular line of development is held to lead through profit-sharing to co-operative production. Mill's language has scarcely ceased to reflect the belief which is in vogue; and the plain average man will still, if you question him, inform you that, "if the improvement, which even triumphant military despotism has only retarded, not stopped, shall continue its course, there can be little doubt that the *status* of hired labourers will gradually tend to confine itself to the description of work-people whose low moral qualities render them unfit for anything more independent; and that the relation of masters and work-people will be gradually superseded by partnership in one of two forms: in some cases, association of the labourers with the capitalist; in others, and perhaps finally in all, association of labourers among themselves."

And yet, were the prophets, who formed these anticipations, to be asked to interpret the present position of affairs, they would probably fail to hide their disappointment. They might, it is true, urge with some cogency that the fulfilment of their predictions was to be gradually accomplished, and was only postponed. Or they might, perhaps, even plead that improvement had not continued its course. But they could hardly disguise, if they were candid, the unpromising appearance of facts; and the commonest honesty would force them to acknowledge that the tendency of speculative thought did not at present incline in the direction which they would wish.

The discussions at recent Co-operative Congresses attest, too plainly to be mistaken, the ominous fact that co-operation has, as yet, been arrested at what the Christian Socialists would consider its initial and subordinate stage, and that it has not proceeded to the higher and fuller development, which they so eagerly contemplated. There is something approaching to pathos in the unwearying persistence with which Mr. Holyoake, for example, in his *Co-operative Movement To-day*, returns again and again to this attractive but disappointing theme, and breaks off abruptly the discussion of other matters to insist on the fundamental importance of co-operative production as an integral part of the original movement. Nor is the evident and natural chagrin of himself and his friends more significant than his candid admission of the conflict of these opinions with those of many of the ablest and most experienced individuals among perhaps the shrewdest body of working men in the country, the directing members of the co-operative retail and wholesale distributive societies. In practice, at least, co-operative production, as it is generally understood, has met with scant recognition at the hands of professed co-operators; and, in the disagreement of views, which is plainly apparent, between warm-hearted enthusiasts for social improvement and hard-headed administrators of co-operative business, it is difficult, after making allowance for the impetus of earnest zeal, which is needed to carry reforms into effect, to put at any low estimate the judgments of practical experience. It is even possible that some injury may have been done to the true welfare of the co-operative movement by the injudicious and inopportune pressure of what must be considered to be, when compared with these practical views, largely academic opinions.

And the practical conclusions thus formed by those, who may perhaps be styled the "men of affairs" of the co-operative movement, have derived support from the later speculations of academic economists. A more exact analysis of industrial society has served to throw into sharp relief the difficulties of co-operative production; and the aspirations of social reformers have come into collision, not merely with the impediments of stubborn fact, but also with the objections of critical thought. The importance of the part played by the employer in the organisation of industry has received an emphasis to which, in Mill's great treatise, it was not yet held to be entitled; and later analysis has distinguished more definitely the management of business from the ownership of capital.

As a striking example of this new emphasis, and an interesting episode in the history of economic terminology, it is worth while to contrast the use of the term *profits* by Adam Smith and, a century later, by the distinguished American economist General Walker. Adam Smith remarks, in a passage[1] of the *Wealth of Nations*, that "the profits of stock, it may perhaps be thought, are only a different name for the wages of a particular sort of labour, the labour of inspection and direction. They are, however," he proceeds to say, "altogether different, are regulated by quite different principles, and bear no proportion to the quantity, the hardship, or the ingenuity, of

[1] Book i. chap. vi.

this supposed labour of inspection and direction. They are regulated altogether by the value of the stock employed, and are greater or smaller in proportion to the extent of this stock." Evidently, in his mind, the interest on capital formed so large and conspicuous an element of profits as to render any other element, if it existed, unimportant;[1] and so far did he push this conception, that in his chapter[2] on "wages and profit in the different employments of labour and stock," he is careful to notice the "deception arising from our not always distinguishing what ought to be considered as wages from what ought to be considered as profit." "Apothecaries' profit," he observes, "is become a by-word, denoting something uncommonly extravagant. This great apparent profit, however, is frequently no more than the reasonable wages of labour." "In a small seaport town," again, he writes, "a little grocer will make forty or fifty per cent. upon a stock of a single hundred pounds, while a considerable wholesale merchant in the same place will scarce make eight or ten per cent. upon a stock of ten thousand." And why? Because, he replies, the grocer must have "all the knowledge that is necessary for a great merchant, which nothing hinders him from becoming but the want of a sufficient capital." He must be a "tolerable judge" of "perhaps fifty or sixty different sorts of goods, their prices, qualities, and the markets where they are to be had cheapest." "Thirty or forty pounds a year cannot be considered as too great a recompense for the labour

---

[1] In book v., chapter ii., article ii., he alludes to that "part" of profit, which is the "compensation" "for the risk and trouble of employing the stock"; but by this he seems to mean what was afterwards distinguished by writers like Mill as *insurance against risk* rather than what they defined as *wages of superintendence*.

[2] Book i. chap. x.

of a person so accomplished. Deduct this from the seemingly great profits of his capital, and little more will remain, perhaps, than the ordinary profits of stock. The greater part of the apparent profit is, in this case too, real wages."

So far Adam Smith: let us now turn to General Walker. We find him [1] laying just emphasis on this very faculty—only exercised on a larger scale—of judging of the qualities of goods, and of the best markets for their purchase (and disposal), as one of the distinctive characteristics of the modern employer; and we find him confining the use of the term *profits* to the reward or earnings of management, and expressly excluding the interest of capital, on which Adam Smith insists. "To the *entrepreneur's* share of the product of industry," he writes, "I shall strictly apply the term profits. This use of the term profits, in my judgment, tends to promote clearer conceptions regarding the distribution of wealth, in the modern industrial state." And he quotes with approval from Webster's dictionary a definition of profit: "'The *profit* of the farmer and the manufacturer is the gain made by sale of produce, or manufactures, *after deducting* the value of the labour, materials, rent, and all expenses, together with the *interest of the capital employed*, whether land, machinery, buildings, instruments, or money." The grammatical construction of this definition, it may be remarked by the way, is not so free from ambiguity as General Walker perhaps imagines. It is at least open to the interpretation that profit is equivalent to the gain made by sale, in addition to, and not apart from, the interest of the capital employed. It might even be argued that the addition of the word

[1] *Political Economy*, part iv. chapter iv. ; *Wages Question*, chapter xiii.

"employed" to the word "capital" hinted at a distinction between capital borrowed from others and capital belonging to the farmer or manufacturer himself, and that, in reckoning his profit, he must deduct for the interest on the borrowed capital, but might include the interest on his own. Perhaps, however, this is too strained an interpretation of the language of the definition; and General Walker's use of the term profits is sufficiently obvious.

But there can be no doubt that into the common use of the term, in England at least, both elements enter—that of the interest of capital, which is emphasised by Adam Smith, and that of the reward or earnings of management, to which General Walker would confine its use. The transference of the emphasis is more important, because it corresponds to a change in fact, which is not so complete as the alteration in thought, which we have traced. On the one hand, the domestic system of industry prevailing in Adam Smith's time did not afford such wide or peculiar scope for the work of business management as that furnished in the large undertakings of the present day; and, on the other, the modern agencies for borrowing and lending capital have rendered less indispensable the possession by the business man himself of all, or the greater part, of the capital used in his business. In this, as in many other cases, the change in theory has reflected the change in practice, although perhaps, in General Walker's writings, it has received an excess of emphasis; and his use of the term profits diverges too widely from the common acceptation to find a permanent place in English economics.

This alteration has had an important bearing on the question of co-operation. It has become apparent that the difficulty, which confronts co-operative production, is not so much the acquisition of capital as the supersession of the employer. Labourers may become capitalists, and in Cairnes' words, bring profits to reinforce wages without overcoming or removing the obstacles, which confront Mill's associations of "labourers among themselves on terms of equality, collectively owning the capital with which they carry on their operations, and working under managers elected and removable by themselves." To accomplish the ownership of capital they have only to save; and co operation, as it has been practised in its distributive societies, has enabled them to save almost without knowing it, and certainly without feeling the burden. Buying their goods at the ordinary market price, and dividing at the end of fixed periods the profits realised in proportion, partly, at least, to their purchases, they receive a sum, which it may seem worth their while to save, in the lump, although, had they saved at the time on each particular purchase, the saving would have appeared too trifling an amount. And the facilities afforded in the co-operative stores and other agencies for the investment of savings have rendered it a task of comparative ease for workmen to become capitalists. Had co-operation achieved no other result, it would merit the warmest approval; and it is advantageous to dwell on these solid incontestable successes when we are reminded of its shortcomings and failures.

But it remains true that co-operative production, in the ordinary sense of the words, has hitherto enjoyed small success; that it has been condemned in practice by co-operative men of affairs, and that this condemnation has even been approved by the critical analysis of some economic reasoners. The great importance and distinctive nature of the functions of the employer, the difficulties encountered, and the capacities needed, in the successful conduct of business enterprise, seem to show how unlikely it is that associations of "labourers on terms of equality, collectively owning the capital with which they carry on their operations, and working under managers elected and removable by themselves," will avoid financial disaster.

And thus, under the combined influence of the practical failure of such schemes, and the damaging criticism of economic theory, the second form of association mentioned by Mill has been steadily giving place to the first in favour with economists, and to some extent also with the general public. Co-operative production, it would appear, has been tried under auspicious circumstances. It has received the gratuitous advertisement of eminent economists. It has been smiled on by public opinion, and commended by statesmen, and yet it has failed. There must, therefore, be flaws inherent in its constitution, and these flaws economic analysis has detected. Profit-sharing, on the other hand, seems to secure the advantages without the drawbacks of the larger scheme. It elicits the interest of the workmen in the undertaking, while it retains the interest and the managing skill and experience of the employer. And so, though it is possible that in the future it will give place to co-operative production, it seems to enjoy a superiority for the present. Such is the comforting conclusion, which has served to solace the keen, but natural, disappointment felt at the comparative failure of co-operative production.

But these pleasing visions have once more been rudely dispelled. Two notable books have made their appearance, which have thrown a flood of instructive light on co-operation and profit-sharing. Mrs. Webb's account of the Co-operative Movement is a timely and original contribution to the discussion of a burning question; and Mr. David Schloss, in his *Methods of Industrial Remuneration*, has executed an analysis of the varieties of industrial payment, which has not, we believe, been surpassed for minuteness and precision of detail. Both writers have brought the powerful battery of a destructive criticism to bear on the claims of profit-sharing.

Mrs. Webb has argued that in its inception in the mind of Robert Owen, as in its later development, the true meaning of the Co-operative Movement has been misread by such advocates of co-operative production as Mr. Holyoake and Judge Hughes. The movement was designed, and has proved, to be frankly democratic in spirit. Any one can become a customer or a shareholder in the store, and partake in its benefits, and, if a shareholder, in its government also. There is a powerful inducement constantly operating on the wills of the existing members to extend the limits of membership in order to benefit by the consequent increase of trade. The store is thus essentially a democratic institution, whereas the establishment of co-operative production would mean the substitution of an aristocratic principle, and the creation of a body of workmen enjoying certain privileges, which they would be likely jealously to preserve from the participation of a larger number. The principle of dividing the profits of the store among the purchasers in proportion to their purchases allows any one to share in the privilege, but the principle of dividing the profits among the labourers, who have produced the commodity, is not open to all, but confined to a restricted exclusive aristocracy. The conduct of some of the small productive societies, which are in existence, affords a discouraging example of the power and reality of these tendencies. They are often, Mrs. Webb has shown, "sweaters" of the labour of others employed as workmen hired for wages.

Again, she has urged that the common use of the term "co-operative production" itself is misleading. The antithesis does not lie between co-operative production and co-operative distribution, but rather between two methods of industrial remuneration and two principles of industrial policy. Co-operators have engaged in the work of production, as well as distribution, with success; and many of the undertakings of the Wholesale Society are productive in character. This argument has been reinforced by Mr. Schloss, who suggests that the difficulty in co-operative production of superseding the employer, on which great stress has been laid by economists, has been overrated. The co-operative retail stores encounter, in their own kind and degree, difficulties of management; and the success of the Wholesale Society has shown that working men are able to cope with the greater risks, and more perplexing changes, of the wholesale markets. They have not displayed such incapacity for business management as the argument, which insists on the importance of the employer, might, if pressed too far, lead the student to suppose. The failure of co-operative production, in the common acceptation of the term, has, Mr. Schloss maintains, been rather due to a vicious system of remuneration; and this faulty method is common to profit-sharing, which economists approve, and co-operative production, which they condemn.

He then proceeds to subject the claims of profit-sharing to a searching scrutiny. He shows by statistics how small is the share of profits actually received by the workmen in the few undertakings, which practise the method. It is, in fact, infinitesimal in comparison with what they receive as wages; and it may be illusory, as, in consideration of such a bonus, they may be content with lower wages than they would otherwise demand and obtain. In order to receive this small, and perhaps delusive, gain, they may be asked to surrender the solid advantage of liberty to strike for higher wages, or to leave the employment of one firm for that of another. Under some varieties of the system they do not receive the bonus in cash, but it is applied to form an insurance fund, the benefits of which will be forfeited by dismissal, or even by voluntary withdrawal, from the employment of some particular firm. In certain cases the system has been introduced with the avowed, or tacit, intention of destroying the influence of the men's union; and, if they are asked in this way to surrender their freedom, they may fairly require in exchange some tangible benefit.

And yet the theory advanced to justify the system to the employer is scarcely calculated to commend it to workmen alive to their interests. For they are told that, in consequence of the stimulus afforded by the share of profits to increased exertion, and care in avoiding waste, they will create extraordinary profits, in which they will only partly share. The profits are confessedly due to their conduct; and it is only in industries, where there is opportunity for this avoidance of waste, and this increase of exertion, on the part of the workmen, that the scheme is considered likely to succeed; and yet the employer is to participate in these additional profits. In the light of this circumstance the plea, often urged, that, if the workmen share in profits in good years, they should also bear a portion of losses in bad, loses most of its cogency; for the profits, in which they share, are of their own creation when they are realised, and they forfeit their share when they are not, although they may have shown just as much care, and displayed no less exertion, and the losses may be due to causes beyond their control. Such arguments are certainly persuasive; and if it can be shown that, by some variety of the existing wages system, the workmen can secure for themselves what, under profit-sharing, they must allow the employer to appropriate in part, the case against the principle, from their point of view, would appear conclusive. This alternative Mr. Schloss discovers in what he terms "progressive wages," by which, while a minimum wage is guaranteed, a bonus is given, proportioned to the quantity, and also, it may be, to the quality, of the output; and with this and similar systems he points out that profit-sharing has, as a matter of fact, been sometimes confused.

Such is, in brief outline, the criticism passed by Mrs. Webb and Mr. Schloss on the principle, whether recommended to co-operators or to private employers, which has found favour with economists and the general public; and, while neither writer is above the suspicion of wishing to establish a case, their criticism is certainly damaging where it is not destructive. They have left the question in a different position from that in which they found it. They have furnished the opponents of the system, which they have reviewed, with an abundant armoury of powerful weapons. They have compelled its champions to fight with their eyes opened to the realities of the position; and the work they have thus accomplished cannot fail to exercise a wholesome influence on the future conduct of the discussion. It may occasion despondency, but it may prevent worse disappointment. It may seem to close one door of advance and improvement, only to open another.

For what conclusions may be drawn from the chapter of economic history which we have been studying? One or two seem of approximate certainty. The first, and perhaps most obvious, is that Mill expressed his prediction in unduly-confident language, and that, at any rate, the period needed for its fulfilment is of secular rather than shorter duration. Neither the "speculations and discussions," nor the "events," of recent years have pointed conclusively in the direction of profit-sharing or co-operative production; and it is more rather than less doubtful, that the "*status* of hired labourers will gradually tend to confine itself to the description of work-people whose low moral qualities render them unfit for anything more independent, and that the relation of masters and work-people will be gradually superseded by partnership in one of two forms: in some cases, association of the labourers with the capitalist; in others, and perhaps finally in all, association of labourers among themselves." It might indeed be urged with equal, or perhaps greater, cogency, that the general tendency of practical experience and speculative thought had been away from rather than towards the general realisation of Mill's two forms of partnership. At first it seemed as if his order of merit, though not perhaps his order of development, were to be reversed, and profit-sharing might succeed where co-operative production had failed. But the practical difficulties, which have confronted co-operative production, are scarcely more formidable than the theoretical defects, which have been revealed in profit-sharing, regarded from the workman's point of view; and the actual record of the successes and failures of the two schemes does not leave much to choose between them. The first scheme — that of co-operative production — has been tried under auspices apparently favourable, and has failed; the other has not yet been subjected to so many trials, but the principle of remuneration, on which it rests, has been adopted in the ventures of co-operative production. This much at least is certain, that, if the wages system is to disappear before either, or both, of these systems, its decease will be delayed or protracted; and this much is doubtful, that either of the systems is, as a prevalent institution, preferable to the other, or to the despised wages system itself.

It may indeed be argued that the causes, which have hindered the success, and limited the adoption, of these new systems, have been largely moral, and that, with moral improvement, such difficulties and dangers will vanish. But the argument is open to two objections. It is profoundly true that social reform is dependent on moral reform, and the reasoning, which insists on the futility of attempting to induce moral improvement by the change of mechanism involved in an Act of Parliament, is not to be readily gainsaid.[1] But it is also true that, granted the moral reform in employers and employed, the wages system itself might work as easily, and with as admirable results, as the suggested alternatives, which do not, and cannot, profess to remove the moral obstacles. The other objection to the argument consists in the fact that the difficulties of these alternative systems are largely economic, and not moral, in character. They are to a great extent, it would seem, flaws inherent in the systems, and not merely defects incident to their working. It is difficult to see how the democratic organisation of the workshop under co-operative production can effectually replace the directing skill and special experience of the employer, where that skill and experience are needed; nor is it easy to imagine how the liberty of the workman

[1] Cf. Essay ii. on this point.

can be fully maintained, or his interests fully secured, under the system of profit-sharing, as it is generally understood and practised. These qualifications are, as we shall observe later, important; but for the present it is enough to urge that Mill's prophecy has been shown to be premature, if not erroneous.

And so our second conclusion is that he unduly depreciated the merits of the wages system, that he underrated its possibilities, and he put too low an estimate on its economic strength. It may be questioned whether the *status* of the hired labourer is so demoralising in itself, or indicative of such low moral qualities in those who belong to it, as he represents it as being, or likely to be. Independence has, without doubt, its attractions, which are sometimes powerful enough to outweigh the consideration of merely material interests; but it may still be questioned whether to be one member of a committee is in itself a higher position, or proves the possession of better parts, than to work under the direction of an individual of trained capacity, and to occupy a subordinate place in a system of superior organisation. It may be easy to magnify the virtues, and to exaggerate the abilities, of the modern employer; and recent writers have not, perhaps, entirely avoided this error. He may not unfrequently be a man of rather unamiable qualities, and may combine a hard disposition with a shrewd intellect and a venturesome temper. He may be practised at driving a bargain; and his dealings with his work-people, as well as his competitors and customers, may reveal this unattractive side of his character. But it is no less easy, and it is, perhaps, more common, to lay excessive stress on such defects, and to exaggerate the hardship of working under a master.

For the economic strength of the wages system is very great. Wages, in practice at least, are a first and not a last charge on the product of industry; and it is the employer, rather than, as General Walker would hold,[1] the labourer, who is in this sense the "residual claimant." The risks of the business are undertaken by him; and to exchange the position of wage-earner for that of member of a co-operative production society might indeed be to surrender a sentimental feeling of dependence for that of responsibility, but it might also mean the substitution of real dependence on the chances and hazards of business enterprise for comparative independence. Under the wages system the employer forms the "buffer," which breaks the shock of the collision, or stoppage, of the industrial train; and the very plea that in bad years the wage-earners, under a system of profit-sharing, ought to participate in losses, if in good years they share in profits, hints at the significant, but undoubted, fact that wages may continue for some time to be paid when profits are *nil* or a minus quantity. To offer co-operation to a labourer seems in many cases to be not unlike giving a sentimental in exchange for a real advantage—a visionary phantom, which may after all elude the grasp, for a solid substantial reality.

For, again, the wages system is capable of greater modification than is often supposed. The most approved parts of the system of profit-sharing, as of that of co-operative production, can, it seems, be grafted on without tearing it up by the roots and planting the other systems in its place. Mr. Schloss has been singularly successful in showing the many varieties of which the wages system is capable; and this is not the least

[1] *Political Economy*, part iv. chap. v.

instructive part of his book. He distinguishes time-wage, piece-wage, task-wage, progressive-wage, collective time, piece, task, and progressive wage, besides different kinds of contract and co-operative work. These varieties are parted from one another by differences, which in some cases are so slight as to be almost unnoticeable, and a trifling change may suffice to transform one into another variety. The fundamental character of the wages system may accordingly be left unaltered, while its details are susceptible of great and manifold improvement.

This consideration leads directly to our third conclusion. Mill's order of development has the specious appearance of being "in conformity with nature"; but that appearance may be only delusive. There are reasons for thinking that nature is characterised by greater diversity. She does not proceed with such rigid unbroken uniformity: she rather allows scope for many different experiments in many different directions. And so there may be room in nature for co-operative production, and also for profit-sharing, without superseding the wages system; and, when they are duly confined to a limited sphere, some of the difficulties detected by later criticism become less obvious and discouraging. As a panacea for social ills neither the one nor the other seems likely to succeed; but, if the scale of their promise be reduced, their performance may prove more adequate.

We must not, it would seem, expect that the general establishment of profit-sharing or co-operative production —were it likely or possible—would inaugurate an era of undisturbed industrial peace.[1] For there is nothing to prove that human nature would, by dint of an alteration in the mechanism of industrial payment or business

---

[1] Cf. Essay vi. below.

PROFIT-SHARING

organisation, undergo a substantial change in temper and character. It is true that the general establishment and successful working of either of the two systems, by which it is proposed to fill the place left vacant by the removal of the wages system, would in reality presuppose a considerable moral improvement, which would be independent of their operation. But some occasion for industrial strife would nevertheless be left. The democratic organisation of undertakings, where the principle of co-operative production is recognised, would leave unaltered differences of skill and capacity, and distinctions of energy and endurance, which would need to be rewarded by varying amounts of wages, if not of profits. So long as the nature of the work performed presented such differences, there must be different classes of workmen; and amity of feeling would be seriously strained when one class thought itself justified to an advance in wages which another class considered unfair. They would both sit, or be represented, on the directing committee; and similar difficulties would arise in the case of the unequal remuneration of individual workmen. Even without such occasions for difference a sufficiently long experience has shown that the proceedings of committees are not unfrequently subject to irritating friction. The proverbial maxim that the best committee consists of two members, of which one is always or generally absent or silent, has an application of its own to the present question. And Mrs. Webb's imputation of an aristocratic taint to the principle of sharing in profits seems here to be pertinent. The tendency of a small body of workmen admitted to such privileges to exclude others from their participation has more than once been illustrated in the history of the co-operative movement; and the wages system, expelled by the front door, has tried to effect its entrance again by the back, and, in doing so, has caused a certain amount of irritation, whether it has succeeded or failed in the attempt.

Nor does it seem to be at all proven that the calmest consideration of interests would prevent the workmen engaged in co-operative production, or profit-sharing, from embroiling themselves, or their masters, in industrial disputes. Under any existing system of profit-sharing their share in the profits bears a ratio which is small, and, by comparison with the wages they earn, insignificant. They might, it is true, were they members of a co-operative society, injure themselves as capitalists and business-managers by asking for higher wages, and pushing the matter to the length of an open quarrel; and they might, were they sharers in profits, forfeit, by leaving their particular employment, the shares set aside for the future and not paid at the time. But it is doubtful whether enlightened selfishness would condemn this course, or disapprove of sacrificing the lesser interest to secure the greater; and it is tolerably certain that the powerful promptings, and subtle influences, of unenlightened temper or sentiment would on occasions lead them to risk the chance.

It is but recently that some instructive cases of industrial dispute have been occupying the public attention, which may serve to illustrate the point on which we have been dwelling. A protracted quarrel between the engineers and the plumbers on the Tyne has shown that the interests of different classes of workmen may collide, and provoke a contest as bitter and determined as any aroused by the hostility of employers and employed; and that even in the same branch of trade, if report speaks true, one union of engineers may try to destroy the influence of another. And, again, the idea, whether tacitly entertained, or tentatively avowed, that masters and men in the coal trade should combine to promote their joint interests at the expense of the public points to the danger of a conflict between the members of a society for co-operative production, sharing in the profits of the undertaking, and their customers, who would also share in those profits on the recognised principles of co-operative distribution. The opposition emphasised by Mrs. Webb between the democratical character of the existing stores and the aristocratical nature of profit-sharing might in this way prove an unpleasant and obstinate reality; and the other side of the shield is disclosed in the charge, not unfrequently made against co-operators by trades-unionists, that they have been so eager to increase the amount of the quarterly dividend that they have treated the workmen in their employment, not better, but rather worse, than an ordinary employer. The charge may be shown to be true or false by *à posteriori* evidence, but the fact that it has been seriously advanced is significant, and the conflict of interests, to which it points, is *à priori* not improbable. All these considerations suggest the conclusion that neither co-operative production nor profit-sharing offers any reliable guarantee for the certain preservation of industrial peace. They might render industrial conflict less frequent than it now unhappily is; but it can scarcely be doubted that the promises made on their behalf must be expressed in less extravagant language, if they are to correspond with their probable, or even perhaps with their possible, performance.

But, if the promises are subjected to modification, the final verdict on these popular schemes may not be so unfavourable as that pronounced by their latest critics. Mrs.

Webb and, to a less extent, Mr. Schloss seem, like Malthus on the question of population, "to have found the bow bent too much one way," and to have been, as he frankly confessed, "induced to bend it too much the other in order to make it straight." Mrs. Webb's contrast between the democratic tendencies of the present constitution of the retail stores and the Wholesale Society and the aristocratic bias of the principle of profit-sharing or co-operative production has undoubtedly the rare merit of originality, and is entitled to a place among those luminous *aperçus*, which admit a new light into a problem hitherto considered under different aspects. She succeeds in placing the question on a fresh basis. She applies to its treatment the novel and powerful instrument of a broad philosophic conception; and the inquiry, which she has made into the views of Robert Owen, shows that the conception does not conflict with some of the original aims of the co-operative movement. But it is doubtful whether she has escaped the characteristic failing of the discoverer, and, in her anxiety to prove a case, has not unconsciously underrated the strength of opposing arguments, and artificially strained the interpretation of some of the facts. In her eagerness to separate the idea of sharing in profits from the co-operative scheme, as designed by Owen, and carried into practice by the distributive stores and the Wholesale Society, she maintains that it was his intention to abolish "profit on price," and that the method of dividing the proceeds of the working of the store at the end of fixed periods is not a division of profits, because the sellers themselves are consumers. But the argument, as Mr. Schloss urges, bears a suspicious resemblance to juggling with words, and looks not unlike an attempt to prove the point by an artificial definition of the term profits. And, when Mrs. Webb examines the recorded instances of co-operative production, her examination, while undoubtedly damaging, is not wholly free from the subtle misleading influence of bias. It might be possible to exhibit a list of failures among the more numerous undertakings conducted on the basis of the present wages system by the Wholesale Society (or by private individuals) similar to those, which she shows as the result of profit-sharing in a comparatively limited sphere; and before it is proved that the principle is irretrievably bad, or doomed to inevitable failure, such a comparison would be needed.

Mr. Schloss, like Mrs. Webb, has made a remarkable and opportune contribution to the discussion of a vexed and perplexing topic; but doubt may be felt in his, as in her, instance of freedom from the temptation to prove a case and of steadfastness in resisting it. The nicety of the distinctions, on which he insists, enables him to remove the disguise from systems, which have masqueraded under the pretence of being genuine examples of profit-sharing, while they are in reality modifications of the wages system. There are, however, cases in which he appears to push these distinctions to an unnecessary or excessive point of refinement; and sometimes he may seem to magnify distinctions into differences, or to discern a difference of kind where there is only a difference of degree. The arguments, by which he shows the unsuspected elasticity of the wages system, might conceivably, were a slight change made, be used to illustrate the possible elasticity of the system of profit-sharing; and the faulty system might thus lose half of its defects without forfeiting the whole of its character. And so eager is he, like Mrs. Webb, to demonstrate the inherent viciousness of the system, that he is perhaps inclined to underrate the difficulty of superseding the employer in co-operative production, and to trace its failure too largely to the method of remuneration common to it with profit-sharing.

And so it may perhaps be possible to steer a middle course for profit-sharing and co-operative production between the Scylla of the earlier prophets and the Charybdis of the later critics, to enable them, if possible, to avoid the rocks, on which they have been wrecked in the past, by discovery in time, and to prevent them from being engulfed in the whirlpool of destruction, to which Mrs. Webb and, at times, Mr. Schloss would seemingly drag them down. There may be a sphere—though it be a more limited sphere than the advocates of either system would allow—for profit-sharing and co-operative production; and the wages system, perhaps improved and modified, may continue to hold its own beside these alternative methods.

The difficulties of management are undoubtedly great, and have grown with the scope of business enterprise and the lapse of time. But they differ in kind and degree in different departments of industry. The training of the co-operative store, and, in a greater degree, the experience of the Wholesale Society, are, together with other important recognised influences of the day, educating numbers of working men to the duties and responsibilities of business management, and are making them familiar with what was once strange and alarming. It is the case, as Mrs. Webb and Mr. Schloss have pointed out justly, that co-operators have engaged with success in the work of production as well as distribution; that some kinds of productive undertakings are attached to the distributive stores; and that the Wholesale Society tries to deal with the more perplexing intricacies of business on a large scale, and has not failed in the attempt. But it must not be forgotten that the difficulty of securing a market is largely removed, and that the business is one of greater routine, and less scope for enterprise or invention, than might, or would be, the case in other productive undertakings. The superintending work of the employer can be replaced more easily than his "engineering" function, as the Americans expressively term it; and the successful enterprises of the co-operative movement have perhaps called for more of the former than of the latter capacity. Yet the one is a training for the other; and within limits, which may afterwards be extended, difficulties of no mean order have been encountered and overcome by working men. Even in private undertakings they are continually rising from lower to higher posts, and the difficulties of management, though they cannot be neglected, are perhaps becoming less formidable.

The problem, therefore, of working men managing industrial enterprise is not, it would seem, insoluble, though it is sufficiently obstinate to suggest that the drift of progress is not towards an uniform or universal system of co-operative production. The question of joint, as opposed to single, management remains; and here once more the answer is that there is room in the field of industry for both. That there are industries suited to joint-stock enterprise is sufficiently obvious; and committees of working men, so far as their class position and abilities are concerned, may conduct contentious business with as much common sense and prospect of agreement, and deal with chances and risks with as much promptitude, boldness, and prudence, as directors chosen from the ranks of merchants and manufacturers. At least there is nothing inherently absurd in such a proposition; but the contrast between their position as wage-earners under the control of a manager and as members of a committee controlling that manager is fraught with more possibilities of conflict and disaster. There are, indeed, analogous arrangements, which are working in practice; and, granted the possession of the right qualities, and the selection of the right individuals, the problem is not insoluble. But it does point to a limitation of the system to cases where the chances of conflict are decreased by the character of the business—by its routine and comparative independence of managing skill and responsibility. In exceptional instances, no doubt, the difficulties, which might actually attach to the business, would disappear under the powerful influence of personal qualities; and in certain industries the difficulties would be reduced, if not abolished, by the normal conditions of the case. Nor, in all probability, is the possession of the requisite qualities so rare, or the existence of the suitable businesses so exceptional, as might be supposed. But the general establishment of co-operative production could not reckon with certainty on their general prevalence, and would deal with the average man and the ordinary business as well as the exceptional business and the gifted individual. Regarded as a general principle the system seems doomed to failure; but, properly limited, it may yet achieve considerable success.

The conclusion, which may be formed on profit-sharing, is somewhat similar. There may be cases, where workmen may be content with "half a loaf rather than none," and disposed to allow the employer to share in the extraordinary profits, which their increased care and zeal have produced. There may be instances, where they may be satisfied with receiving their share in the shape of a deferred annuity or the like, and not in hard cash; and the forcible inducement to save without knowing or feeling may be as salutary here as in co-operative distribution itself. In certain cases, where there is scope for avoiding waste or displaying greater energy, such a method of remuneration may stimulate to an increased output, and may thus recommend itself to an employer, and a feeling of attachment may arise between him and his workmen, which would not be secured to the same extent by any less complete modification of the wages system.

But it may be possible to go further. It may be possible to allow workmen to leave the business, if they wish, or to strike for higher wages, if they choose, and yet to retain, and receive at once, if necessary, their share of the profits. It does not seem incompatible with the successful working of the system that they should continue to be members of an union; nor do its principles necessarily condemn the bestowal of the whole of the extraordinary profits upon them, while the employer enjoys compensation in an increased improbability of a strike or withdrawal of his men, or in the pleasure of a new or added feeling of joint interest in the welfare of the business. Even in a business, where the opportunity for extraordinary profits did not seem to present itself, these considerations might induce trial of the system, at any rate in part.

But, on the other hand, it remains true that the share of profits must, in most cases, be so small in comparison with wages as to render the improbability of dispute less weighty an influence in leading the employer to introduce the system; and the desire to limit the freedom of the men to strike for higher wages will be as powerful a motive, in all probability, with him in determining the details of the system as it may prove with the leaders of the men in advising their constituents to reject it. Like co-operative production, profit-sharing seems to have only a limited sphere of operation; and, like it also, it does not promise to supersede the wages system. Mill's confident prophecy is destined to pass into the category of unfulfilled predictions unless it surrenders its universal character; for without such limitation it is the expression of a pious aspiration rather than a solid and reasoned belief.

V.

CO-OPERATION IN ITS RELATIONS TO TRADE UNIONISM AND SOCIALISM.[1]

I HAVE been asked to take as the subject of my address to this society the relations of Co-operation to Trade Unionism and Socialism. The subject, it need hardly be observed, is of vast dimensions, and, were it to be adequately treated, would require not one, or even two, but several lectures. For these three terms—Co-operation, Trade Unionism, and Socialism—represent the most prominent phases of what is sometimes conveniently, if ambiguously, called the "Labour Movement." Not very long ago a book was published with this title, written by an Oxford resident,[2] in which the author with admirable skill represented Co-operation, Trade Unionism, and Socialism as the three agencies, which, operating in their separate spheres of action, would combine to effect the inevitable transformation from the existing to the future economic order. It is impossible not to doubt whether the society of the future, any more than that of the present, will admit of being exactly compressed within the neat limits of a consistent philosophy; and we need not now venture far into the dangerous and uncertain region of prophecy.

[1] An address to the Oxford Co-operative Society (March, 1896).
[2] Mr L. T. Hobhouse.

Nor is it certain that the author of this book did not reach his results by a process, which was legitimate, but open to the possibility of inadequacy, or even of error; for he selected for special emphasis certain incidents of the agencies, which he was examining, and declared that such and such a characteristic constituted the essential principle of Co-operation, of Trade Unionism, and of Socialism respectively. The danger of this process lies in the possibility that other characteristics may be equally deserving of notice, or at least cannot with safety be omitted from any complete view of the case. I must confess that one of the chief difficulties, which I myself have encountered in dealing with the subject, has arisen from the different interpretations given to two at least of the three terms we are considering. Trade Unionism seems to possess a tolerably precise and definite meaning, which is generally accepted; but Co-operation is certainly employed by different writers and speakers in different significations; and on the Protean varieties, which Socialism assumes in the hands of its supporters and opponents alike, it is needless to dwell.

Let us, therefore, commence by making an attempt to define the three terms as broadly as possible. Trade Unionism may be termed the endeavour to promote the interests of the workmen in a trade by organisation for defence and attack; Co-operation may be defined as combination, not for the purposes of defence and attack, but for those of mutual self-help; and Socialism may be understood as the employment of the collective authority of the State for certain economic ends in lieu of individual action. The definitions, which we have given, may not be considered fully satisfactory, but they do not err on the side of narrowness. If anything they are too comprehensive; but they can hardly be accused of emphasising one particular feature of the movements defined, to the neglect of others. In the course of discussion we may have occasion to enter on more detailed distinctions, but at the outset we may be content with such broad definitions. Let us proceed to examine into some characteristics, which the three agencies thus described possess in common.

In the first place, then, Co-operation, Trade Unionism, and Socialism agree in being movements, which are primarily intended for the improvement of the position of the working classes. It is true that both Co-operation and Socialism comprise among their adherents members of other classes, and that they are directed to larger ends than those which concern the working classes alone. But Co-operation, in the form in which it has as yet achieved practical success in this country, has been, primarily at least, a working-class movement; and the economic investigator generally interprets the term, when he seeks exactitude, as excluding rather than including such middle-class enterprises as those Army and Navy Stores, before which, in the height of the London season, you may see rows of carriages waiting, which certainly do not belong to the "working classes" in the ordinary acceptation of the term. We are not pronouncing at present on the correctness or error of the distinction, though it may be confessed that not a little confusion of thought in economic reasoning on the history and future of the Co-operative Movement seems to have been begotten by neglect of differences, which may appear comparatively unimportant. At any rate, for our immediate purpose, we may take it that Co-operation means primarily that working-class movement, which has created the various retail distributive stores to be found in many industrial centres, which has led to the formation, and successive development, of those Wholesale Societies, which supply the retail stores, and which, with less or greater success, has been connected with the institution of various productive enterprises—sometimes recognising, and sometimes deliberately rejecting, the principle of distributing part of the profits among the workers actually engaged in the production of the commodities in question. Understood thus, the Co-operative Movement, although it has received support from the members of other classes of the community, and may number in its own ranks some, who belong to the lower middle rather than the strictly working classes, is yet primarily a working-class movement.

Of the intimate connection of Trade Unionism with the working classes it is unnecessary to attempt any formal or elaborate proof; and Socialism, if its aims are more ambitious, and embrace the whole of society, certainly proposes, as interpreted by its leading expositors, to influence the distribution of wealth in favour of the working classes as opposed to the present owners of property. As working-class movements, then, Co-operation, Trade Unionism, and Socialism are significant of the spirit of the times. They are significant, because they have grown, and have not diminished, in power and influence. But they are also significant for another reason, which we may proceed to notice. They are significant, because they have met with considerable sympathy and support from the members of other classes of the community. That sympathy has been begotten, not so much of any timidity or wish to conciliate a powerful party, which now constitutes in many civilised countries a majority of the electorate, as of a genuine interest in social improvement, and a sincere abhorrence of remediable suffering. It cannot be denied that the growing political importance of the working classes has brought with it an increased attention to their wishes and demands; and such a result is in accord with the ordinary operation of the usual motives, which influence the conduct of reasonable men. Nor should we underrate the power of determining their lot, which has now been placed in the hands of the working classes; for every thoughtful observer must be anxious that the acquisition of power should be accompanied by a feeling of actual responsibility. But it may unhesitatingly be affirmed that the three agencies we have described have received an impulse and direction from the disinterested zeal and kindly feeling of other classes of the community; and as unhesitatingly may it be asserted that with all the additional political power that the working classes may obtain, and probably will secure, in the future, they will find it difficult to overcome resistance, tacitly or openly offered to their demands by the middle and upper classes, unless they have first enlisted the support of some at least of the most capable and energetic members of those classes. It is, then, significant of the spirit of the times that these three agencies—Co-operation, Trade Unionism, and Socialism—should have received the aid, which they have undoubtedly derived, from the active sympathy or silent favour of the members of other classes. It is characteristic of the English temper that this should be the case. It is a fresh illustration of that apparent disregard of logic, which on many occasions has sufficed to preserve us from danger;[1] and, so long as this quality continues to characterise the mass of the English community, it may disappoint impatient reformers, and may even delay beneficial progress, but, as it has been in the past the despair of Continental Socialists, so it is likely in the future to substitute permanent, if gradual, advance for that

[1] Cf. Essay i.

revolutionary speed, which generally results in inevitable reaction.

Of the fact that Co-operation, Trade Unionism, and Socialism have received valuable assistance from other classes of the community besides that working-class, which they primarily concern, no serious doubt can be entertained. In its early days Trade Unionism had, it is true, to wage a bitter and protracted struggle. It had to contend with the penalties and obstacles of the law, and the pronounced and persistent opposition of influential opinion. But it is no less unquestionable that in later years it has been powerfully aided by that same opinion enlisted on its side; and it is matter of historical fact that the pressure of opinion has effected the removal of legal disabilities, and, in not a few struggles with employers, the representative organs of opinion — the newspaper press—have extended their active and avowed support to the side of the unions, and censured the attitude, and condemned the action, of the masters.

In the case of Co-operation the sympathy and aid of the members of other classes have been even more prominent. Indeed there is perhaps no movement of our times, which has enjoyed greater advantages in the expressed approval of public men and the warm commendation of economic writers. That approval and commendation, it must be confessed, have been directed especially towards that side of the movement, which has been least successful in practice;[1] and it is by no means certain that the other sides, through no fault of their own, have not secured, by unfulfilled pretences, an admiration and eulogy scarcely intended for them. But of whole-hearted devotion to the co-operative cause not a few examples may be found in

[1] See the previous Essay.

men like Mr. Vansittart Neale, who belonged by education and position, not to the working, but to the upper classes; and of genuine and deliberate eulogy many passages might be quoted from economic works of recognised authority, and from the utterances of eminent public speakers.

The support thus extended to Co-operation has been coincident in some cases with leanings to Socialism— not indeed a Socialism of the Continental type, aiming at revolution, nor a Socialism, like that of Marx, based on an elaborate system of dialectical reasoning, the subtlety of which cannot easily be denied, however severely its accuracy be impugned. The Socialism, which has found favour, has been inspired more largely by a feeling of repugnance aroused by the misery and poverty that are to be found under the existing economic order, and by an ardent desire to substitute improved social conditions. It has not indeed despised small reforms, but it has not remained content with them alone; and it has thought that in the concentrated authority of the State a remedial power might be discovered, which would cope successfully with difficulties too great to be overcome by individual effort or voluntary combination. Such, in general terms, was the Socialism of the English Christian Socialists—of Kingsley and Maurice and others—and they were some of the most earnest advocates and zealous friends of the Co-operative Movement.

Even at the present day in England the most influential support is accorded to philosophic Socialism — to Socialism, that is, as a system—by the educated rather than the working classes; and it is certainly the case that such improvements of a socialistic character as have been effected in English legislation, like the Factory Acts, have been generously advocated, and eagerly pressed, by members of the upper and middle as well as by those of the lower classes. On the whole, there can be little doubt that the three agencies of working-class improvement—Co-operation, Trade Unionism, and Socialism—have so far illustrated, and accorded with, the general spirit of the age, that they have derived material assistance from the action and sympathy of others besides the working classes alone.

There is another circumstance common to these movements, to which attention may be drawn, before we proceed to consider their differences. It is broadly correct to say that they have enlisted in their support the highest ability, and the most forcible character, to be found among the working classes themselves. It is sometimes urged by opponents of Trade Unions, that they comprise in their ranks no more than a minority of the working classes; and it is argued that they possess no sufficient claim to speak for that majority, which is unwilling, or unable, to take part in their organisation. Similarly it is contended with great plausibility by economic observers, who have no perceptible bias for or against Trade Unionism, that its ability to influence the general course of wages must be discounted by the consideration that in many trades it does not pretend to embrace even a majority of the workers. In some trades, it is true, the organisation is more nearly identical, at any rate, with the skilled workmen engaged in the industry. But in others Unionism is confessedly weak, and in yet others it does not exist at all. Such considerations must, no doubt, be taken into account in any candid inquiry into the economic power of Trade Unions; but, on the other hand, it must not be forgotten that, if they comprise a minority alone, it is a minority, which by its compactness, training and prestige is likely to exert an influence disproportionate to any mere calculation of numbers; and it is also a minority, which certainly includes some of the highest ability, of the most statesmanlike wisdom, and of the boldest and most determined energy, of the working classes.

In a similar manner it can hardly be doubted that some of the most thoughtful and educated intellect, and generous and high-minded zeal, of those same working classes evinces an inclination to Socialism. It is not, in their case, any more than in that of the upper and middle classes of this country, a Socialism of a violent or revolutionary type. It is a Socialism of a more philosophic temper, and a more merciful and righteous attitude. It is a Socialism, which does not seem always to have realised its full consequences, and appears to be founded more in emotion than reason. In this, and not in any violence of intention or action, appears to lie its real danger. The economist may be forgiven for thinking that motions in favour of the nationalisation of land, and of the yet more comprehensive programme, that would transfer to the hands of the State the disposal of the instruments of production, which have been passed at recent Trade Union Congresses, have partaken of the nature of abstract resolutions, begotten, it is true, of a real disapproval of the more obvious evils of the existing economic order, but intended rather as an expression of sentiment than as a preliminary to actual practice. We may perhaps go further, and assert that the agitation in favour of an Eight Hours Day, to be established by legislative compulsion, has achieved no small part of its undoubted success from the same cause. And we may believe that, when the occasion arises—if it should arise—for giving practical effect to some of these socialistic aspirations, the qualities of cautious and courageous wisdom, and of sane and sober common sense, which have in the past conducted to victory over formidable difficulties in the case of Trade Unionism and Co-operation, and even now have made their appearance in the form of outspoken disapproval on the part of some of the older unions of the more extreme proposals of their younger brethren, will assert themselves, and lead to safe conclusions. Yet it cannot be denied that it is to the more thoughtful and generous working-men that socialistic aspirations have mainly appealed. It is they, who have been most impressed by the evils of the times, and most anxious to find a remedy in a quarter, which certainly promises the employment of a more powerful authority than can be elsewhere discovered, but has too often disappointed by imperfect fulfilment the eager and confident hopes, which it has excited.

We are indulging in no idle flattery when we assert that our own movement—that of Co-operation—has drawn its strength from some of the ablest and noblest members of the working classes. It is true that, like all movements, it has had its sordid and its petty side. It is true that, like all movements, it has disappointed some high expectations, which were formed by some of its earlier supporters. But the fact remains that it is a considerable and acknowledged success, that it has steadily grown from small beginnings to great achievements, and that it has comprised in its ranks the flower of the working classes of this country.

But, if these three agencies agree in being, primarily at least, working-class movements; if they have in common obtained support, and met with approval, from the members of other classes of the community; and, if they have included among their adherents the most intellectual, the most high-minded, and the most forcible, individuals of the working classes themselves : in what do they differ from one another? The writer, to whom we referred at the beginning of this discussion, considers that each will play its part in the society of the future ; and we may agree with him in this conclusion. No reasonable man can expect that that society will be absolutely uniform.[1] It will assuredly present, not one, or two, but many types. We may expect to see there Trade Unionism, possibly furnishing new developments, Co-operation, probably not entirely similar to its present form, and some further extension of authority on the part of the State, and some greater substitution of collective for individual action, which may be called Socialistic. Our only complaint against the writer, to whom we have alluded, is that he selects one phase of each of these agencies, and declares that that is essential, and will, while the others pass away, survive to take its place in the society of the future. For instance, he regards Trade Unionism as necessary to protect the interests of the wage-earning producer ; Co-operation, as represented in the distributive societies, where the profits are divided among the consumers in proportion to their purchases, as destined to grow so as to comprise the vast majority, if not the whole, of the consumers of the nation; and Socialism, whether municipal or imperial, as required to shield the interests of those producers, who are unable to defend themselves by organising Trade Unions, and to secure for the great body of consumers, represented by the State, the unearned gains arising from the ownership of land and of capital. This conception, no doubt, forms a neat and consistent philosophic system, and may well attract; but it may be doubted whether it does not

[1] Cf. Essay i. above.

assign undue exclusive prominence to certain conspicuous facts.

For instance, it may be questioned whether it is an adequate account of the Co-operative Movement to take into consideration the retail distributive stores or the Wholesale Society alone. In its origin, at least, the co-operative creed was very much wider. It aimed at the regeneration of the whole social and industrial order.[1] It is not too much to say that many of its early adherents aspired to remove altogether the necessity for Trade Unionism and Socialism. Some of its pioneers were, it is true, themselves Socialists; and the name of Robert Owen has been deservedly held in high honour alike by English Socialists and by English Co-operative workers. But Co-operation is broadly distinguished from Socialism, because it definitely and avowedly relies on self-help, and not on the help of the State. Socialism, however elastic be the interpretation given to the term, puts in the forefront of its programme the employment of the power and authority of the State—it may be to assume control, or possession, of the instruments of production—it may be to influence the distribution of wealth in favour of the labouring classes—it may be only to substitute collective for individual action in cases where experience or expediency dictates. It may vary from an ambitious to a humble programme, and may attract or alienate accordingly; but in its many forms it yet retains this distinguishing characteristic, that it substitutes in greater or less measure the State for the individual. Co-operation as distinctly relies on self-help. It is separated from the violent revolutionary Socialism of the Continental type, because it proceeds by peaceful methods. But it is also separated

[1] Cf. the previous Essay, and also that which follows.

from the more moderate Socialism of the English pattern, because it does not appeal for assistance to the State. It proposes no interference with the rights of property, and no disturbance of freedom of contract. It is in accord with Socialism in seeking to transform society, and to benefit the labouring classes. But it aims at a peaceful, automatic transformation, and it directs the labouring classes, not to deprive others of wealth, but by their own exertions to increase their own possessions. It invites them, not to abolish property, but rather to become property-owners; and it has been blamed by unfavourable critics for allowing the high aims of its earlier exponents to degenerate into a petty longing to increase the quarterly dividend.

Co-operation, as we have noted, started with an ambitious programme. It aimed at the regeneration of industry. It sought to introduce a new "heaven on earth"; and it was welcomed by economists and favoured by statesmen. The reason for this sympathetic reception, however, was to be found, not so much in that side of the movement which has achieved success, as in that which, it must be admitted, has hitherto been attended by comparative failure. On this side it was thoroughly opposed to the principles of Trade Unionism. There can be little doubt that writers, like Mill, thought that in Cooperation they had discovered the effectual remedy for industrial disputes; and it is curious, and not uninstructive, at this interval of time to look back, and to study the language habitually employed[1] about Trade Unionism by authors of culture and repute.

They afford an illustration of public opinion, which has passed away with the facts, which gave occasion to it; and

[1] Cf. Essay vi. (for the language used by Mr. W. R. Greg).

they point to the considerations, which led economists and public men to approve of Co-operation. It was not the prospect of working-men becoming their own shopkeepers, and securing the profits of the retail, or even of the wholesale trade; but it was the idea that, by forming co-operative partnerships, and superseding the employer, they would check the occurrence of industrial strife, because they would remove its occasion. In this way they would displace Trade Unionism as they would supplant Socialism. Trade Unionism supplied machinery, more or less effective, for defence against the attacks of employers, and for assault on their profits secured, as the workmen held, to the detriment of their own wages. But Co-operation, by enabling them to become their own employers, would obviate the necessity for Trade Unionism. Such, undoubtedly, were the anticipations formed; and such was the new "heaven on earth," which Co-operation, according to these fond visions, was to inaugurate in the industrial world. Remarkable as has unquestionably been the development of the other sides of the movement, and admirable as are its consequences in encouraging thrift and checking the evils of credit, it was not these, but the first, which enlisted the sympathy of statesmen, and received the commendation of economists.

But what has been the actual fulfilment of these ardent and confident hopes—these eager and grand anticipations? Co-operative production, thus interpreted, has as yet achieved but small success, while Co-operative distribution has won extensive and admitted triumphs. The consequence is that Trade Unionism has still a part to play, and it has itself exhibited fresh developments. At first the explanation of the comparative failure of Co-operation, in the wider conception formed by its early adherents, and by enthusiastic supporters outside its ranks, was found[1] in differences between the work of distribution and production. That such differences exist is undeniable; and economists maintained that workmen, who were capable of overcoming the real, but comparatively minor, difficulties, which confronted efforts to supersede the retail shopkeeper and the wholesale dealer, might yet themselves be overcome by the more serious obstacles, which would resist an endeavour to supplant the employer. He performed functions, for which in the modern industrial world a special training, and peculiar abilities, were needed. He might appear to receive a large remuneration compared with the wages of his workmen; but it measured rightly, and did not exceed, the importance of his services. If the workmen attempted to fill his place with a salaried manager, they would be compelled to offer a larger stipend than they might naturally consider to be necessary; and, if they tried to dispense with skilled management, they would steer for the rocks, and be doomed to shipwreck. In the effort to avoid such difficulties economists recommended as a substitute for complete Co-operation, dispensing with the employer, a system of profit-sharing, under which he would remain at his post as the director of industry, and yet the workmen would be more closely attached to the success of the concern by a bond of partnership consisting of a share in the profits. Latterly this system has in its turn been subjected to criticism; and it is significant that the practical managers of the distributive retail and wholesale societies, and of the productive undertakings connected with them, have been so far from regarding it with unqualified admiration that they have been reluctant to counsel or

[1] Cf. the previous Essay.

approve its adoption. In the meantime a new conception of the aims of the Co-operative Movement has been brought into prominence. It may perhaps be traced by prophets wise after the event in the inner history of the early period of the movement itself; and it may have directed the thoughts of some of its original pioneers; but it certainly had not penetrated to the economic mind, or perceptibly influenced popular opinion. The conception may be correct, and deserve approval, but it is scarcely that for which public sympathy was originally elicited.

According to this conception,[1] the distributive stores, and the Wholesale Society, represent a democratic organisation, anxious to extend its privileges to fresh comers, while the principle of giving a share in the profits to the workers engaged tends to engender a narrow exclusive spirit, and to beget an aristocratic selfishness. The essential principle of co-operation, according to this conception, is the distribution of the profits among the consumers; and the co-operative ideal is found in the extension of the sphere of the Wholesale Society and the retail stores to the whole of the nation.[2] Workmen are to share in profits, not as wage-earners, but as consumers; and it is not co-operative production, in the sense of workmen attempting to perform the business of production as well as distribution, which has broken down, but co-operative production, in the sense of giving a share of the profits to the actual workers in the undertaking.

The important consideration in the present connection is the light thrown on the relations of Trade Unionism

---

[1] See the previous Essay for the exposition of this view by Mrs. Sidney Webb.

[2] Cf. the evidence of Mr. Mitchell before the Labour Commission, and also Mr. B. Jones' *Co-operative Production*.

and Co-operation by this fresh conception of the meaning and aims of the Co-operative Movement. If co-operative production, in the sense of industrial partnership—whether completely accomplished by the workmen managing the business, and distributing the profits, or partly effected by the employer remaining in supreme control, and granting a bonus on wages—be the ultimate goal of the Co-operative Movement, it might seem to remove any necessity for Trade Unionism; and the two agencies might appear fundamentally opposed. Such seems to have been the idea of economists, and of the general public.

If, however, co-operative production in this sense be doomed to a limited success — and certainly such has hitherto been the case — a sphere would remain open for Unionism in protecting the interests of workmen in those cases where co-operative production had not been adopted.

If, again, co-operative production in this sense be, not merely a chimera impossible of universal, or even of limited attainment, but a positive error due to misdirected effort, and the essence of Co-operation consist in the practice recognised by the distributive stores and the Wholesale Society of assigning a share in the profits to consumers in proportion to purchases, then the sphere remaining open for Unionism would be yet more extensive; for the workers in co-operative undertakings as well as in those private businesses, which survived, might seek defence in the resources of organised union.

Accordingly, upon the conception formed of the object and scope of the Co-operative Movement will depend the estimate of the place left for Trade Unionism, and the view of its relations to Co-operation.

But we may go further. For we may suppose that

co-operative production, in the sense of imparting a share of profits to the actual workers, is realised; and yet opportunity may remain for the action of Trade Unions. It is by no means certain that the general introduction of profit-sharing, even if marred and limited by no aristocratic exclusiveness, would result in complete industrial peace. It should always be borne in mind that the share of profits thus distributed, as a French writer has aptly remarked, must be rather the condiment to give savour to the meal—the pepper, salt, and mustard —than the substantial portion of the meal itself. The question of wages must of necessity appear the larger and more immediate concern of the workman, and the question of a share in the profits must seem, by comparison, problematic, unimportant, and remote. In their anxiety to gain an immediate and considerable advantage in wages, the workmen may conceivably, in accordance with the most rational principles of enlightened selfishness, incur a problematic loss of profits, and may demand and support organisations, such as Trade Unions, which will assist them in securing the nearer and more obvious aim. Disputes have not been unknown in establishments conducted on profit-sharing principles. Strikes have occurred in the productive undertakings of the Wholesale Society on the part of workmen, who, as members of retail distributive stores, were indirectly interested in the avoidance of loss to the business in which they were working; and, while human nature remains unaltered in its broad characteristics, such conflict of interests must sometimes occasion the natural consequences.[1]

[1] Cf., for a fuller development of this argument, and that of the following paragraph, the previous and the succeeding Essay.

CO-OPERATION AND TRADE UNIONISM 115

But side by side with this altered conception of the Co-operative Movement, which has contributed to reduce the antithesis formerly erected between Trade Unionism and Co-operation, Trade Unionism itself has undergone new developments. With the recognition of its legal standing, illegal tendencies have largely passed away; and no one, except the most bigoted opponent, would apply to it to-day the language commonly used a quarter of a century ago. The friendly-society side has advanced more definitely to the front; and on this side, at least, Unionism has something in common with that promotion of thrift, which has played a large part in the history of the Co-operative Movement. But, even regarded on the trade-society side, a new spirit has passed over the scene. Organisation implies representation, and with effective representation has come the possibility of peaceful negotiation. In not a few trades the existence of powerful unions, together with strong associations on the part of employers, has led to systematic arrangements for the preservation of industrial peace.[1] Of course this aspect of the Trade Union movement may not always be prominent. The aggressive warlike attitude may sometimes take the place of the peaceful disposition, but the more frequent establishment of conciliation and arbitration boards is a recognised fact of the times; and those, who have earnestly sighed for the inauguration of an era of industrial peace, have found that the path to that goal does not lie exclusively through co-operative partnerships.

The logic of events has, therefore, shown that Trade Unionism and Co-operation are not mutually exclusive; and latterly, perhaps, a more pronounced disposition has

[1] Cf. Essays ii. iii. vii. and viii.

been evident on the part of the adherents of either agency to recognise claims made upon it by the other. It has, for example, been suggested that Trade Unionists might possibly employ some of their funds in assisting efforts of co-operative production; and, with more practical effect, it has been urged that Co-operative distributive stores, Co-operative Wholesale Societies, and Co-operative productive establishments, might set an example to private employers in the treatment of their workmen. Even more daring venturers in the region of speculation have hinted that in the wages paid by co-operative establishments to their workers might be found a standard by comparison with which private employers might know whether they themselves were, or were not, acting justly—were, or were not, paying "a fair day's wage for a fair day's work." And it may also be noticed that later investigation has shown that the wages system itself is far more elastic than was once imagined.[1] It is capable of great modification apart from the formal adoption of the principles of co-operative production as generally understood. In different ways the uniformity of time or piece wages may be exchanged for various encouragements to better work; and Co-operation may be expected to give a fair trial to these different systems, where opportunity offers, and to join hands with Trade Unionism in advancing the interests of workmen.

We have completed the task which we essayed. We have tried to indicate some of the reasons for which Co-operation may be connected with, and distinguished from, Trade Unionism and Socialism. It is possible that we have been able to render scant justice to a subject of vast importance, and that we may seem to have applied

[1] Cf. the previous Essay.

the dissecting knife of the economic surgeon rather than any kinder instrument. But we have succeeded in our object, if we have shown that it is difficult to lay down hard and fast lines of demarcation, or to pronounce definitely on the particular sphere in the movement of society, which each of the three agencies may occupy. The more the economic student reflects on the complex character and multifarious details of society, the firmer becomes his conviction of the value of truths, which may seem to be truisms; and we may conclude by insisting on one of those truths—on the desirability of what we may call the catholicity of social reform. Some reformers may have attached their faith exclusively to one of the three agencies, which we have now been considering. We cannot expect to shake this confidence; and we would not damp their enthusiasm. We would only ask them to keep before their minds the possibility that equally enthusiastic workers may be contributing, with them, to the sum of human progress.

VI.

METHODS OF INDUSTRIAL REFORM.[1]

IN England, as in the rest of the civilised world, there is, at the present moment, a lively and general interest in social and industrial reform. The columns of the daily and periodical press, the discussions at meetings and congresses, the speeches of candidates at municipal and parliamentary elections, and the announcements of publishers' catalogues, afford abundant proof of the intensity and the wide diffusion of this interest. The atmosphere is charged with eager hope and with confident enthusiasm.

That such a tendency is of good augury for the future will only be denied by the soured cynic, whose opinion is as little deserving of credit as that of the visionary fanatic. For it is better that men should desire and anticipate progress, even at the cost of illusion, than that they should shrink from experiment, and abandon themselves to the cowardice of despair. Yet it cannot be doubted that certain dangers beset such a disposition of mind, and to one such danger we may direct our attention for a few minutes.

It has often been observed that social reformers are

[1] An address delivered to the London Branch of the Christian Social Union, and afterwards published in the *La Riforma Sociale*. (September, 1894).

prone to regard their own pet proposal as the sovereign remedy for the ills they are combating, and to dismiss the schemes of others as erroneous or futile. It is so easy to concentrate, and it is so difficult to distribute, enthusiasm with impartial wisdom. It is so tempting to construct some magnificent comprehensive proposal, which will embrace the whole of society; and it seems by comparison so tame and commonplace, so ineffective and puny, to attempt with modest perseverance to accomplish some slight improvement in some particular portion of the race of man. And thus the reformer, who has taken the world for his province, is disposed to resent the intrusion of similar ambitions, and to despise as merely parochial the petty schemes of unpretending workers.[1]

The most superficial observation alone is needed to throw doubt on the validity of such an opinion. A brief study of past history will reveal the shattered hopes and broken promises of adventurers, who have trodden the path before; and it must be sadly confessed that the record of social reform is, to no small extent, a pathetic tale of high aspiration and bitter disappointment. So far the cynic is justified in his mistrust of progress. But, if a reason be sought for these discouraging failures, it is often to be found in the extravagant scale on which the projects were planned and attempted; and it is a careless and one-sided view of history, which will fail to discover the solid and substantial triumphs won by humble and honest workers. It is here that the cynic is mistaken. The failures have attracted attention by the very magnitude of the promises, which have been put forward; while the successes, though numerous, have escaped notice through the very diversity and minuteness of their manifestation.

[1] Cf. Essay i. above.

Recent research into the nature and constitution of society has served to bring into relief its complex and manifold character. The analogy, which one school of thought has sought to establish between society and the human organism, has thrust into unmistakable prominence the significance of a gradual process of minute development—of slow modification and adaptation to environment—in lieu of any sudden and complete change. And the modern forms of Socialism, with all their eager ambitious aspirations, incline to evolution rather than revolution—to a gradual transformation, based on the nature of things, rather than an abrupt and arbitrary reform achieved by the action of bold and resolute individuals. This evolution, they admit, may be assisted, but it cannot be forced, any more than it can finally be prevented. The different aspects, again, which society presents to the student as he passes from one epoch, or class, or country to another, have been emphasised by the comparative and historical methods of investigation introduced of late into various departments of thought. It is true that analogies as well as differences have been discovered, and that broad common lines of evolution have been traced; but it is equally true that attention has been directed to important distinctions of detail, which had been overlooked. And, on minute and candid examination, it appears that projects of vast and uniform character, designed for speedy and general realisation, are, by the very conditions of the case, exposed to imminent risk of failure; and that it is necessary to study carefully different methods of possible adaptation to a changing environment. The point, on which it seems especially desirable to insist, is the necessity of catholicity in social reform, and the advantage of attacking the problem simultaneously on different sides. We must be prepared for the total or partial failure of schemes, which at first have seemed certain to succeed; and we may be surprised at the unexpected triumph of reforms condemned *à priori* as impossible of attainment. In illustration of this conclusion we may proceed to examine into certain facts of the recent industrial history of this country.

If an English economic student were asked to-day to name the chief agencies of *voluntary* industrial reform, he would probably select, as the most potent and obvious, Trade Unionism and Co-operation. If the same question had been put twenty or thirty or forty years ago, he might have returned the same answer; but it is not unlikely that he would have drawn a significant distinction. The hopes and sympathies of the reformer would then have inclined towards Co-operation; and he would have regarded Trade Unions as necessary, perhaps, but as necessary evils. Now the position of affairs has been somewhat reversed. The confidence felt in the future of Co-operation has sensibly declined, while a function of Trade Unions has come into prominence, which has enhanced the importance of the place they may occupy in industrial life, no less on account of intrinsic advantages to themselves than of the benefits, which they may confer on society at large. And thus, with the lapse of time, the relative estimate of these two agencies of industrial reform has been, if not wholly reversed, at least considerably altered. Unsuspected merits have been discovered in the one, while defects, not previously observed, have revealed themselves in the other. The fact deserves, and will reward, closer inquiry.

It is difficult to gauge the extent of the change, which has been effected, without referring to the periodical

literature of some thirty years ago. Those, who are acquainted with that literature, will be ready to allow that the writings of Mr. W. R. Greg reflected the educated thought of his day. In an Essay on the "Intrinsic Vice of Trade Unions," contained in a volume, entitled *Political Problems for our Age and Country*—which was written not long after the publication of the Report of the Royal Commission, appointed in 1867 to inquire into the Sheffield outrages—Mr. Greg used these words[1]:—
"It is needful also . . . that the purposes for which these combinations of workmen were originally formed, or at least to which they are now directed, are *essentially* injurious and unjust; that they are hostile to the interests of the community at large, as well as to those of the artizans themselves; and (what is more to the present purpose) that the objects they have in view *can, from their very nature, only be secured by proceedings intrinsically illegal and oppressive*, commencing by intimidation and 'social pressure,' practically and naturally advancing to assault and battery, vitriol-throwing, blinding, maiming ('laming,' as it is technically termed), and logically and actually leading up to murder, whenever the parties are sufficiently bent upon their ends, and sufficiently exasperated in their feelings to *insist* upon success." In a subsequent essay Mr. Greg passed a high eulogium on what he distinguished as "Industrial and Co-operative Partnerships," which was in marked contrast with his criticism of Trade Unions. "How," he observed,[2] discussing what we should now term *profit-sharing*, "*this* form of partnership, or genuine and fair co-operative system, can be made to work, is a mere matter of detail."

[1] Page 112. [2] Page 151.

Such was the deliberate language of a writer of acknowledged authority, who kept himself abreast of the current of popular opinion. Indeed he was often in advance of that opinion; and it cannot be doubted that in the passages quoted he was expressing the approved judgment of the cultivated and educated thought of his day. Yet at the present time the same language would appear to many—perhaps to most—Englishmen to be curiously exaggerated, though there may be quarters where something similar survives. What then are the reasons for this significant change?

They do not lie so much in the fact that, with the legal recognition of Trade Unions, secured some twenty years ago, the era of illegal violence seems to have passed away; although we must still be prepared at times of excitement to hear of wrong, or doubtful, action on the part of men new to the power, and ignorant of the conditions, of responsibility. Nor do they consist solely in the circumstance that the friendly-society side of Trade Unions— a side, which enjoyed the warm approval of Mr. Greg and others—has developed so largely as to thrust the trade-society side into the background. The accounts of any important union will certainly show that the sums spent on the support of its members during disputes with employers are but a fraction of those paid for relief in sickness and in other benevolent directions. The combination of the two objects in the same society has probably exerted a restraining influence on the leaders of the unions for the very reason, for which Mr. Greg himself objected to it—the danger, namely, that money, accumulated with patient sacrifice for beneficent objects, might be rapidly dissipated in initiating or maintaining a strike. Even the newer unions, more recently formed among unskilled labourers, which at first were disposed to lay exclusive stress on what Mr. Greg would have distinguished as the trade-society side, have more recently exhibited a tendency to imitate the older unions in the matter of friendly benefits.

Nor, again, is it merely the case that the latest economic investigation has discovered an important, and, in the opinion of some inquirers, a necessary, function for Trade Unions in the determination of wages. In Mr. Greg's time the idea was generally held that Trade Unions were useless, because, on the one hand, the interests of masters and men were identical, and, on the other, the unions would not be able to resist the potent forces of competition. This opinion has certainly been modified; and it may even be thought that the common view inclines now too far in an opposite direction. For, if it is true that the interests of employers and employed are identical, it is no less true that they are also opposed.[1] They are identical in the *production* of wealth; for the ultimate source of remuneration of either party is found in the total amount of wealth produced, and, the larger that amount, the greater also is likely to be the share falling to either. But here the identity of interests ceases. It is unquestionably to the interest of the employed, that the employer's profit should be such as to induce him to bestow all his energy and skill on his business undertaking, to introduce the best and newest machinery, to procure materials in sufficient quantity and adequate quality, and to devise and adopt the most improved methods of organisation. It is equally to the interest of the master that his men should receive sufficient wages to maintain themselves, and to rear and

[1] Cf., for further consideration of this point, Essay viii. below.

METHODS OF INDUSTRIAL REFORM 125

educate their children, according to an efficient standard of life, and that they should be able to enjoy a healthy amount of leisure and recreation. So far, the interests of both parties are identical, but beyond this point they necessarily diverge; and the divergence may easily occasion dispute.

For in the *distribution* of wealth it cannot be doubted that, the greater the share of the one party, the less will be that of the other; and hence it is natural, it is even inevitable, that difficulties should arise from time to time; and it is unreasonable, without careful inquiry, to accuse one side or the other of wilful and gratuitous dissension. Either may be censured for carrying matters so far as to injure production materially; and in that case they will inevitably injure themselves. If the employed prevent the outlay of the necessary capital, and hinder the exercise of the requisite business capacity, they naturally must suffer by their conduct; and, if the condition of the labourer be degraded, the employers cannot escape participation in the injurious consequences. By such action either party, aiming at immediate advantage, is careless of ultimate harm.

In the *distribution* of wealth, therefore, a real divergence of interests may arise between masters and men; and the formation of an union to protect the welfare of the men is rather a recognition of actual fact than the gratuitous introduction of an unnecessary element of strife. The most recent economic research has tended to confirm the advantages, which the men claim to derive from such associations. They may be unable to triumph over adverse influences. They may not succeed in preventing an influx of labour into their industry, attracted by the promise of increased wages. They may secure an advance of wages for themselves at the cost of loss to their fellows, who possibly may be consumers of the goods raised in price in consequence of this advance in wages, or producers of the materials or machinery, which are used, or be otherwise employed in some auxiliary industry. They may compel the *entrepreneurs*, or the capitalists, baffled of the expectation of finding relief in an increased price for their products, or a reduced price for their raw material or machinery, to abandon the business, or remove it to other districts or countries. All these are possibilities; but it is none the less true that Trade Unions give the workman, bargaining with the employer, an advantage, which he would not otherwise possess. He secures the benefit of combined forces and accumulated savings, and is enabled to hold out for a reserve price. Such at least is the present opinion of many English and foreign economists;[1] and it is strengthened by the comparison of a single employer to a strong combination—a combined mass of capital and business capacity — which has been made by Professor Marshall.[2] From this point of view Trade Unions may be regarded as supplying a means of opposing one combination to another, and of placing the contracting parties on an equality.

All these considerations have been brought into prominence since Mr. Greg wrote; and they have unquestionably contributed to produce a change of opinion on the merits and defects of Trade Unions. But they are not perhaps of such importance as the point on which we may now proceed to dwell. Mr. Greg regarded Trade Unions as fundamentally trade-societies, constituted essentially for the object of waging perpetual or intermittent strife:

---

[1] Cf. Essay ii. [2] Cf. *Economics of Industry*, bk. vi. ch. xiii. sec. 4.

it never occurred to him, or his contemporaries, that they might be instruments of industrial peace. This possibility, however, has lately become more evident; and to a certain extent it is due to the changes we have noted above. The comparative disappearance of violent methods on the part of the unions themselves, and the development of mutual and friendly benefits, accompanied by unwillingness to dissipate funds in the costly luxury of a strike, the realisation by the workmen of the power of an union in influencing wages, and the conviction on the part of the masters that to seek at all costs a larger profit may result in "killing the goose that lays the golden eggs," have combined to produce this result. But in the last analysis it rests on the diffusion of a belief, which with every candid and instructed student only needs accurate statement to carry conviction, and on the uniform testimony of a wide general experience, that representation forms the only basis of successful negotiation, confirmed by the special history during twenty-five years of a particular industry, the conditions of which *prima facie* might have seemed least adapted to occasion, or exhibit, favourable results.

It is unnecessary to demonstrate formally the principle that disputes in industry, as in every other department of human activity, can only be settled, or prevented, by negotiation between the parties at issue, and that the negotiators should, if possible, be few in number, and must be representative.[1] Thus far every thoughtful man, whether he be, or be not, favourably disposed to Trade Unions, would probably give his assent. But he is likely to accept with more reserve the next stage in the reasoning,

[1] Cf., for fuller development of this reasoning, the author's *Industrial Peace*.

in which it is affirmed that Trade Unions supply the most effective machinery available for the representation of the men. Yet, as a matter of actual fact, they have certainly fulfilled this function, and it would be difficult, if not impossible, to discover adequate or suitable substitutes. Without organisation effective representation seems impossible; without representation a successful settlement of disputes is little more than an idle chimera; and without such settlement industrial peace cannot supersede industrial war. It does not seem possible to impugn the successive portions of this argument, and, if we remove the intervening part, it is reduced to the dictum that Trade Unions are an essential condition of industrial peace.

Mr. Greg, no doubt, would have been surprised at this conclusion; and yet it rests on no fanciful foundation, but on prosaic fact. Important testimony on the matter has been collected by the Labour Commission. We may here[1] refer especially to that of the witnesses in Section A., which was occupied with "Mining, Iron, Engineering, Hardware, Shipbuilding, and Cognate Trades." In some of these industries the relations between masters and men have been characterised by the existence, and pursuance, of a method of procedure, which is eminently rational; and the results attained are marvellous. We may select some of the most remarkable. What has perhaps especially been shown is that the general public entertains an exaggerated idea of the frequency of industrial disputes. It is always hearing, as it thinks, of strikes and rumours of strikes; and it is certainly the case that the infancy of an union is often accompanied by obstinate and vexatious quarrels. Hence it is only natural that in England at the present moment,[2] when

[1] Cf. also the following Essay.   [2] *i.e.* 1893 and 1894.

unskilled workmen, hitherto unorganised, have endeavoured with success to construct combinations, strikes should attract and receive attention. Nor can it be denied that a new form of dispute has recently come into prominence, though it was not unknown before. It is not very long ago that a quarrel arose on the banks of the Tyne between engineers and plumbers, when either union advanced a claim for the exclusive assignment to its members of a certain description of work. Disputes of this nature usually arise when, as in shipbuilding, the industry itself is undergoing change, and the work of different classes of workmen is nearly allied, or wholly identical. But nevertheless it remains doubtful whether the general public does not exaggerate the frequency of industrial disputes, and fail to appraise at their true value the many cases, in which they are prevented or peacefully adjusted.

Some prolonged and bitter struggle, like that in the coal trade of the Midlands, or some important movement among a mass of workmen, such as the dock-labourers of London, attracts the attention of newspaper-reporters, and is described with abundant and picturesque detail, while the minor disputes of daily, or hourly, occurrence, which at their first inception, or within a brief subsequent interval, are peacefully adjusted, escape unobserved, and the institutions, which have contributed to accomplish these satisfactory results, rob the newspapers of "good copy" and the general public of reading, which, if melancholy, is perhaps not uninteresting. As in many cases of social reform, failures attract attention, while successes pass unheeded; and one of the most useful functions of a Royal Commission, such as that upon Labour, consists in the diligent and authoritative collection of information respecting neglected or forgotten facts.

It may not be unprofitable to dwell for a while on some of the detailed evidence laid before the Commission on this question of industrial strife. Much has been written in the daily press on a recent strike in the Durham Coal Trade; and it cannot be denied that this was a bitter and protracted struggle. But the serious and notorious character of the conflict should not make us forget that, for twenty years, a committee of masters and men had, with little friction and discontent, settled countless disputes arising in the case of particular mines, and that for twelve years the general rate of wages had been regulated by means of sliding scales amicably arranged by both parties. In the Northumberland Coal Trade, again, a strike occurred in 1887,[1] which dragged its weary length across the space of seventeen weeks: but it succeeded twelve years of uninterrupted peace, and since 1873 a Joint Committee of masters and men had existed in that district, which rivalled, if it did not surpass, that of the Durham trade. In the manufactured iron industry of the North of England, where formidable difficulties arose from the fluctuating nature of the trade, and the rough uneducated character of the men, there was a record of industrial peace, extending over a quarter of a century.[2]

Similar instances may be discovered in other industries, varying in details of constitution, and in measure of success. In fact, there is now in existence a considerable literature dealing with ventures in conciliation and arbitration; and the student may compare different systems, and determine the reasons why an experiment, successful in one quarter, fails in another, and note the slight, yet important, improvements, which the special requirements

[1] Cf. Essay iii. above for an account of this dispute.
[2] *Ibid.*; and also *Industrial Peace*, chap. iii.

METHODS OF INDUSTRIAL REFORM 131

of a particular industry have discovered for the benefit of others. Some, for example, prefer conciliation, because, they say, the question under dispute is examined by those, who possess a practical knowledge of the actual conditions of the industry. Others find arbitration effective where voluntary agreement has failed; for, they argue, the fact of its existence exerts an indirect pressure on the parties involved, inducing them to avoid or limit the cases, in which resort to a third party is necessary, and it appears to be the only mode of escaping from the deadlock, which occurs in the absence of such provision. Some, again, approve of sliding scales, by which wages vary according to the selling price of the product, and they recommend improvements in the construction and working of those scales; while others, for various reasons, criticise the general character, and the particular details, of these various expedients for securing industrial peace. Such divergent opinions have been brought together by the Labour Commission. They deserve, and they will reward, the careful and impartial study of industrial reformers; and they correspond, to some extent, at any rate, to the varying characteristics of different industries. Two facts, however, stand out prominently from the mass of particulars. The first is the solid success achieved in this department of industrial reform. The second, and not less important, is the large, if not indispensable, part taken in the matter by Trade Unions.

It is true that in the evidence given before the Commission suggestions are advanced for investing with a legal sanction the awards of arbitrators, and the decisions of boards of conciliation; but, when the precise *modus operandi*, or the probable results, of such legislation are considered, the suggestions seem to be lacking in solidity of basis, and to experience no little difficulty in meeting the objections of opponents. In fact, by the bulk of the witnesses the idea of such intervention is emphatically rejected; and in any case, in view of results attained by voluntary initiative, despite of some discouraging failures, it seems premature to have recourse to the sanction or compulsion of law.[1]

In some industries, indeed, a pecuniary fine has been actually imposed for breach of a voluntary agreement concluded by the leaders of the union with the representatives of the masters, and for infringement of the decisions of arbitrators. The statement on this point of the secretary of the Boilermakers and Iron-Shipbuilders' Union may be said to constitute an epoch in the history of industrial relations. It should be noted that in this industry no board of conciliation or arbitration had been regularly constituted; but the secretary stated[2] that "for many years" no dispute "on a large scale" had arisen. He added: "We do not believe in them" (*i.e.*, in disputes), "and our experience is that ninety-nine out of every hundred can be amicably settled, if there is a desire on the part of employers and the representatives of the men to do so." The annual percentage of the total income of the Union expended on disputes during the previous ten years amounted, according to his figures, to little more than three and three-quarters.

But the particular case, to which special attention may be drawn, is this; and the actual words used by Mr. Knight may be quoted. "We had a case," he remarks,[3] "at Hartlepool a short time since, where a vessel was

---

[1] Cf. Essays vii. and viii., and also *Industrial Peace*, chap. iii.
[2] Q. 20,681.   [3] Q. 20,718.

in for repairing, and the men knew that the vessel was in a hurry and thought there was a very good chance to get an advance in their wages, so they went to their foreman and made a demand for two shillings a week advance. The foreman, knowing the arrangement between our Association and the Employers' Association, refused to give the advance, and at once wired to me at Newcastle, and by the orders of the council I sent back to say that the employer was to give the men the advance as asked for, because we did not want to stop the work, as the ship was in a hurry, and we wanted to get her off. The employer gave the men the advance as asked for, and we at once sent to the firm, requesting the firm to tell us the amount of money they had paid to the men as advances of wages on that job. When the job was completed those particulars and details were sent to us at Newcastle, and also the names of the men who were engaged upon the job, and who had made the demand. As soon as that was done our council ordered the members, who received the money, to refund that again to the Society, and we sent a cheque from the head office to that firm equal in amount to the advances given."

This is a plain unvarnished tale; but perhaps it is more convincing than the most elaborate argument, and it demonstrates the nature and extent of the authority, which may be exercised by the leaders of a powerful union, in inducing their constituents to maintain loyally an agreement concluded in their behalf. The power, it is true, like all other power, may be abused; but recent events in certain industries, such as the Durham and Northumberland Coal Trades, tend to show that the more serious and immediate danger may lie in refusal on the part of the men to listen to the counsel of their leaders, and in the angry reckless use of the right, vested in themselves by the democratic constitution of the unions, of deciding the question at issue by a plebiscite. In any case the evidence collected by the Commission establishes these significant facts. In the first place expedients for preventing, and adjusting, disputes attain their object more completely in those industries, in which the organisations are older and more powerful. In the second place it is difficult, if not impossible, to discover any satisfactory substitute for Trade Unions as an instrument for the authoritative representation of the men. Mr. Knight stated[1] in his evidence that "a marked improvement" had "taken place amongst employers of labour in their treatment of trade organisations. In most cases employers now recognise trade unions and treat with them as such, which is an enormous advantage to both parties, for which we are thankful"; and he remarked[2] at another stage of his evidence that there was "scarcely a non-society man in the whole of" their "districts. I suppose," he added, "95 per cent. of the men are in our Society, and in some of the districts there is not a single non-society man."

Mr. Lindsay Wood, who, as a master, gave evidence on behalf of the Durham coal-owners, admitted[3] in his turn that the result of strong organisation on both sides in that trade had been to "secure harmony between employers and employed." The "existence of official relations between employers and employed" had, he freely allowed,[4] "done very much to diminish friction and to prevent strikes"; and one observation, which he made, was specially significant in its bearing on the general question,

[1] Q. 20,698.   [2] Q. 20,725.   [3] Q. 1789.   [4] Q. 1786.

METHODS OF INDUSTRIAL REFORM 135

and in anticipation of events, which were then impending in the trade.[1] "I think," he said,[2] "that the fault we are suffering from at the present moment is the want of discipline of the members of the association"; and, in answer to a question whether he would like to see associations stronger rather than weaker, he replied,[3] "I would if I have to deal with the association." It would be easy to multiply examples of testimony pointing in the same direction; but we may confine our attention to the evidence relating to the Board of Conciliation and Arbitration in the Manufactured Iron Trade of the North of England, which is especially noteworthy, because this Board may be fittingly regarded as the illustration *par excellence* of success in such matters.[4]

Mr. Trow, the eloquent representative of the men, and the secretary of their union, was himself a member of the Labour Commission, and many of the questions put by him to different witnesses were not uninstructive. He also gave evidence, in the course of which he observed:[5]— "It is necessary that the Commission should understand how truly the men believe in the system" [of arbitration and conciliation, established in that industry], "and how honest and faithful they are in carrying out its awards." And, when asked whether a non-union man could be chosen as a representative on the Board of Arbitration, he replied[6] that he would not be selected, "because we should consider there was nothing binding upon him, as he represented nobody, and it would be unfair upon us to sit

---

[1] A strike followed, in which a conflict between the views of the majority of the men and the opinions and advice of the leaders became apparent, as on an earlier occasion in Northumberland (see Essay iii.).

[2] Q. 1787.   [3] Q. 1788.   [4] Cf. Essay iii. above.
[5] Q. 15,159.   [6] Q. 15,399.

with him before the employers and pledge a man who represented nobody but himself."

The evidence that we have quoted should suffice to convince impartial students that a new and useful side of the work of Trade Unions has been discovered in the prevention and adjustment of industrial disputes. We must not indeed entertain exaggerated hopes, or we shall be doomed to painful disillusion; but we are certainly not in error, or in conflict with fact, when we describe Trade Unions as possible peacemakers. This conviction has slowly, but steadily, permeated public opinion, and has contributed to give to the Unions a different position from that which they held in Mr. Greg's day. But an important conclusion is suggested respecting the probable direction of industrial reform. At one time it seemed that an obstinate deep-rooted antagonism, proclaimed and accentuated by Trade Unions, existed of necessity between employers and employed, and that the effectual remedy consisted either in establishing a partnership between master and men by some system of profit-sharing, or in enabling the workmen to start a business on their own account under some form of co-operative production. A further possibility has now been discovered; and, though some may regard it as an unsatisfactory compromise, and hold that profit-sharing or co-operative production is the true and final remedy, on the other hand these systems, once considered unimpeachable, have disclosed serious defects, and in actual practice, it must be confessed, have not afforded much ground for encouragement.

Here, again, an illustration is offered of the manner in which the fondest and most cherished hopes of social reformers may prove delusive, or be realised in a different shape from that which was once expected.[1] In this country there are co-operative retail stores, and there is a Wholesale Society, established for providing, and, in some degree, for producing, articles of consumption. These stores fill a wide sphere of activity, and have continually grown in importance. They proceed on the judicious system of cash payments, and they generally aim at supplying articles of genuine quality. They are not, however, constituted on the same pattern as those Army and Navy and Civil Service Supply Stores, so familiar in London, where goods are sold at lower prices than those commanded in the ordinary shops. In the workmen's co-operative stores, on the contrary, the goods are sold at the current retail prices, and, at certain fixed periods, the profits accruing are divided among shareholders and customers in proportion to their purchases. Anyone, who will, may become purchaser, and shareholder—may participate in the benefits, and join in the administration, of the store. The members are eager to enlarge their numbers, for such an increase involves additional trade and augmented profits. The store is thus, as Mrs. Sidney Webb has shown in her work on *The Co-operative Movement in Great Britain*, a democratic institution, with an excellent record in the past, and great promise for the future. As is not unfrequently the case, incidental advantages, of which the first promoters took little account, have, with the lapse of time, grown in relative importance, and shown themselves pregnant with useful consequence.

Among others of this nature may be placed the encouragement of saving. For it has been possible for men and women to save without being aware of the process until it is accomplished. They save when they purchase

[1] Cf. the previous Essay, and also Essay iv.

their goods; for, while they are paying the current price across the counter, a portion of the quarterly dividend is being reserved for their benefit; and it may reach a figure sufficient to induce investment, facilities for which may be offered by the store itself. This result, which is placed beyond question, was at first incidental, and its full possibilities were hardly suspected.

But the earliest, most ardent, and prominent promoters of Co-operation, among whom the Christian Socialists were numbered, entertained wider views, and cherished larger hopes. They would have considered the results actually achieved petty and unsatisfactory; for in Co-operation they aimed at a reformation of society in general, and of industry in particular. They fondly imagined that working men would become their own employers, and not merely capitalists, as the movement has rendered them. They looked, in fact, for what is commonly known as co-operative production. So far these eager and amiable hopes have, to a large extent, proved illusory. In actual practice it cannot be maintained that co-operative production has achieved remarkable success. The number of such enterprises, in this country at least, is small. The opinion of many of the most expert administrators of co-operative business is apparently opposed to the principle of giving a share in the profits to the employed as such, and adheres to the ordinary wages system. And lastly, critics, such as Mrs. Sidney Webb, in her *Co-operative Movement in Great Britain*, and Mr. David Schloss, in his *Methods of Industrial Remuneration*, have urged[1] that the exclusive attention given to the particular difficulty of superseding the employer has diverted notice from others, which are not less formidable. The business of

[1] Cf., for a fuller statement of these arguments, Essay iv. above.

production, they maintain, has been attempted, and successfully accomplished, by working-men co-operators; for the Wholesale Society, and many of the retail stores, not only sell, but manufacture; and it is the principle of remunerating the actual workers by means of a share in the profits, which condemns co-operative production, as the term is generally understood, in the judgment of practical co-operators, and conflicts with the democratic character of the movement. It introduces an aristocratic taint; for, unlike the privileges of the retail store and the Wholesale Society, which are open to all, participation in profits is limited to a select number, who, in all probability, will not desire to extend the advantages to others.

This indictment, if valid, implies the censure of a system, which secured the preference of writers, impressed by the difficulty of finding a satisfactory substitute for the employer in the direction of co-operative business; for the principle of remuneration, which they favoured, is common to co-operative production, and to their own proposals of profit-sharing. *Prima facie*, no doubt, this last method of industrial reform offers no inconsiderable attractions. It seems to effect a happy combination of the old ability and experience of the employer with a new incentive to diligence and activity on the part of the employed. But it has not escaped damaging criticism. The profits shared are, and of necessity must be, small in proportion to the regular wages which are paid; and sometimes, indeed, they form a substitute for the higher wages which, in the absence of the system, would have been given. The reasons, for which the system is recommended to the approval of the master, are not likely to render it peculiarly welcome to the men. Its upholders claim that, in virtue of it, his profits will increase, consequent on the greater energy, diligence, and care exhibited by the men; and thus confessedly the men will only enjoy a part of the profits that they have admittedly produced. In consideration of this imperfect participation they may be asked to surrender freedom to strike for an advance of wages, or in resistance to a reduction; and, if the bonus be given, as is often the case, in the form of a deferred annuity, or of insurance against loss through illness, or as a provision for surviving and dependent relatives in the event of death, such advantages may be forfeited, if the employment for some reason or other is left. Such conditions are not unlikely to appear to Trade Unionists to be serious defects, if not fatal irremovable obstacles; and it is idle to think that they will be disposed to regard with favour a system, under which an existing independence is sacrificed for advantages that may prove hypothetical.

From another point of view some doubt may be felt of the high anticipations formed of co-operative production and profit-sharing. The two methods have been put forward as certain guarantees against industrial war; for it is supposed that workmen will not strike against their companions in co-operation, and that they will not risk, by putting pressure on an employer, who has admitted them to partnership, a diminution of the profits in which they are going to share. Trade Unions, it is urged, may act as defenders of workmen's interests in the event of industrial war; but the occasion for warfare is removed by co-operative production and profit-sharing. There is undoubtedly some truth in these arguments; but objections are not lacking.[1] For it is easy to show

---

[1] Cf. Essay iv. above.

METHODS OF INDUSTRIAL REFORM 141

that there are opportunities for dissension among co-operators, and between master and men engaged in a profit-sharing enterprise. An inequality in the remuneration of different classes of workmen, or of different individuals of the same class, is a sufficient pretext; and the quarrel between the engineers and the plumbers on the Tyne, to which we alluded previously, is certainly not uninstructive in this connection.

Nor is it difficult to see that the security offered by the supporters of co-operative production and profit-sharing may be adequate in some cases, and inadequate in others. They rely on the identity of the interests at stake. But anyone, who does not rest satisfied with superficial appearance, must reflect on the advantage to be expected, on the one hand, from an advance of wages, and the loss to be sustained, on the other, by a reduction of bonus; and, in the majority of cases, he will acknowledge that the wages are large, and the bonus is small, and that the wages are immediate, and the bonus belongs to a more or less distant future. If the metaphor be not pressed too far, we may say that most men can discern the wages with the naked eye, but that the profits require the microscope or telescope of the trained economist. Nor can we forget that cases may arise where passion and prejudice may blind men to their real interests. The hope, then, of suppressing industrial war by means of co-operation and profit-sharing cannot be confidently entertained; and, if Trade Unions may with some reason be expected to assume the *rôle* of peacemakers, we may feel doubt in which direction the student may look with greater security for industrial reform.

Prophecy, however, is proverbially fallacious, and the

wise will venture on it with very great caution; but from this study of the history of the past we may, perhaps, deduce the lesson that it is probable, and it is certainly desirable, that industrial reform should develop, not in one, but in many directions.[1] We have dwelt on the favourable side of Trade Unions, which recent events have brought into prominence, and on some disadvantages of co-operative production and profit-sharing; but we may none the less readily admit that Trade Unions are not free from defects, and that profit-sharing and co-operative production are capable of conferring great benefit on the industrial world.[2] For the different systems are not mutually exclusive. We may hope to witness many successful experiments in the future in many directions. What we may now reasonably ask is an open mind and a catholic temper—a willingness to test reforms which promise well, and a firm resolve that preconceived opinions shall not interfere with the lessons of experience. We need enthusiasm indeed, for the difficulties confronting us are great, and nothing but intensity of purpose, aided by strong conviction, can overthrow them. We also need prudence to avoid delusion, and prevent dissipation of resources. But, above all, we require diligence in the study of facts, and promptitude in profiting by their teaching. Without these our enthusiasm is only too likely to evaporate in fanciful chimeras, and our caution to take refuge in timid, ineffective indolence.

[1] Cf. Essay i.   [2] Cf. Essay iv.

VII.

THE REPORT OF THE LABOUR COMMISSION.[1]

THE publication of the final report of the Labour Commission has brought to a close an inquiry which is probably the most elaborate that has ever been instituted by the Government of this country. It is with feelings of mingled gratitude and despair that the economic student has, during the last few years, watched the steady accumulation on his shelves of the literature issued by the Commission. He cannot fail to be grateful for the energy, which has collected together such a mass of information; but he may well despair at the prospect of coping with it, even when aided by the various indexes, summaries, and digests prepared by the Secretary. A few figures taken from the Report[2] of that official upon the work of the office will illustrate, more forcibly than any words, the immense character of the inquiry. Sixty-seven Blue Books—some of considerable bulk—one hundred and eighty-two sittings, five hundred and eighty-three witnesses, and a correspondence amounting to forty-eight thousand, eight hundred letters and reports sent by post, and thirteen thousand, five hundred received, indexed, and filed, are figures to which

[1] A Paper read before Section F of the British Association, at Oxford, 1894, and published in the *Economic Journal* for September 1894.
[2] Fifth Report, part ii. pp. 1-25.

it would be difficult, if not impossible, to discover a parallel; and we are prepared to learn that the Commission has proved the most costly that has ever been undertaken, and has absorbed some fifty thousand pounds.

What then, we may ask, is the outcome of this vast inquiry? A brilliant article from a well-known pen has appeared in one of the monthly magazines,[1] in which the writer sums up her opinion by selecting as her title *The Failure of the Labour Commission*. But it may be doubted whether the title does not involve a *petitio principii*; for our verdict upon the results of the Commission must depend on the expectations we have formed. If, like Mrs. Webb, we hold that society is disorganised, and in need of radical reform, if we interpret every sign of the times as pointing in one direction, if we look forward to the certain substitution of a collectivist *régime* for the present industrial order, we shall naturally be impatient of any questioning of the expediency, or practicability, of proposals of a collectivist tendency, such as the legislative introduction of an Eight Hours Day, and we shall be inclined to dismiss such questioning as an exercise of dialectical ingenuity. Nor shall we be disposed to remain satisfied with the idea that a remedy, effective over a tolerably wide and increasing range, for some of those maladies, which are regarded by collectivist writers as symptomatic of fatal disorder, can be discovered and applied by voluntary effort, unaided and unhindered by State-interference; and we may set aside the idea as idle and antiquated. A Majority Report, which is content for the most part to present a summary of opinions put forward on either side of a disputed question, like the

[1] *Nineteenth Century*, July, 1894.

Eight Hours Day, and, impressed by what voluntary experimental effort has already achieved in the prevention of industrial conflict, is not prepared to regard as necessary, or to recommend as desirable, the intervention of the State in the *rôle* of compulsory mediator, may well appear tame and impotent beside a Minority Report, which contemplates organic changes in the constitution of society, and makes no attempt to conceal the positiveness of the opinions, which those, who have signed it, have formed, not unfrequently, it would seem, without any very manifest disposition to hear, or examine, what may be urged on the opposite side of debatable questions. It is scarcely unjust, and it is not untrue, to remark that the Majority Report aspires at least, whether it attain success or not, to be judicial; and that the Minority Report proceeds from men, whose judgment of the demands of a popular policy may be shrewd and acute, and their experience of the feelings and hopes of certain important classes of workmen wide and intimate, but whose bias is unmistakable, and whose language is that of advocates rather than judges. Where the points at issue are fine and complex, judges may hesitate where advocates may be sure; and Mrs. Webb, we imagine, would be the last to deny that she is a convinced advocate of radical change, and that her sympathies accord with the signers of the Minority Report.

It is, it must be admitted, a task of some difficulty to define the proper functions of a Commission. The cynic would probably affirm that its primary object is to avoid inconvenient legislation—to appear to gratify a demand by inquiring into its reasons. No doubt the immediate effect of the appointment of a Commission may be thus described without serious inaccuracy. It certainly results in the temporary, and sometimes in the permanent, postponement of legislation. But the further question arises whether such a consequence is not fraught more often with benefit than injury. When a popular cry has once been effectually started, it not unfrequently happens that it is caught up, and passed on, with undiscriminating enthusiasm. But the proposal, once subjected to searching examination, is found to involve unsuspected dangers and to present unimagined difficulties. It is undoubtedly the function of a Commission to bring these dangers and difficulties to light; and such an end can be attained in few more effective ways than by the pertinacious interrogation and cross-examination of the advocates of the proposal. This examination may be conducted by a small body of experts, skilled only in the elimination of irrelevant matter, and interested, not in the triumph or defeat of a cause, but in the ascertainment of truth and the refutation of unsound argument; and a Commission constituted on this basis is perhaps the ideal form. But it is hard to find Commissioners of the calibre and temper required, and the more popular mode of representing various interests, though it may lead to an inconclusive report, does secure the rigorous scrutiny of enthusiastic plans by hostile critics, while their supporters enjoy an opportunity of bringing out their merits. It may be plausibly argued that in the case for proposals of organic changes in the industrial arrangements of society it is even more important to realise the difficulties than to know the advantages of any suggested course of action; and a Commission representative of different interests and opinions rarely fails to achieve the first of these ends. No critic of the Labour Commission would deny that its members represented the most varied interests. No student of its voluminous publications could fail to acknowledge the vast extent of the

REPORT OF THE LABOUR COMMISSION 147

ground, which had been traversed, or the great diversity of opinion that had been elicited. No reader of the Majority Report would venture to complain that it did not present a full and accurate statement of the views of the advocates and opponents of industrial changes. The signers of the Minority Report themselves affirm[1] that the "summary of the arguments used by witnesses for and against particular proposals" has, so far as they can judge, "been intelligently and impartially performed." They apparently consider such a summary of secondary importance, and they do not think that the conclusions drawn by the majority are either adequate or accurate; but with the fairness of the summary itself they have no quarrel.

With regard to one of the most important questions, which came within the scope of the Commission's investigations, it may be doubted whether in presenting such a summary they have not rendered the most useful and opportune service in their power; and, whether the summary is, or is not, the result[2] of an exercise of dialectical skill in the conduct of the examination of some of the witnesses by some of the Commissioners, it is at least in strict accord with the traditional practice of Royal Commissions. They are expected to bring into close juxtaposition the opposing arguments put forward on either side of debated questions; and this function is considered as important as that of drawing conclusions and offering recommendations. The latter must almost of necessity either be biassed by the predilections of individual Commissioners, or must attain unanimity by vague generalities; but the former duty can be satisfactorily discharged without the intrusion of bias or a recourse to vagueness. Perhaps the most debatable,

[1] Fifth Report, part i. p. 127. [2] As Mrs. Webb argues.

and certainly not the least important, question that came before the Commission, was that of an Eight Hours Day; and it was pre-eminently a question that required the treatment we have endeavoured to indicate. It cannot be denied that the cry for a further limitation of the hours of labour has attained a wide popularity; but it can scarcely be doubted that the enthusiasm, which has been excited, is undiscriminating. Nor can it be disputed that, whatever opinion may be honestly entertained of its expedience or feasibility, it is a question on which legislative action should not be hastily or carelessly taken. It is a question, the precise meaning of which is not free from uncertainty, and the consequences are hard to determine. If the arguments in favour of it be sound, they will stand the test of severe examination; and, if they be faulty, the dangers and difficulties of the proposal will be brought into naked prominence by such a process. It is one of those cases where a "leap in the dark" is a hazardous venture; and, if the Commission has done nothing else, it has served to throw some light on the darkness.

No doubt some further inquiry might have been made with advantage into the actual experience of the working of an Eight Hours Day; and we may regard the omission to make such inquiry as a defect. But we may also hold that the meaning attached by various advocates to the proposal, and the possible consequences that might follow on its adoption, required and deserved the most searching examination, and that the time of the Commission has not been wasted in consequence. It has certainly shown that there is considerable difference of opinion among working-men on the necessity or advisability of introducing an Eight Hours Day by legislative sanction, and that in the trades and districts, which desire

REPORT OF THE LABOUR COMMISSION 149

it, a minority of no inconsiderable strength is opposed. It has also shown that the proposal is urged by different classes of workmen with different, and even conflicting, aims—that some, like the coal miners, regard it as a means of raising wages by limiting production, while others, like the transport trades, hold that the output will be maintained by employing the unemployed. It has shown, once more, that various difficulties attach to the methods suggested for bringing the change into effect, and that, whether we allow a trade an option to assent or to be exempt, it will not be easy to determine the limits of a trade, or to ascertain its wishes, and that similar obstacles will arise, if we substitute districts for trades, or supplement trades by districts. In short, the Commission has shown, as we might expect, that the proposal has not yet been thoroughly considered; and, if this be the case, it would naturally seem to follow that the legislation, for which we are ripe, is only that of a tentative and experimental character.

It is in a similar spirit that the Commissioners deal with the larger question of extending the sphere of public employment. They are content to present a summary of opposing views, and to recommend minor reforms on existing lines; and they do not share the confidence felt by the signers of the Minority Report in the inevitable approach, and certain success, of collectivist organisation. Which report reflects the more accurately the present state of general opinion can hardly be doubted; and, if the Commission represented varied interests, it was to be expected that the majority should arrive at a cautious conclusion — inclining in a negative direction — on schemes, which pointed to the reorganisation of society on a new basis. With regard to many minor reforms, such as the improvement of the sanitary condition of domestic workshops, the increased efficiency of inspection, and the provision of better cottage accommodation for the agricultural labourer, they do not appear to be in fundamental disagreement with the minority, although they are inclined to emphasise less strongly the evils of the existing state of affairs, and to be less drastic in the remedial measures, which they suggest.

But, after all, the main subject, to which the attention of the Commission was directed, was the means of preventing industrial quarrel; and the consideration of the conditions of labour, of the limitation of the hours of work, of irregularity of employment, of a Labour Department and Labour Statistics, of the employment of women, and of agricultural labour, must be regarded as subordinate to this main subject. It is only so far as they bear upon it that these questions fall within the scope of the inquiry. The Commission—to quote the actual terms of appointment—was instructed to "inquire into the questions affecting the relations between employer and employed, the combinations of employers and employed, and the conditions of labour, which have been raised during the recent trade disputes in the United Kingdom; and to report whether legislation can with advantage be directed to the remedy of any evils that may be disclosed, and, if so, in what manner." The Minority Report expressly assigns as its reason for discussing the organisation of society on collectivist principles the belief that the "fundamental cause of disputes between employers and employed is to be found" "in the unsatisfactory position occupied by the wage-earning class" under existing conditions. What, then, is the conclusion of the Commissioners on this question of industrial quarrels, and of their prevention? It is scarcely inaccurate to say that they found themselves confronted by such a remarkable development of voluntary effort that little, if any, room was left for new suggestion. Even the Minority Report, with some apparent inconsistency, is content here to assign to the State the *rôle* of counsellor rather than dictator. But the Commission has rendered valuable service by placing on authoritative record what has been already achieved, and establishing some important conclusions not hitherto generally recognised. For it is the business of a commission not merely to collect and sift opinion, but to ascertain and arrange facts. On this question, at least, it cannot fairly be accused of a failure to amass material. The examination of witnesses—both employers and employed — from each industry in succession by the three separate committees, into which the Commission was divided, supplemented by returns received to inquiries made of the various associations of employers and employed, has resulted in an exhaustive survey of the conditions of English industry in this respect; and the reports prepared by the Secretary on the aspect of industrial affairs in the other countries of Europe, in the United States of America, and in our Colonies and Dependencies, furnish material for comparison between our own position and that obtaining elsewhere. For student and legislator alike such a survey must prove of the highest value; and it is the more valuable because, unlike the evidence of experts, which, rightly or wrongly, the Commission seems to have adopted a general policy of excluding, the facts are derived from first-hand information.

What, then, are the main conclusions that may be drawn from this mass of material? The first and most obvious is that a number of experiments have been made in the past, and that more are being made in the present, with a view to the preservation of industrial peace. The second is that, in spite of some disappointment, considerable success has attended those experiments. The third is that the main conditions of success are now ascertained; and the fourth and last is that little room is left for the intervention of the State.

The first two of these conclusions will come as a surprise to many students, and to the general public. The magnitude of some recent conflicts has tended to obscure the facts; and the newspaper reader, fresh from the interesting perusal of a graphic account of the incidents of some gigantic struggle, like the coal dispute of 1893 in the Midlands, written by the vivid, and sometimes perhaps imaginative, pen of a special correspondent, is apt to believe that the chronic condition of industry is one of warfare, or at least of intermittent strife, with brief intervals of peace. But, although the scale of the conflicts may have grown, there is reason for thinking that their frequency has diminished.[1] The evidence given before the Commission certainly points in this direction. A quarter of a century of unbroken peace in the Manufactured Iron Trade of the North, the continued existence, in despite of obstinate general strikes in either district, of Joint Committees for the adjustment of local disputes in the Northumberland and Durham Coal Trades, the recovery of money given as wages to men at Hartlepool, who had struck for increased pay against the wishes of the executive of the Boilermakers and Iron-shipbuilders, and the repayment of the money to the employer in question,[2] the maintenance of the Sliding Scale in the

[1] See Essay vi. above.
[2] *Ibid.* for a full description of this incident.

South Wales Coal Trade, and the successful formation of Conciliation Boards in connection with various Chambers of Commerce, and of Wages Boards in different industries, are pieces of testimony established by unimpeachable evidence, and indicate the steady development of conciliatory methods. No doubt the rise of the New Unionism, as it is termed, has been accompanied by a recrudescence of aggressive, if not violent, action. But the New Unionism seems to be only repeating the general experience of infant Unionism in the past. It is not until the men are secured in their adherence to an union by the undoubted fact of its success and permanence, and by the enduring bond of friendly benefits, that they are ready to be represented by negotiators armed with plenipotentiary authority; and it is not until this stage has been reached that employers are disposed to enter with confidence into relations with the officials of the union. Already the New Unionism is falling into line with the Old on the question of friendly benefits; and it does not evince disapproval — but rather the reverse — of conciliation. The tendency seems to incline towards industrial peace.

A more ominous feature of the times perhaps is the rise into prominence of "demarcation disputes."[1] These occur between different classes of workmen, and are occasioned by changes in the methods of industry, which render doubtful what kind of work belongs to what description of workmen. A peculiar obstinacy seems to attach to such disputes, and from the nature of the case they are not easy to adjust. They suggest, however, the reality of an inherent conflict of interests between different classes of workmen, which may reassure those alarmed at the

[1] *e.g.* that between the engineers and the plumbers on the Tyne, mentioned in Essays iv. and vi.

prospect of employers and employed combining to injure the public, or of large federations of different trades establishing themselves over a wide area, or of the ultimate issue of such tendencies in the collectivist organisation of industry. They show that, for the present at least, the individualist taint has not disappeared from ordinary human nature.

But we may proceed to ask : What are the ascertained conditions of the preservation of peace? They may be summed up in one word—organisation.[1] Twenty-five years ago this might have appeared a paradox:[2] to-day a Royal Commission indorses the paradox as its deliberate opinion, supported by irrefragable evidence. The actual language employed by the Commissioners deserves quotation. "With regard to those industries," they remark,[3] "which are carried on on a large scale, and require the co-operation of great bodies of more or less skilled and trained workmen, the evidence received by the Commission points to the conclusion that, on the whole, and notwithstanding occasional conflicts on a very large scale, the increased strength of organisations may tend towards the maintenance of harmonious relations between employers and employed in a manner suitable to the modern conditions of industry. The belief was expressed both by employers and workmen that, where a skilled trade is well organised, good relations tend to prevail, and countless minor quarrels are obviated or nipped in the bud." Such is the express conclusion of the Commission ; and, if it had done nothing else, it would have rendered a service of no mean order by placing this opinion on record. For there

---

[1] Cf. Essay iii.
[2] Cf. the remarks of Mr. Greg quoted in the previous Essay.
[3] Sec. 90.

are still sections of educated society, to which the conclusion may occasion surprise; and they may be yet more astonished to learn that it is indorsed by employers as well as by workmen.

We must not, it is true—and the Commissioners do not fail to utter the warning—be too sanguine or hasty in the inferences we draw from such an opinion. The contests, which accompany the infancy and weakness of a new union, the magnitude and severity of the conflicts, which occasionally occur in the maturity and strength of an old union, the consideration that unionism embraces but a minority of workmen, and is sufficiently strong to exercise a restraining influence in but a minority of trades, the dependence of its ability to prevent conflict upon its power to exclude non-unionists from employment, the greater difficulty, which seems to attend the formation, and maintenance of the authority, of strong associations of employers, the dilemma, which has presented itself in connection with the undoubted decline in popularity and efficiency of the sliding-scale, turning on the circumstance that the very establishment of some such permanent arrangement may seem to render unnecessary the continuance of the union which has effected it, and may incline the men to withdraw their support and to stop their subscriptions, are facts, which the Commission has brought into prominence, and they certainly serve to discount any excess of sanguine expectation.

But the broad truth remains that organisation is a condition precedent to the systematic preservation of peace, and that in not a few industries conciliatory arrangements have followed as the result. The Secretary's Report on the position of the Colonies, the United States, and Foreign Countries in the matter, shows clearly that as yet we are far in advance; and the reason is found in the comparative weakness and immaturity of organisation in other countries. An important conclusion follows regarding the *rôle* which the State may properly assume. If voluntary experimental effort has achieved so much, it might be suspected that little room would be left for the State; and, with all their collectivist tendencies, the Minority Commissioners do not differ materially from the Majority in the expression of such a belief. No doubt, whether the means adopted for the preservation of peace be occasional or enduring, and whether it proceed by *conciliation*, or mutual agreement between the parties concerned—a method, which appears to meet with the widest approval—or by *arbitration*, or the reference of the quarrel to a third person for decision, or by a mode of adjustment, which the Commissioners distinguish as *mediation*, where a third party intervenes, not to decide the matter at issue, but only to persuade the disputants to settle it for themselves—in all these cases, after the decision has been secured, the question of its enforcement remains, and it is here that the aid of the State is most persistently invoked. Different methods have been suggested, only to reveal the inevitable difficulties, which attend their application.

The State, it is urged, may give a legal sanction to the awards of arbitrators and the decisions of committees of conciliation, or it may itself establish courts for the adjustment of industrial disputes. In either case it is difficult to see how it will avoid prescribing the rate of wages—a power, which it once possessed, but few would wish to see revived. In either case it is not easy to determine the manner in which its authority can be enforced. If the penalty for breach of agreement be a money fine, who is to pay it? And, if it be imprisonment, who is to be imprisoned? At present the law does not recognise collective bargaining between associations of employers and employed. The individual workman is considered to make an individual contract with the individual employer, and the remedy for breach of contract, if such there be, lies with, and against, the individual. Those *conseils de prud'hommes* existing in France and Belgium, which have been so often quoted as precedents for England to follow, concern themselves, not with the determination of the general rate of wages for the future, but with the interpretation of particular contracts in the past, and are occupied with the redress of minor grievances and the adjustment of individual quarrels.[1] The position of existing legislation in England is so far similar that, while there have for long been on the Statute Book provisions for legalised conciliation and arbitration[2]—which apparently have never been exercised —they do not contemplate any binding sanction attaching to collective arrangement by associations of workmen and employers of the rates of wages for the future. The further question indeed arises whether those bodies should not be allowed to exercise an option of becoming legal entities, and thus rendering themselves liable to the payment of a pecuniary penalty for a breach of agreement. A suggestion to this effect has received the tentative support of some members of the Commission; but it may be doubted whether it provides an effective escape from the difficulties of the situation. It would probably be regarded with little favour by Trade Unions, at present protected by the state of the law from vexatious litigation by discontented members. And, if the association itself were

[1] Cf. Essay iii. [2] Cf. *Industrial Peace*, chap. iii.

thus rendered liable to a pecuniary penalty, it would still be confronted by the difficulty of recovering the money from individual workmen, who, coincidently with refusing to abide by an agreement, had left the union. The dilemma remains that either the union is so strong that its moral influence is adequate to secure adherence without assistance from the law, or that it is so weak that legal aid would fail to enable it to reach discontented and recalcitrant workmen. We are brought back to the conclusion that the State must play the part of counsellor and encourager rather than that of compulsory peacemaker. Even if it assumes the innocent *rôle* of mediator as a regular function, it may endanger that reputation for impartiality, on which the success of occasional mediation depends.

In the face of these considerations we cannot wonder that the Commission came to the conclusion [1] that "at the present stage of progress it would do more harm than good either to invest voluntary boards with legal powers or to establish rivals to them in the shape of other boards founded on a statutory basis, and having a more or less public and official character." It is significant that the Minority Report should appear to be in practical agreement with the Majority in this respect. Speaking of boards of conciliation, the Minority Commissioners remark: [2] "We see no advantage in giving them any legal functions or compulsory powers. Their decision can only be effective in so far as it brings to bear the common public opinion of either side." Sir

---

[1] Sec. 302.

[2] Page 145. Apparently the Minority Commissioners view *with favour* only the application of conciliation to the "proper interpretation of an existing agreement."

John Gorst, in his separate Report, would apparently proceed somewhat further in invoking the active intervention of the State; and the dislike of the Minority for legislation is, no doubt, founded on a rooted distrust of the present industrial order, and a confident belief that disputes are inherent in it. Yet the aversion shown is deserving of notice, whatever be the conception of society on which it is based, and however inconsistent it may seem with other articles of the collectivist faith.

Such, then, appears to be the chief outcome of the vast inquiry on which the Labour Commission has been engaged for the last three years. On the main subject referred to them the Commissioners have placed upon record the past progress, and the present position, of conciliatory methods for preventing, and adjusting, industrial disputes; and, from the very nature of the facts, they could scarcely fail to arrive at the conclusion that it was best to leave to voluntary effort what voluntary effort had accomplished with such success. In the disapproval of the intervention of the State both Majority and Minority were agreed, and the Commissioners could do nothing more than advise the encouragement of further voluntary experimental effort. On another important question, which occupied a prominent place in their investigations, they found a vagueness and uncertainty prevailing, which seemed to render legislation of dubious expediency; and they contented themselves for the most part with recording the arguments advanced on either side of this debatable question. Here the Minority parted company from the Majority, because they regarded the legislative limitation of the hours of labour as one important step towards the collectivist organisation of society. Holding this opinion, they naturally did not agree with the

Majority in acknowledging the great improvement, which had been effected in the condition of the larger proportion of the occupants of the ranks of industry; and they laid emphatic and exclusive stress on certain unpleasant phenomena, which they regarded as symptoms of radical disease. On the advisability of various minor reforms, however, they agreed with the Majority, although in some cases they desired to advance further, and by more rapid stages.

If, then, the report of the Majority may seem by the apparent paucity, caution, and pettiness of its recommendations, to contrast with the magnitude of the inquiry and the easy confidence of the Minority, it is because they were not prepared for organic changes in the constitution of society; and they were ready to recognise that improvement might be accomplished, and had been effected, by the steady progress of experimental methods, sometimes, no doubt, assisted and inspired by the State, but, at least in connection with the question, which formed the primary subject of their considerations, devised and applied by voluntary effort. The Commission was, it is true, appointed in a large degree because the public held that industrial conflict was increasing in gravity and frequency, and that something must be discovered to arrest its prevalence. The report of the Majority proves that the tendency inclines in the other direction, and that a machinery, not indeed free from a liability to break down on occasions, or universally applicable, but one which has worked with remarkable success in different conditions, has been discovered by experience, and has proved effectual, for the preservation of industrial peace. This may seem a lame and idle conclusion to impatient reformers, but it is not unlikely to recommend itself to the approval of sober common sense.

VIII.

THE RELATIONS OF ECONOMIC SCIENCE TO PRACTICAL AFFAIRS.[1]

AT the Oxford meeting of the British Association a report was presented on the "Methods of Economic Training in this and other Countries,"[2] the general conclusion of which pointed to a deficiency in this country in the organisation of instruction, and in the recognition given by the examinations of the Universities, of the public service, and the legal profession. In the spring of the following year, Mr. Goschen, presiding at a dinner of the Economic Association, commented[3] on the inopportune contempt of the practical man for economic reasoning at a time when many of the questions engaging public attention were economic in character. The phenomena thus noted may possibly be connected, and a disregard of economic reasoning explained by a lack of systematic economic instruction. At any rate, the members of this Section will scarcely feel more certain of the fact that the questions of the day are largely economic in character than of the illumination obtained by an acquaintance with

---

[1] Presidential Address to the Economic Science and Statistics Section of the British Association at Ipswich (1895).
[2] See *Report of the British Association for* 1894.
[3] See *Economic Journal* for June, 1895, vol. v. No. 18, p. 301.

Economic Science and Statistics. They may not succeed in winning the attention of the practical man; but they are not unlikely to find solace in the flattering conviction that the loss is on his side, and not on their own. The proceedings of the Section in this and in previous years will prove beyond dispute that, whether or not the practical man troubles himself to ascertain or to follow the opinion of the professors, the professors are not seldom busy in the consideration of the practical questions of the day.

I make this assertion with the more boldness, because it requires no extraordinary keenness of vision to detect signs in the practical man of a disposition hardly consistent with the scorn he is prone to bestow. I believe that, in spite of what we may regard as his worse impulses, he manifests a growing inclination to seek counsel—and even imperatively to demand guidance—on social and political problems from economic professors. I do not know how otherwise to explain the fact that a well-known firm of London publishers has issued, and, I imagine, found it profitable to issue, a series of books on social subjects, which now numbers upwards of eighty volumes. Many of these books may not be scientific in character; but so large an issue, taken in conjunction with other significant circumstances, such as the recent revival of a desire for economic lectures on the part of the clients of University Extension, does afford some presumption in favour of a fresh growth of popular interest. Indeed, I have heard more than one practical man complain, not that it was unreasonable to look for guidance in economic matters from economic experts, but that, with every disposition to hear the advice of professors, it was impossible to obtain it. This complaint may, or may not, be founded on reality; but the professors may be pardoned, if they regard

RELATIONS TO PRACTICAL AFFAIRS 163

it as a sign of a more wholesome condition of mind. The complaint may be due to the fact that the guidance sought is not such as the professors can offer, and that the advice, which they are able and ready to give, is considered inadequate or superfluous.

I am going to address myself to the audacious task of endeavouring to indicate, by actual example, the guidance, which the economic professor may furnish to the practical man on the questions of the day; and I have prefaced my attempt with these observations, to show that I am aware of the hazard and difficulty attendant. Were I to seek for an appropriate metaphor to describe my venture, I might find it by saying that I was about to disturb a hornets' nest; and, if I am fortunate enough to escape with the scornful neglect of the practical man, I am afraid that the professor may be less compassionate, and that his sting may prove as venomous. I may, perhaps, plead in excuse that it is at once the traditional privilege and the inherited duty of occupants of presidential chairs to devote their observations especially to that part of their science, with which they have been most closely connected. I have certainly endeavoured on the one hand to bestow a considerable portion of my time on the scientific study of economics as expounded in systematic treatises; and, on the other, my occupation as College Treasurer has forced me into intimate contact with the hard facts of at least one department of practical life. I would not for one moment claim that this dual experience gives me any title to speak with authority on the relations of economic science to practical affairs; but it has determined the grooves, in which my thoughts have mainly run, and, so far as I may presume to a special acquaintance with any department of economic speculation, it is with that which concerns the bearing of theory on practice. Without unbecoming arrogance, I may, perhaps, think that I possess in not very disproportionate measure the failings of the practical man and the academic professor; and in this capacity I undertake the task before me.

Before considering some particular questions of the day, we may determine the general character of the guidance offered by economics in matters of practice. I believe that in this connection economists must disclaim a pretension to strict neutrality. Much, no doubt, may be urged in support of the claim, and considerable advantages might follow from its successful establishment.[1] The cool examination of heated questions in the dry light of science might seem the appropriate occupation of the academic professor. From the serene heights of tranquil speculation he might complacently look down on the heat and turmoil of affairs, and, standing apart from the conflict himself, refuse to assist any combatant. But the strict maintenance of this attitude is a " counsel of perfection " and a practical impossibility. The student must be more or less than human, who, dealing with a department of knowledge so intimately related to the welfare of humanity, can avoid, as the result of his scientific inquiry, forming a favourable view of one course of conduct, and an adverse opinion of another, and endeavouring to promote the former, and to hinder the latter, both by advice and by act. He cannot be content to observe the connection of cause and effect without trying to set in motion the cause or to restrain its action. He cannot acquiesce in the speculative solution of a problem without being impelled to embody his theory in practice. He cannot contemplate the misery due to bad economic

[1] Cf. Essay xii. below.

arrangements without seeking to devise and apply a remedy; and, viewing the matter historically, the practical object of benefiting their fellow-creatures has been at least as powerful a motive with great economic thinkers as the speculative aim of enlarging the boundaries of knowledge. They have been reproached for hardness of heart and dulness of imagination, and the popular account is prone to regard them as dry and unfeeling; but the description is a travesty of the facts, and their errors have probably been due as often to excess as to lack of enthusiasm. The recurring contrast of wealth and poverty, of careless ease and careworn want, of lavish indulgence and narrow penury, has awakened as responsive a chord in their hearts as in that of the most ardent and generous socialist; and it is impossible to run over the conspicuous names on the roll of economic worthies without being impressed by the warmth of their zeal for social reform, and the intensity and persistence of their anxiety to remove or mitigate human suffering. The "economic man" of popular description, whether or not he occupy a place in economic theory, is no portrait of the economist of actual historical fact. The name of "dismal science," so often misapplied, was suggested not so much by the suppression of human interest as by the apparent destruction of cherished hopes. The science was "dismal," not, as popular usage interprets the phrase, because it was dry and uninteresting, but because it seemed to counsel despair; and even then the title partook of caricature.

Nor do I think that in this connection an attitude of strict neutrality is desirable, if it be possible. The besetting sin of the academic temper is indecision, and few errors are more mischievous in practical affairs. An obstinate regard for neutrality may easily beget indecision, and from that moment the economist becomes ineffectual for practice. I must confess to the belief that the practical man has a right to demand an opinion on economic points from the academic professor, and that the professor has a claim to take part in the guidance of economic affairs, which is derived from his scientific study. He is an expert, and it is no less his duty than his privilege to discharge an expert's functions. He cannot, as it seems to me, properly evade the one or abnegate the other. He may be careful in forming his judgment. He may conscientiously endeavour to assign its due weight to every circumstance. He may remember, and insist, that in many practical problems other aspects besides the economic must be considered. But the economic is often of great, and sometimes of paramount, importance; and on this he cannot disown the responsibility of making up his mind without, as it seems to me, forfeiting his own self-respect and his usefulness to others. From that moment his neutrality vanishes. He may, and probably will, incur an opprobium, which he might have avoided by a refusal to adopt a decisive opinion. He may sacrifice a quiet and ease, which he might have retained. But, whether our aim be the correct conduct of affairs, or the due recognition of economic science, I cannot doubt that he has chosen the better part. To insist on a strict neutrality for economists in matters of practice seems to me idle and misleading. It is idle, because the economist is human, and economics is concerned with some of the most important interests of human welfare. It is misleading, because it is the duty of the economic expert to offer guidance on economic points, and there are at all times few practical questions which do not present an economic side. Certainly at the present juncture, when the pressing problems of the hour are in many cases distinctly and admittedly economic in character, to attempt a divorce between theory and practice is especially inopportune. It is an impossible endeavour to saw a man into separate quantities; and I would claim for the appropriate description of every great economist the epitaph on the tomb of the German socialist, " Ferdinand Lassalle, thinker and fighter." We need not abandon the thought, but it should stimulate, and not paralyse, the action; for the one is not fully complete until it is realised in the other. Economics is indeed a science, and on that ground claims a recognised place in the programme of this Association; but it is essentially, as I think, an applied, and not a pure, science, and the economist has only fulfilled part of his mission when he has solved a speculative problem. I am aware that this contention may not be admitted by many academic professors and practical men, but I believe that it is in accord with historical tradition, and admits of logical justification.

Yet, if an attitude of strict neutrality be impossible and ineffective, the opposite extreme of dogmatic assertion is as undesirable as it is dangerous. The older economists have been often charged with an error of this nature, and it cannot be denied that the accusation rests on a basis of truth, though it has sometimes been couched in exaggerated form. Certainly the modern economist is inclined to state his opinion with less assurance, and for that very reason he has lost some of his influence on practical affairs. For the practical man has a sneaking affection, and even respect, for dogmatic assertion. At any rate, he desires a plain, direct, and concise answer to his questions, and it is not easy to distinguish between an avoidance of dogmatism and an appearance of indecision. Nor can it be denied that, as a discipline of the mind, a study of the more abstract reasonings of some of the older writers, which generally presented the semblance, and sometimes offered the reality, of a precise, defined, consistent whole, is both wholesome and stimulating. Legal authorities now pronounce inadequate Austin's "Lectures on Jurisprudence," but I must confess that I look back to my first acquaintance with them as an epoch in my mental history. I believe that they acted as a tonic and purgative, clearing away obscurity and stimulating intellectual effort. If I may say so, the effect of reading such an author as James Mill is not unlikely to be similar in the case of the young economic student; and for that reason, were there no other, I should personally regret the exclusion from a systematic economic course of the study of some of the more rigidly abstract reasonings of some of the more strict of the older economists. Such study may be regarded as a propædeutic, through which the student should pass; and he will lose, and not gain, by its omission. The regimen may be somewhat severe, and the diet, so far as the moment is concerned, not very nutritious; but the system is braced, and the digestion strengthened.

The fact, however, is that the more famous of the older economists themselves were less abstract and precise than they are represented in common opinion. They took a keen and constant interest in the practical questions of their time. Their speculative opinions were largely influenced by the prominent facts of their day. The acumen of later, and even contemporary, criticism has discovered gaps in some of their reasonings and inconsistencies — which perhaps do them honour—in some of their arguments. Recent economic analysis[1] certainly endeavours to bring within its range a larger number of facts, to be more explicit in stating and repeating the assumptions on which it proceeds, and to be more cautious in establishing conclusions and definite in limiting their application. But the change is largely due to the increasing complexity of the facts; and the difference in the mode of approaching and method of handling a question is one of degree rather than kind. The particular problems, which confronted the older writers, admitted more often of a plain dogmatic answer; and, if the deliberations of the later economist be more comprehensive and protracted, his conclusions need not on that account be indecisive. Indeed, with the lapse of time, the necessity and advantage of expert advice have grown more obvious and urgent.

What then is the general character of that advice? The answer may seem a truism, but it is surely this. As in other departments of study, the mission of the scientific economist is to discern, and to assist others to recognise, the unseen. He is not content with a superficial view. He endeavours to penetrate below the surface of affairs and discover the invisible forces. He employs telescope and microscope to bring within the range of vision what is distant or unnoticed. He compels the practical man to pay attention to something more than the obvious and immediate consequences of the policy he is pursuing; and the chief advantage of economics, as part of a scheme of general education, seems to consist in inducing a habit of mind which will not be satisfied with superficial explanation. And it induces this habit in matters with which men and women are brought into close and necessary contact

[1] Cf. Essay xiii. below.

in the ordinary routine of everyday life. They may flatter themselves that common sense alone is needed to deal with such matters, and that no scientific training or aid is required. Economics dispels this subtle and dangerous illusion, and furnishes an instrument, which at once controls, and strengthens, common sense. Nor is this claim for economics as a discipline of the mind and as a guide in matters of practical conduct by any means novel. It was put forward with prominence by Bastiat, whose writing is sometimes regarded as an illustrative example of the application of orthodox economics to the treatment of an important practical question. It has been recently adduced by the Duke of Argyll, who, dissatisfied with what he considers orthodox economics, attempts to supply its defects by disclosing the "Unseen Foundations of Society." The arguments and conclusions of Bastiat may not be accepted, the criticisms of the Duke may be refuted, by contemporary economists, who may claim the title of "orthodox," if they desire an epithet which seems to bring as much opprobrium as honour; but they would certainly agree with the earlier exponent and the later critic, who, curiously enough, have not a little else in common, in regarding the mission of economics as an endeavour to see, and to reveal to others, the unseen.

That such a description is no barren truism, that economics thus conceived may shed illumination on dark or obscured problems, that it may prove, in Bacon's language, not merely *lucifera*, but also *fructifera*, may, I think, be shown by a brief consideration of some typical questions of the day.

I. Few are more prominent than that of industrial strife. We deplore its occurrence, and are ready to welcome any promising means suggested for mitigation or prevention.

Nor does popular opinion refuse to economics a voice in the matter, but, on the contrary, its authority is continually invoked. What, then, in accordance with the principles we have sought to establish, is the guidance which it can offer? Are there any common beliefs which it may show to be superficially founded? Few assertions certainly are more frequent than that the interests of employers and employed are harmonious, and that disputes involve a disturbance of this fundamental harmony. On the other hand, few facts are more obvious than that employer and employed regard their interests as essentially antagonistic, and from this antagonism the disputes have arisen. Economics is able to show that either view expresses a portion, and only a portion, of the truth; and by the systematic mould in which its reasoning is cast, brings into clear relief the relation of the complementary truths.[1]

In the *production* of wealth the interests of the parties harmonise, for, with the modern organisation of industry they require the services of one another, and, the more efficient they respectively are, the larger is likely to be the wealth produced. It is the interest of the employer that the wages earned by the men should be adequate to maintain, and, if possible, to increase, their efficiency; and it is the interest of the employed that the profits of the *entrepreneur* should encourage enterprise, and induce a sufficient supply of capital. For production—and this is a point which economics, and economics alone, can duly emphasise—is the ultimate source of the wealth distributed. The larger the amount produced, the larger, *cæteris paribus*, is likely to be the share of either party in distribution; and in any event it is certain that a decreased production must

[1] Cf. Essay vi. above for a similar line of reasoning.

issue in effects on distribution, the burden of which will fall, though in varying measure, on either party. The influence thus exerted on distribution by production is one which workmen seem especially likely to forget, and many of the common arguments in favour of "making work," or providing "employment for the unemployed," proceed from ignorance or neglect of this consideration.

On the other hand, it may be urged that employers are not very keen to recognise the influence, whether for advantage or drawback, of distribution on production. No doubt the division of economics into separate departments tends to make even the student forget their mutual connection. We do not remember constantly that production and distribution are simultaneous, and are only distinguished for purposes of convenient analysis. Yet one of the most important advances of recent economics consists in the emphasis given to the influence of distribution on production; and we see more clearly than our predecessors how the poverty of the poor, by begetting inefficiency, may cause their poverty, and high wages may imply, not a high, but a low, cost of production. Either of these truths may be pushed to excess; but they are certainly fraught with important consequences, and have an intimate bearing on the question before us. But, like the influence of production on distribution, the telescope of the economist is needed to bring, and retain them, within the range of ordinary vision.

The full and constant recognition of these truths conduces to a more comprehensive conception of the possible results of industrial disputes. We can see, on the one hand, that a victory for the moment may not prevent defeat in the long run, and that loss, which is obvious at the time, may issue in ultimate gain. When we remember that to discern these distant results the naked eye of the plain observer seems incompetent without the aid of the economic organon, we are as ready to recognise the likelihood of industrial conflict as we are anxious to devise the means of preventing it. For in the *distribution* of wealth the apparent interests of the two parties are antagonistic, and, given the amount produced, the larger the share of the one, the less will be that of the other. The frank recognition of this possible antagonism is the first step towards the prevention of its natural consequences. The imminence of the possibility supplies the strongest motive for removing unnecessary hindrance, and furnishing likely assistance, to a pacific agreement. And, whatever the final consequences of a dispute to the interests of either party, the existence of friction and irritation is beyond question an injury and hindrance to production. The loss thus occasioned is immediate as well as distant, and may be considerable ; but, if the telescope of the economist is generally needed to bring sufficiently close the ultimate effects of industrial disputes, his microscope is sometimes required to magnify the results of friction to dimensions, which will attract, and retain, the attention of the ordinary observer. By discovering these deeper considerations beneath the superficial appearance of affairs, economics may furnish useful guidance in the prevention and adjustment of industrial disputes.

For to what conclusion do these considerations lead? To the discovery of some machinery, which may prove not unacceptable, and yet, by imposing delay on the outbreak of strife, may allow the two parties to hear what either has to urge, and to consider the possible consequences of the action they are proposing to take. Such a machinery may be discovered in boards of conciliation and courts of arbitration.[1] The fact that both sides should be organised on a sufficiently responsible basis to send accredited representatives, the fact that, thus meeting one another, they are compelled to seek and adduce reasons for their own position and to listen to the arguments in support of their opponents, the fact that delay and deliberation are recognised preliminaries to the commencement of war—these facts may not appear important in themselves, but they offer a chance of pacific adjustment, and afford opportunity for the consideration of ulterior issues. They prevent the apparent interests of the moment from winning an undisputed victory over the less obvious interests of the future; and they do not allow an advantage in distribution to be secured without thought of the effects on production. On the other hand, the antagonism of interests incident to the distribution of wealth, when the production is regarded as a given quantity, suggests that the machinery may on occasions break down, and that the arrangements should properly consist of different stages and provide supplementary resources; for arbitration may succeed in adjusting a dispute to which conciliation has proved incompetent, and conciliation may conceivably be useful where arbitration has been ineffectually tried. Such antagonism also suggests that voluntary adhesion is likely to be more abiding than compulsion, and more conducive to the permanent interests of peace,[2] and that to prevent the occurrence, or reduce the likelihood, of industrial conflict, a traditional standard of settlement, changed in grave emergencies or serious vicissitudes alone, should be established in the trade and recognised as fair.

For economics, as it seems to me, can do little more han point out those ultimate and obscure consequences,

[1] Cf. Essay ii.   [2] Cf. the previous Essay.

which are concealed by immediate superficial appearances; and it is not in possession of a precise principle or rule, which can be definitely applied to the determination of industrial disputes. Could it, indeed, furnish such a rule, the arguments[1] in favour of the legal bestowal of compulsory powers on courts of arbitration and boards of conciliation would gain considerable strength; for it must be remembered that the questions before them are not the interpretation of past contracts, such as are habitually submitted to the Continental *conseils de prud'hommes*,[2] but the establishment of agreements for the future, and it is difficult to force parties to agree when you do not supply a principle of agreement, nor does it on the whole seem likely to conduce to conciliatory relations to declare that, while you will not compel masters and men to agree, you will compel them to abide at all hazards by the agreement to which they may come. For these reasons, tempting as it undoubtedly is to invoke legal compulsion, I believe that the State can do little more than supply facilities for voluntary agreement, and, exercising, perhaps, some gentle persuasion, leave the pressure of public opinion to induce recourse to machinery thus provided. Such I take to be the drift of competent experienced opinion and the probable scope of effective legislation;[3] and such, as it seems to me, is the kind of guidance, which economics can offer on this practical question.[4]

II. In a town like Ipswich we are forcibly reminded of another question of the day—I mean agricultural

[1] Cf. the previous Essay.
[2] Cf. Essay iii.
[3] The Act recently passed may be generally described as intended to exert a "gentle persuasion."
[4] Cf. also the following Essay.

depression. From the Reports of the Assistant Commissioners to the Royal Commission on Agriculture it would appear that Suffolk shares with its neighbour, Essex an unenvied pre-eminence among districts, which have suffered, and that the present condition of this important industry borders here on despair. In the actual words of Mr. Wilson Fox, the Assistant Commissioner, agriculture in Suffolk " is well-nigh strangled."[1] Can economics throw any light on this lamentable situation? If there is one theory, which is supposed to be more remote from fact than another, it is the theory of rent.[2] It is the fashion, even with professed economists, to regard it as unduly abstract; and in a recent address[3] to a learned society, connected with this Section by no distant ties, the President selected the theory as a conspicuous example of older formulæ laid aside. The account of the theory given in that address is open to question, but the ground of rejection is worthy of note. Lord Farrer, it would seem, condemns the theory because it is a "formula useless for practical purposes." This criticism raises the question we are now considering, for we are trying to ascertain the guidance, which economic science can furnish in practical affairs. That it has an important, and, indeed, a necessary, relation to practice we have asserted in positive terms, but the relation is not, as we think, that which Lord Farrer apparently assumes. For economics does not furnish precepts or formulæ immediately applicable to practice; but it supplies systematised knowledge, the possession and employment of which will afford assistance in the direction

[1] Cf. Report, p. 82.
[2] Cf. Essay x. below.
[3] Cf. *Journal of the Royal Statistical Society*, vol. lvii. part iv. December, 1894, pp. 595, etc.

of practical affairs. The theory of rent is not, then, a maxim of conduct, but a rational explanation of fact. Conceived thus, in my own experience as College Treasurer, I have been struck by its pertinence, not its inadequacy. It has certainly seemed to me that, on a broad view, the tenant considers the rent to be properly that which is left when, on an average of years, he has reaped a fair profit and paid his labourers the wages they command. The landlord, so far as I have been able to discover, occupies in his eyes the position—to use language differently applied[1] by General Walker—of a " residual claimant"; and such, also, as I read the theory, is the place which he fills therein.

Nor is it difficult to interpret part of the present depression in conformity with the theory of rent. I must take leave to dissent from Lord Farrer when he asserts that the formula, even in its older shape, paid no regard to situation or to means of transport; and I am disposed to affirm that the emended statement of recent text-books, in which these considerations, with others mentioned by Lord Farrer, receive explicit recognition, is not so much a departure from the older form as a development and extension of it.[2] But, taking the two points of fertility and situation alone, it is the agreement, and not the conflict, of what has happened with what the theory might have led us to expect that is likely to impress. It can hardly be doubted that one of the most remarkable changes of recent years has been the development of the means and reduction of the cost of transportation. This change implies a loss of the advantage derived from proximity to the

[1] *i.e.*, to the wage earner. Cf. *Political Economy*, by F. A. Walker, part iv.
[2] Cf. Essay x. for a fuller statement of this argument.

market in the case of commodities, which admit of conveyance from a distance. Interpreted in the language of the theory of rent, English land, as respects certain products, has forfeited part of the natural protection afforded by its situation near to the market. With the partial loss of this advantage has also disappeared part of another, for the diminution in the cost of transportation has opened European markets to the virgin soils of America and other countries; and with regard to products, which admit of conveyance from a distance, the fertility of English land, whether it be due to the skill of generations of comparatively high farming or to natural qualities of soil, has lost part of its advantage. In the language of the theory of rent, the forfeiture of these two advantages involves depression in the sense of a decrease of rental; and, as it seems to me, the adequacy rather than deficiency of the theory is evident as a rational explanation of fact.

Nor is it useless for practical guidance. The fact, which it establishes, is a connection between cause and effect, and not a maxim of conduct; for the laws of economics, like the laws of every science, are, as it has been aptly expressed, statements in the indicative and not the imperative mood. But the possession of the scientific knowledge of the causal connection is more likely than its absence to conduce to prudent practice. In the instance before us the conclusion seems inevitable that, so far as the depression is due to foreign competition, and the virginity of competing soils, and facility of transportation, continued attention to products, which must be conveyed to their market quickly, is likely to be more profitable in an old country like England than the continued production of commodities, which can be raised to greater advantage on newer soils, and be easily transported from considerable distances. I am aware that this is a hard saying, that necessary conditions of cultivation, sometimes neglected, must be taken into account, and that such a change as is often contemplated in such discussions may mean a painful and difficult departure from traditional habit, and an apparent sacrifice of inherited or acquired skill. It is easy to talk glibly of the English farmer abandoning the cultivation of cereals, at any rate as a staple product, and turning his attention to vegetable and dairy produce, to fruit-raising, and poultry-rearing, and bee-keeping, and the various other modes of making a fortune, which are put forward for his edification. But the lesson of economic theory is plain, so far as the depression is due to foreign competition, and the maintenance of a Free Trade policy is assumed.

I do not discuss the latter question, because it is far too large to be adequately treated in a paragraph or two, and is excluded from practical politics by the leaders of political parties, but it is certainly a question on which economics may reveal the unseen.[1] Among those invisible facts may, perhaps, be placed a circumstance often neglected in popular discussion. In many arguments on agricultural depression the landed interest is treated as strictly separable from the rest of the community, and a fall in rent is regarded as the loss to a particular class of an advantage enjoyed apart from exertion.

If I may say so in passing, some of the abundant popular use made in recent years of the conception of rent as an unearned increment seems to me to afford an example of the misapplication of theory to practice.[2] For, in not a few instances, what has happened is this : a theory, resting on nice distinctions, has been crudely applied to practice, and the distinctions employed to

[1] Cf. Essay xii.   [2] Cf. Essays i. and x.

prescribe a definite policy, without regard to their nicety. In other words, the theory has been used as a precise maxim, which could be straightway embodied in practice, and not as a scientific conception, the knowledge of which might protect the practical man from hidden pitfalls.

In England, at least, so far as agricultural land is concerned, the landlord is usually a partner with the tenant; and, whether or not the system be better than that of occupying ownership, it is certain that part of the rent is a return for expenditure, and not a payment for natural qualities of soil or situation; and to this extent a fall in rent is likely to operate as a discouragement or preventive of the fresh and continuous expenditure needed to maintain the land and the buildings in a state of efficiency. I cannot doubt, in view of evidence given before the Commission on Agriculture, and of other signs, that the depression must have already produced deterioration in this respect, and thus have injuriously affected the economic position of the general community.

Nor is the landed interest strictly and entirely distinct. In an old country different classes are connected with one another by ties hard to disentangle, and impossible to sever without injury or danger. The educational endowments of the country, as a melancholy personal experience has taught me,[1] cannot regard agricultural depression with the complacency of disinterested observers. The effect on certain public institutions, like some of the London hospitals, is notorious; and it can scarcely be doubted that, though the prudent management, by which they are characterised, may have led many of the great insurance companies to write down their landed invest-

---

[1] Cf. Papers read by the author to the Royal Statistical Society in February, 1892, and January, 1895.

RELATIONS TO PRACTICAL AFFAIRS 181

ments, and withdraw from them as they are able, yet they have been, and are, largely interested in the fortunes of landed property, and, perhaps especially, in the rentals of landlords, on the security of which they have made advances. With the stability of the insurance companies is linked the preservation of, perhaps, the bulk of the savings of the professional classes. In short, in an old country, a strict separation between the interests of different classes is only true with large deductions.

III. But economics also raises and solves the doubt whether depression in agriculture can be attributed to foreign competition alone. It is a significant fact that, according to authoritative accounts, many of the competitors of the English farmer have not escaped the distress from which he has suffered; and in England the depression, in spite of constant reductions and abatements, has exerted an influence on profits scarcely less grievous than that on rents. These circumstances certainly lend weight to the contention that the fall of prices—which is not peculiar, though perhaps especially discouraging, to agriculture—is partly due, to state the matter in the least controversial shape, to a change in the general relation between the supplies of gold and the monetary work that it is required to perform. To the discovery of a cause like this, hidden from superficial view, and to the indication of the manner in which it may affect the position of agriculture and other industries, economics, by virtue of its mission to discern the unseen, is peculiarly competent. I do not propose to enter now at any length on the vexed question of the currency, but it is certainly a prominent practical question of the day.[1] It is a question on which the economist may claim to

[1] Cf. Essay xi.

speak with authority, and the practical man may demand, as he may be expected to follow, the definitive guidance of expert opinion. On this question, perhaps, in particular, the unassisted vision of the naked eye may form erroneous conclusions, and derive no little profit from the use of the optical instruments provided by the economist.

I cannot preface what I propose to say more appropriately than by a quotation from Jevons. In that pamphlet on *A Serious Fall in the Value of Gold*,[1] which has attained the rare dignity of an economic classic, commenting on the alarmist anticipations of Chevalier and Cobden, he remarks that the alteration in the value of gold, consequent on the discoveries in California and Australia, would probably be "most gradual and gentle." "Far from taking place with sudden and painful starts, flinging the rich headlong to a lower station, and shaking the groundwork of society, nothing is more insidious, slow, and imperceptible. It is insidious because we are accustomed to use the standard as invariable, and to measure the changes of other things by it; and a rise in the price of any article, when observed, is naturally attributed to a hundred other causes than the true one. It is slow because the total accumulations of gold in use are but little increased by the additions of any one or of several years. It is imperceptible because the slow rise of prices due to gold depreciation is disturbed by much more sudden and considerable, but temporary, fluctuations which are due to commercial causes, and are by no means a novelty." I propose to apply briefly these remarks of Jevons to some aspects of the controversy,

---

[1] Cf. *Investigations in Currency and Finance*, pp. 78, 79.

which has arisen on the cause of the fall of prices of the last twenty years.[1]

It is, for example, sometimes asserted that the influence of credit on prices is so considerable as to reduce to unimportance a decrease in the available supplies of gold. It may at once be admitted that the modern extensive development of credit obscures the relation between the metal and prices; but it does not destroy it, and, according to the view we have been trying to emphasise, the mission of economics is to remove this veil of obscurity. In this instance it may show that the relation is not unreal because it is indirect; that credit, expanding and contracting of itself owing to increasing or diminishing speculative activity, is yet limited and controlled in its movements by the changing dimensions in the basis of cash on which it rests; and that, through the bank reserves, meeting or restricting the demands for petty cash, and permitting an expansion or causing a curtailment of credit, the supplies of the standard metal exert an important influence on prices.[2] Economics may thus furnish a rational account of the *modus operandi*, and statistics supply corroborative evidence. This evidence, indeed, may be said to amount to ocular demonstration; for no one, who has studied with moderate attention the course of a curve of general prices[3] over a period of time, drawn in accordance with the graphic method of statistics, can have failed to distinguish the different character of the fluctuations thereby shown—to have separated the more obvious and pronounced fluctuations of credit, marking

---

[1] Cf., for a fuller treatment of this subject, the author's *Money, and its Relations to Prices*.

[2] Cf. Giffen's *Essays in Finance*, second series, ii.

[3] Such as that constructed by Mr. Sauerbeck.

the flow and ebb of confidence, from the minor passing changes due to some temporary accident of demand and supply on the one hand, and, on the other, from the general trend of the curve indicating a growing abundance or scarcity in the available supplies of the standard metal. This is a broad influence, the operation of which is only discernible on a comprehensive view; but the graphic method of statistics brings it within the range of ordinary vision, and the reasoning of economics discloses the connection of the phenomena. The influence of credit is apparent on the surface, but the deeper influence can be detected beneath; and, if the general level of one credit cycle be higher or lower than another, the change points to the presence and action of some less obvious cause. In a modern commercial society, with its development of banking and credit, we are able to observe and to measure cause and effect. At the one end of the process we possess statistics of the production of gold, and can frame estimates of the amount and character of extraordinary demands.[1] At the other end we can employ, in the form of index numbers, as they are called,[2] a means of measuring changes in general prices, which is certainly adequate to show the direction of the change, if it is not competent to indicate its precise amount. For the connection between cause and effect we look to economic reasoning, which here, as elsewhere, enables us to discern the unseen.

A similar test may be applied to the adequacy of some

---

[1] To some extent also this is true of the changes in the ordinary demands, but the stress of the argument may be laid on the extraordinary demands.

[2] Cf. those compiled by the *Economist*, Mr. Palgrave, Mr. Sauerbeck, Dr. Soetbeer, and Sir Robert Giffen.

other causes. It is sometimes said that a complete explanation of changes in general prices can be discovered in the particular circumstances of individual commodities, without any reference to a common cause. The answer is evident on the principles we have been endeavouring to establish. Those particular circumstances lie on the surface, and the common cause is only apparent if we penetrate beneath. Here, again, economics is aided by statistics. Economics can recognise and explain the operation of a common cause in enhancing or diminishing the effect of particular circumstances, and statistics can offer corroborative evidence of the presence of such a cause. For the very meaning and intention of a statistical average is to eliminate the influence of particular causes, and therefore the testimony of those index numbers, in which an attempt is made to exhibit the average change in prices, is adequate to establish the influence of some common cause, if the basis on which they are constructed be sufficiently comprehensive and typical. It can scarcely be doubted that this criterion is satisfied in the case of some of the best known varieties. The presence of that common cause, it must be remembered, does not imply the absence of other contributory or counteracting causes; and the inquirer in the region of the moral and political sciences is always beset by difficulties arising from the plurality of causes. But, if he can establish the presence of a common cause competent to produce the effect, and can point to the effect which has been produced, the argument for the connection between the two attains that high degree of probability, which is all that we can expect to reach. In the instance before us statistics may show the presence of this common cause and the occurrence of the effect, and economics may indicate the competence of the cause to produce the effect. We know that until recently the production of gold had declined from the level reached in the middle of the century, and we are aware that a series of extraordinary demands[1] had coincided, while various index numbers are in general agreement in exhibiting a fall in prices, though the degree of the fall shown in each case may vary.[2] The economic theory of supply and demand may, then, be used to establish the connection between cause and effect; for, if the supply of a commodity declines while the demand for it increases, a rise in its value, and a fall in the value of articles compared with it, become inevitable. Such has been the position of gold during the last twenty years.

It may be noticed that the possibility of a plurality of causes increases the likelihood of the action of some common cause; for, under the conditions, we cannot expect the apparent effects of this cause to be immediate or universal. The presence of counteracting or modifying circumstances, of opposing or contributory causes, will delay in some cases a process accelerated in others, will minimise here an effect which is accentuated there. The apparent change due to the cause is only likely to be general and not universal, to be gradual and not immediate. The assertion that a fall in prices, if due to an alteration in the available supplies of the

---

[1] *e.g.*, on the part of Germany, the United States, the Austro-Hungarian empire, and Russia.
[2] An index number may be briefly described as a mode of showing the average change in prices, by comprising in one grand total the percentages of rise or fall shown in the recorded prices of certain selected typical commodities.

standard metal, should be immediate and universal, cannot be sustained when economics, penetrating beneath superficial appearance, reveals the interaction of different causes; and, if the testimony of index numbers points to a general change, it is no sufficient answer to affirm that it is not universal. On grounds of economic reasoning we should expect a slower movement of retail than of wholesale prices, of the prices of articles of minor than of those of more general consumption, of wages than of prices generally.

The mention of wages suggests another point neglected in some current discussions, but brought by economic reasoning from obscurity into prominence. It is sometimes asserted that the fact that wages have not fallen is a proof that monetary causes have not produced the fall of prices. But, apart from the known tendency of wages to move more slowly than prices, such an assertion overlooks the possibility of a simultaneous change in distribution. Economic reasoning points to the probability of such a change in favour of the wage earner, and to the effect that it would produce; and statistical evidence corroborates that reasoning.[1] If such a change be proceeding, we should expect wages to rise; and the fact that they are stationary tends to prove, not to disprove, the existence of a monetary cause of the fall of prices. A failure to give explicit recognition to this possibility is due to neglect of the plurality of causes, and is akin to another argument sometimes advanced.[2] This maintains that, if it can be shown that the country has progressed, or not receded, in wealth, in the development of trade and manufacture,

[1] Cf. the investigations of Sir Robert Giffen in England, of M. Leroy-Beaulieu in France, and of other inquirers in other countries.
[2] Cf. Essay xi.

in the prosperity of the mass of the community, it is thereby proved that the fall of prices has wrought no injury. But it may be answered that the progress might have been greater in the absence of the fall, and other forces may have prevented the cause in question from producing its full effect. Here, again, economic reasoning may aid in discerning what is invisible to the unassisted eye.

Few truths, indeed, are slower to receive, and more likely to lose, popular recognition than those which lay stress on the mutual action of different causes. We are told, for instance, that the fall of prices is due to circumstances connected with improvements in the production and transportation of commodities; and it must be admitted that such a common cause is not, like particular causes affecting individual commodities, eliminated in the general average of the index numbers. But the one common cause—that of improvements in production—does not exclude the operation of the other—that of a change in the available supplies of gold. Taking a broad view of the whole century, it would certainly seem that the movement of improvement has set steadily in one direction; but that the movement of prices has first declined, and then advanced, and then declined again. It is possible that the movement of improvement may have been accelerated and retarded at different times; but the change in the movement of prices, which requires explanation, is not a variation of degree, but a reversal of direction. And this reversal coincides with similar changes in the available supplies of the standard metal. If the disturbances in America at the beginning of the century, with the known diminution in production, were followed by a fall, if the Californian and Australian discoveries of the middle of the century were accompanied by a rise, and, if the notorious extraordinary demands since 1873, statistically computed by Sir Robert Giffen,[1] coming on a supply which until the past few years was diminishing, coincided with a fall again, it seems impossible to doubt that, although improvements in production and transportation may have been contributory causes, an important influence has been exerted by the monetary supplies. With the aid of the economic telescope and microscope forces too remote or obscure to be detected by the naked eye are thus brought within the range of ordinary vision; and the action of the standard metal on prices is one of those forces, for, in Jevons' language, it is "insidious, slow, and imperceptible."

Such is the guidance, which, as it seems to me, economics is able to offer; and in this question of the currency, as in the others of which we have treated, it is surely not destitute of practical import, for the detection of a monetary cause of the fall in prices is so far an argument for the adoption of a monetary remedy.[2] Such guidance, also, I believe, economics can furnish on many other questions coming to the front; and, in offering this, it cannot be accused of an excessive or defective estimate of its claims to popular recognition. I am convinced that, as the years elapse, its aid will be sought with increasing urgency, and that it will discharge, with a fuller consciousness of its high prerogative, its important but difficult mission of seeing for itself, and disclosing to others, the unseen.

[1] In evidence given before the Gold and Silver Commission, and, more recently, before the Commission on Agriculture.
[2] Cf. Essay xi.

IX.

THE RELATIONS BETWEEN INDUSTRIAL CONCILIATION AND ECONOMIC THEORY.[1]

THE treatment, which I have ventured to give in this Paper to the subject of the Relations between Industrial Conciliation and Economic Theory, may appear to be confined within narrow and definite limits. It may seem to involve nothing more than an inquiry into the connection which exists, or may exist, between practical expedients adopted with some success in some industries for the peaceful settlement of wages, and that limited part of theoretic economics, which is concerned with the determination of the rate of wages.

And yet, narrow and definite as are the limits prescribed, the subject almost of necessity presents some points of wider interest and of larger importance than might at first be supposed. It necessarily involves the examination from an economic standpoint of the nature and consequences of those combinations, which seem to be occupying, and to be destined to occupy, a more and more prominent position in the industrial world as time moves on. For the adoption, and the continued observance, of industrial conciliation appear to presuppose some sort of organised representa-

[1] A Paper read before Section F. of the British Association at Bath, 1888, and printed *in extenso* in the Report for that year.

INDUSTRIAL CONCILIATION 191

tion ; and organised representation is but another name for combination.

The subject, again, almost of necessity compels the consideration of some of the chief changes, which have taken place in the economic theory of wages, as it appears to have been conceived by Ricardo, and as it is now generally accepted. And lastly, it has certainly some bearing on the relations between economic theory and practice.

I may be permitted to preface my examination of the question by a brief account of the circumstances, which originally induced me to attempt it. Some time ago two able and indulgent criticisms appeared of certain views I had put forward.[1] These criticisms led me to reconsider those views with some little care, and it is the general results of that reconsideration, which I now submit.

The first of these critics—who, I may remark in passing, was a strenuous adherent of the "historical" method—observed that the work he was criticising was the "outcome of common sense working upon historical and statistical material *unaided*[2] by economic theory." The other critic, who lent his support rather to the abstract or deductive method, rejoined that the "*neglect*"[2] of that theory was the "one grave defect" of the book. Now, it appeared to me, perhaps not unnaturally, that both these criticisms were wrong. It seemed to me impossible to discuss with adequate completeness the facts and principles of industrial conciliation and arbitration "unaided" by economic theory ; and, on the other hand, I hoped that I had not been guilty of the sin of "neglect" of that theory. I was of opinion, in opposition to my first critic, that such knowledge of theory as I might have possessed had "appreciably helped" me in the discussion of industrial conciliation ; that it had

[1] In *Industrial Peace*. [2] The italics are my own.

"supplied" me with "points of view"; that it had given me "guidance in the arrangement of material"; and that the "facts of real life and the theories of economists" had not "been kept, as it were, in two separate compartments of" my "mind." And yet I could not agree with my other critic, when he asserted that "Political Economy does supply the principle" on which an arbitrator should act, or a sliding scale proceed; and that that principle was that he, or it, should endeavour to award such wages as would be obtained if "combination on either side were absent." This criticism appeared to me to be nearer the truth, but I did not think that it had succeeded in reaching it. And so I was led to reconsider the attitude I had adopted.

I am afraid that I can only explain my meaning, and define my attitude, by quoting the three passages in the book, to which my critics referred, where the relation of economic theory to methods of industrial conciliation is considered.

The first of these passages occurred at a place[1] where the nature of what I ventured to call "irregular negotiations" between masters and men in industrial disputes was examined. The passage ran in these terms: "Nor, be it noticed, does there seem to be any economic standard which can be called into requisition in such disputes; for, as Professor Sidgwick has pointed out, where two combinations meet one another, political economy is perforce silenced."

In the second and longest passage,[2] it was argued that the "principle," on which an arbitrator should act in adjusting industrial disputes, "could hardly be supplied by Political Economy. . . . As Jevons has shown in his *Theory of Political Economy*, in all bargains about a single *indivisible* object"—and I lay special stress, for reasons

[1] Page 14. [2] Page 54.

which will appear later, upon the word *indivisible*—"there may arise a 'deadlock,' because neither party can read the mind of the other, and discern the exact length to which it is prepared to go in pushing demands, or accepting concessions. Nor, indeed, did they possess the gift of clairvoyance, would the problem be necessarily solved. For, even then, there might be no definite point fixed in the mind of either. After alluding to this passage in his *State in Relation to Labour*, he" (*i.e.* Jevons) "proceeds to point out that the existence of *indivisible* combinations in trade disputes"—and here again I would emphasise the word *indivisible*—"usually reduces them to a bargain of this 'indeterminate' nature. To avoid a strike it may be the interest of either party to relinquish, or, at least, to relax, its demands; but theoretic economics cannot resolve the problem. It is, in mathematical phraseology, 'indeterminate.'"

The third and last passage occurred [1] where the introduction into a sliding scale of such elements as the cost of materials, and the state of the labour market, was under consideration "From an economic point of view, indeed," it was argued, "there is considerable reason for having regard to them, but it is the traditions of the trade which are of the greatest importance. For the existence of combinations on either side banishes, as we have noticed, to a very great extent, all economic considerations, so far at least as the determination of the exact basis of the settlement is concerned." And then, later on, in the same paragraph, it was urged that "the negotiations into which" the two parties "enter can hardly be reduced to a question of pure economics, nor is there any economic touchstone which can be brought into requisition to decide

[1] Page 93.

the matter." And then the next paragraph began with these words: "In a certain sense, indeed, it may be said that the regulation of wages by selling prices does rest upon an economic basis, however the particular details of that basis may be arranged."

These, then, are the three passages to which my critics seemed to refer; and I should summarise the argument, to which they were intended to give expression, in some such way as this. What I maintained was, that, while the general nature of the principle on which a sliding scale may be based, or an arbitrator or conciliation board proceed, may, and indeed must, possess an economic complexion, yet the particular application of that principle—the special relation between wages and prices, adopted as the starting-point of a peaceful arrangement—is not strictly determinable by economic theory. A treatise on industrial conciliation cannot then be written "unaided" by economic theory; and yet it is none the less true to maintain that "theoretic economics" cannot resolve the problem involved in the determination of the *exact* basis of a pacific settlement.

For what is the fundamental assumption of "theoretic economics"? The answer, which would, I imagine, be at once returned to this question, would be, that the fundamental assumption of any scheme of theoretic economics is competition. That competition may be hindered in its action by qualifying circumstances—by the *vis inertiæ* of custom, or some other obstacle—but we may, nevertheless, maintain that the hypothesis, which presents itself at the outset before these qualifying circumstances are taken into consideration, and the hypothesis, which is revealed in the last analysis, when these circumstances have been successively abstracted, is undoubtedly com-

INDUSTRIAL CONCILIATION 195

petition. The term "competition," however, stands in need of fuller explanation; for, for the purposes of "theoretic economics," the objects, or interests, about which the competitive forces play, must be, in theory at least, susceptible of continuous subdivision. This was what I meant when I followed Jevons in arguing that "the existence of *indivisible* combinations" in trade disputes usually "reduced" them to a bargain of "an indeterminate nature."

The proposition just laid down seems to admit of more than one easy and simple test. We might take, for instance, Jevons' own conception of "final utility." Few economists would deny that that conception is now an accepted part of economic theory, and that it is one of the most fertile conceptions of modern economics.[1] There are signs of its extension—along with the increasing amalgamation of the theory of exchange with that of distribution—from the theory of exchange of material commodities to that of exchange of services. It has been applied to the determination of interest; and it is connected with the theory of rent. But it cannot be accepted, save on the assumption enforced by Jevons himself,[2] that "more or less of a commodity" can "be had, down to infinitely small quantities."

Take once more the law of Diminishing Return—the overthrow of which, as Cairnes once pointed out,[3] would involve the re-writing of the greater part of economic theory—and what do you find? Here, again, the assumption seems to be fundamental, that "doses" of capital and labour—to use the elder Mill's suggestive expression—

[1] Cf. Essay xiii. below.
[2] *Theory of Political Economy* (2nd edition), p. 130.
[3] *Logical Method* (2nd edition), p. 36.

can be applied to the cultivation of land in infinitely small quantities, and that the returns to those "doses," when a certain point of cultivation has been reached in a certain stage of civilisation, diminish also, *cæteris paribus*, by infinitely small degrees.[1]

Or take again—though I do not lay much stress on this—one variety of the application of the "graphic method" to economics. It seems impossible to represent, as some economists have done with conspicuous success, economic theorems by geometrical curves, unless we assume the possibility of division into infinitely small quantities.

This possibility, in fact, is the underlying basis of a theory of competition, and in the final analysis of any such theory it cannot fail to appear. The theory may be only hypothetically true, although it may be a more accurate and serviceable representation of fact than is sometimes maintained. The conditions of the hypothesis must always be remembered; and it may be the case, in some instances, that the quantities, into which the commodity or service is capable of division, are only infinitely small in comparison with the great mass of the commodity or service under consideration. But this possibility does not prevent the theory from being hypothetically true; nor, on the other hand, does it obviate its failure to apply in entirety to cases where this capacity of infinite divisibility is lacking.

One of these cases occurs whenever a combination of sellers meets a combination of buyers. The commodity

[1] The analogy between marginal increments on the side of production and those on the side of consumption has been drawn by Professor Marshall in his *Principles of Economics*. Cf. Essay xiii. below.

INDUSTRIAL CONCILIATION 197

or service offered by either party in exchange for that supplied by the other is, *ex hypothesi*, whole and indivisible. There may possibly be—as we shall endeavour to illustrate later—a maximum as well as a minimum limit, beyond which it may respectively be the interest of neither party to go. But no theory of competitive economics, based as it is on the possibility of infinite subdivision, will enable us to determine the precise point between these two limits, at which it is for the joint interest of the two parties to stop; for the commodities or services they are exchanging are, by the very terms of the existence of the combinations, incapable of that infinite subdivision. On the one side we have, roughly speaking, a combined mass of labour offered for sale; on the other, we have a combined mass of remuneration—be it expressed in terms of nominal, or real wages or earnings—and, by the very conditions of the combinations, neither of these two masses is capable of infinite divisibility. If a combination of buyers alone or a combination of sellers alone existed, this capability might be impaired, but it would not be paralysed. The one commodity or service offered in exchange would retain it, and the other would lose it. And hence it is that Professor Sidgwick has discussed,[1] as a part of economic theory, the action of monopoly or combination. But the combination he considers is, as he himself expresses it, only one-sided; and the combinations, which we are now discussing, are found on both sides. And yet the existence of these combinations seems, we must remember, to be a necessary condition of successful conciliation, or arbitration, or sliding scales; for there must be organised representation on either side, if there is to be any authoritative or binding agreement, and

[1] *Principles of Political Economy*, book ii. chap. x.

organised representation is but an alternative expression for combination.[1]

Nor does my critic show a way of escape from this conclusion; and, if I put my own interpretation on his language, and supply the missing parentheses, the difference between us may be reduced to the narrowest limits. Let me quote his words: "As a matter of fact," he argues, "political economy does supply the principle—which is, that the arbitrator should endeavour to award such wages as would be obtained, if combination on either side were absent. If he fixes them appreciably above or below this level, economic theory shows that his award will have very soon to be revised. So, too, economic theory shows that, if a sliding scale has the effect of making the wages paid under it differ much from competitive wages, it must break down."

Now, looking at the matter for a moment from a practical standpoint—although, for the immediate purposes of this discussion, this mode of regarding the question is chiefly important for the side-light it may throw on the theoretical aspect—my critic's argument does not carry us very far. For where is the arbitrator to discover this ideal standard? If he confines his consideration within the limits of the two organisations, which are represented before him, he manifestly can discover no such standard. He cannot arrive at anything save a particular relation between wages and prices, which is held by both parties to be fair; and the fact that they both consist of combinations, whose express purpose is to secure better terms than could be obtained by individual competition, establishes a strong presumption against the belief that any standard could have become traditional, which was determined

[1] Cf. Essay iii.

merely by the influences affecting competitive wages. Nor, for the very same reason—and of this point the history of industrial conciliation supplies more than one striking and instructive illustration—will they be inclined to accept an appeal to the standard of wages prevailing outside the limits of their own, or at least of some, combination; for, by doing this, they would virtually nullify the *raison d'être* of their own organisation.

Nor, indeed, is it possible for the arbitrator himself to penetrate, as it were, beneath the stratum of combination and to reach that of pure competition. Within the limits of the combinations before him he cannot do this; for he cannot strip off so much, and declare that what is left is what would be the case "if combination on either side were absent." He cannot, in fact, isolate the competitive wage from the action and inter-action of the two combinations. The rate of wages is the result—to use a metaphor with which students of logic are familiar—of chemical rather than mechanical action, and the effects of the causes are intermixed.

Nor, again, can he succeed in this aim by having recourse to the labour market outside these limits; for he cannot really pass beyond the influence of the forces originating within them. The so-called competitive market itself must be influenced by the action of the combinations. If you have a strong buyer and a strong seller—and what are combinations but strong buyers and sellers?—at any particular time in a market, they will, for good or for evil, affect the market price; and, if the permanent condition of affairs be that of a strong buyer confronting a strong seller, they will, for good or for evil, exercise a permanent influence on the market price, however wide the area of the market may be.

This conclusion conducts naturally to the consideration of the question from the point of view at present of the most immediate importance—that of theoretic economics. And here I am prepared—and the previous course of the argument has tended to this result—to accept my critic's opinion, subject to my own interpretation and commentary. I readily allow that, if an arbitrator fixes wages at too great a distance above or below a competitive "level," in time the action of what we may perhaps call *external* competition—modified, indeed, and retarded by combination—will bring about a reversal of his decision. I do not see how he is to ascertain this competitive "level," save by examining into the past history or present condition of a market—be it within or be it outside of the limits of the organisations represented before him—where combinations have influenced wages. Nor do I think that it would be easy to determine the exact distance, which would be "appreciable" enough to upset his award. But, subject to these reservations — the latter of which is, I admit, more important from the practical than the theoretical point of view—I accept my critic's conclusion. And, in the same way, it may be the case that, "if a sliding-scale has the effect of making the wages paid under it differ much from competitive wages, it must break down." But here, again, it is true—from the standpoint alike of theory and of practice—that these "competitive wages" themselves will be influenced by the reflex action of the powerful combinations; and that the exact amount of difference, which, for the purposes we are now considering, ought to be characterised as "much," would be hard to determine.

The truth may be expressed in some such way as this: combinations cannot entirely free themselves from competitive influences, any more than competition can nullify the presence and action of combinations. Competition prescribes, at any particular time in a market, what we may follow Roscher[1] in calling a maximum and a minimum limit to wages; but "theoretic economics," based on two-sided, or at any rate on "one-sided," competition, cannot determine the exact point between these two limits at which two combinations will, or should, agree on a price. "The existence," then, "of combinations on either side" does "banish," "*to a very great extent*," all economic considerations, "*so far at least* as the *exact* basis of a settlement is concerned."

I do not maintain, as my critic seems to imagine, that, "by means of arbitration and conciliation and sliding scales the wages paid in a trade can be somehow or other removed from the arena of competition"; but I do maintain that it is impossible to determine by any theory, based essentially on the unrestrained freedom of any fresh combatant to enter the lists, or of anyone already within the arena to withdraw, the exact issue of the contest when, in place of this unrestricted freedom, you have the comparatively rigid and unvarying forces of two rival combinations.

Metaphors, however, are proverbially liable to break down at some important point; and therefore I will endeavour to make my meaning plain by an examination of the general nature of the change, which has passed over the theory of wages in modern economics. The old theory of Ricardo[2]—so much maligned and so often misunderstood—was so far true that, looking at the matter chiefly from a statical point of view, and remembering that Ricardo used the term "profits" in what would now be

---

[1] Cf. *Principles of Political Economy*, book iii. chap. iii. § clxv.
[2] So far, indeed, as Ricardo can strictly be said to have *formulated* any definite and complete theory of wages.

regarded as a loose and inexact sense, if you had a definite total amount of wealth produced, and a definite share of that total were taken for the landlords in rent, the remainder would be all that could be divided between the capitalists and the labourers, and, if wages gained, profits must lose. Looking at the matter, then, in this way, it would not be difficult to obtain from Ricardo an idea of a "competitive" maximum limit of wages. That limit would consist in the amount of wealth left when the capitalists had secured the rate of profits prevailing in the country—the rate, that is, prescribed by the return yielded by the land on the margin of cultivation to the capital and labour applied to it.[1] Nor, again, would it be easy even now to discover any other "competitive" minimum limit than that presented in Ricardo's idea of the cost of production of labour.

Wherein, then, did he fail? He failed in neglecting to lay stress on the causes, which might extend the maximum limit. Nay, he rather looked forward—and we cannot say that this pessimistic forecast was unwarranted by the circumstances of the times, when the law of Diminishing Returns seemed to be applying to England with terrible reality—to a contraction than to an extension of the maximum limit. Neither he nor Malthus—as M. Leroy-Beaulieu has insisted with characteristically French epigrammatic force[2]—was a "geographer." Their horizon—so far

---

[1] And so Ricardo may really be said to agree with later writers in finding the maximum limit to wages in the productivity of industry, however much he may differ from them in the narrowness and rigidity with which he may have conceived that limit. It must be admitted that it would be more accurate to represent him as limiting profits by wages rather than wages by profits; but the statement in the text may be regarded as consistent with the *broad* outlines of his reasoning.

[2] In his *Essai sur la Répartition des Richesses*.

as the future was concerned—was bounded by the circumstances of their own country, and on those circumstances they founded their generalisations of the future.

In the second place, Ricardo may be said to have failed by neglecting to give sufficient emphasis—and to repeat the emphasis at each successive stage in the argument—to the elasticity of the expressions, "the cost of production of labour," and "the average rate of profits." It was to a large extent in consequence of this that he failed to examine the distance by which, at any particular time, and in any particular condition of the labour market, the extreme point of the maximum limit might be parted, as Roscher has urged, from the extreme point of the minimum, and the causes, which might contribute to bring wages further away from the one extreme and nearer the other. He identified, in short, the maximum and the minimum; and this is not misleading when we consider only the question of "natural," or, as we should now call them, "normal" wages. But it is misleading to give so rigid a character as a rapid perusal of Ricardo might suggest to this identified maximum and minimum; and, with the exception of some brief passages, he did not examine at all into the causes affecting what we may term "market wages."

A later and more comprehensive analysis—assisted in its turn by the altered and altering circumstances of the times—has endeavoured to supply these deficiencies. It has shown how the maximum may be extended as civilisation advances, as invention and knowledge progress, as distribution itself reacts on production by increasing the efficiency of labour, and generally aiding in the augmentation of wealth. It has replaced the suggested rigidity of the Ricardian conceptions by elasticity; and it has also investigated the causes of market wages as distinct from, and yet connected with, normal or natural wages. It has shown how the strength the workmen have gained by the aid of public sympathy and of legal enactment has affected both the market and the normal wages, and has elevated alike what we have called the competitive minimum and the competitive maximum limit. And it has also shown—and this is, perhaps, the most important point—how the power of combination has enabled the workmen to raise wages in the market at any particular time from the extreme of the minimum towards the extreme of the maximum. They have become strong sellers, and they have secured the advantage, which will always accrue to strong sellers in a market. They have not emancipated themselves from the influence of competition, but they have retarded and modified its action.[1]

In time, no doubt, the influence of competition would effect—as Ricardo, confining his examination almost exclusively to normal wages, held—an identification between the competitive maximum and the competitive minimum limit. But the reflex action of the market wages might cause this identification to be made at a higher or a lower point in the area covered by these two elastic expressions. It might raise the old minimum nearer to a new maximum, it might depress the old maximum nearer to a new minimum. And—as Marx in his discussion of the iron law of wages has shown, although strangely enough he neglected to draw the natural inference from his argument—it would take time to do this; and during the interval the market influences would bring about many fluctuations in market wages, while the moment the identification had taken place —nay, even while it was going on—new market influences would be at work producing new fluctuations. The identi-

[1] Cf. Essays ii. and vi. above.

fication, then, is theoretical, and refers to normal wages, and the theory of market wages allows us to suppose at any particular time, in any particular market, an interval between the lowest possible point of the competitive minimum and the highest possible point of the competitive maximum. The minimum, in short, which is to be found, as in Ricardo's time, in the cost of production of labour, is an elastic idea, and may cover a wide area; and the maximum, which is also to be found, as in Ricardo's time, in the average rate of profits, is also an elastic idea, and may also cover a wide area. There is nothing, then, to prevent us from supposing that in the labour market at any particular time—and still more in any particular trade—there may be a competitive maximum and a competitive minimum limit of wages—the former lying at the point, where more wages would mean such a low rate of profit, that there would be a pressing danger that the requisite business management and enterprise would fail to appear, and the requisite capital cease to be forthcoming, and the latter being found in a similar way at the point, where more profits would mean such a low rate of wages that there would be an imminent prospect that labour of the requisite efficiency would not be available. Nor are we debarred from examining the causes, which may influence the fluctuation of market wages between these two points, and the market wages, we must remember, will in their turn exercise a reflex influence on normal wages.

Our combination of workmen, then, enjoys the advantages of a strong seller in the market, and within the competitive minimum they may be conceived to have set up, as it were, a minimum limit of their own. Were they not confronted by a rival combination of masters, they might conceivably make this minimum coincide with the competitive maximum. But they are confronted by this combination, which in its turn endeavours to set up, as it were, a maximum limit of its own within the competitive maximum. Were it unopposed, it might, in the same way as the combination of the men, effect a coincidence between this maximum and the competitive minimum. But, as the case stands, neither of the two combinations is unopposed. Neither of the two can secure the terms, which it might otherwise have obtained. A compromise is inevitable, and on the one side or the other a greater or less concession must be made. The point, at which the agreement is effected, will lie between the competitive minimum and the competitive maximum—understanding by these terms the extreme points of the area covered by the elastic expressions "the cost of production of labour" and "the average rate of profits." But it will probably coincide with neither; and no theory of pure competition, based as it essentially is on the possibility of infinite sub-division, will enable us to determine at what precise point between these two extreme competitive limits the two combinations, dealing as they are *ex hypothesi* with commodities or services incapable of infinite sub-division, will come to an agreement, and effect an exchange. All that we can safely infer is that the point of agreement will not lie outside these limits, unless indeed either of the two parties is blind to its economic interests.

I have endeavoured to reply to the argument advanced by one of my critics; and, without undue presumption, I may claim to have answered the other by implication. For, while I have tried to show that theoretic economics cannot determine the exact basis of industrial conciliation,

I have incidentally indicated the reasons for my opinion that it may have something to say about the general character of that basis. Combinations are, as we have seen, in some degree subject to the influence of competition, which prescribes the extreme limits, within which they act; and it is probable, therefore, that economic theory, based as it is on competition, may not be entirely foreign to a treatise on industrial conciliation, based as it is on combination.

The fundamental principle, indeed, of the most advanced form of industrial conciliation—a sliding scale—is the concurrent variation of wages and prices. This is an economic principle; and I do not know how it can be satisfactorily or completely investigated without the aid of economic theory. And so I have endeavoured to show[1] that the practice hitherto followed in connection with the construction and operation of those scales is "in a measure in accord" with the modern economic theory of wages. I do not think that it is at present possible to effect a complete reconciliation between the economic theory of wages and the factors entering into the determination of a scale; but, if we make such allowance for the consequences resulting from the presence of rival combinations as the previous course of the argument has indicated, our emphasis would rather be laid on the points of agreement than on the points of difference.

For there is the broad fact of a concurrent variation of wages and prices. That is an element common to the scale and the theory. It is true that the prices in the theory are in the present or the future,[2] while the

[1] *Industrial Peace*, p. 94.
[2] The modern theory of wages looks to the general output of industry, or the selling prices of the particular goods.

prices in the scale are in the past[1]—that the former are "realisable," while the latter are realised. But this difference arises from a practical necessity, which may be regarded as one of those conditions, which generally attach to the putting of theory into practice, but do not on that account make the theory untrue to the practice. You must ascertain the variation that has taken place in prices before you can determine what variation should be made in wages; and your particular practical mechanism for ascertaining prices does not allow you to do so until they have actually been realised. The fundamental principle, then, on which the sliding scale and the theory of wages alike are based, is not affected by this difference; nor is it—if the period of ascertaining the prices be frequent—a difference of any great magnitude. And here it is relevant to add that the competitive forces, on which the theory of wages rests, have, as a matter of actual fact, been adduced and accepted as a reason for the more frequent ascertainment of prices.

It is true, again, that the economic theory of wages takes into account the question of the supply of labour, and the demand for its services, and that this element is not explicitly recognised in a sliding scale. But, here again, the difference is in reality less considerable than might be imagined, and is only such as the previous course of the argument might lead us to expect. The economic theory of wages is based on competition, and the sliding scale on combination. But, as we have seen, combinations are not entirely emancipated from the influences of competition; and it may fairly be argued that, as a matter

[1] By a sliding scale changes in wages are to follow ascertained changes in prices; and the same principle is broadly recognised in other varieties of industrial conciliation.

of actual fact, competition is implicitly, if it is not explicitly, taken into account in the construction and operation of a scale.

In the construction this is the case; for the basis, from which a scale starts, is, as Professor Munro has said,[1] "historically" connected with competitive influences, so far as they have not been modified by combination. The general basis, again, is only the centre of a number of particular local arrangements, which in their turn start from a time when competitive influences were at work through the medium of combination, prescribing a maximum and a minimum limit to wages.

Nor are the facts different from this when we turn our attention to the operation of a scale; for, should particular local circumstances conspicuously alter, the intervention of a joint committee of masters and men may be solicited to alter the particular local arrangements, without interference with the average wage, which forms the basis of a scale; and, should the general circumstances of the trade themselves conspicuously alter, or those of the labour market, experience has shown that the basis originally adopted in the scale may be liable—more than once—to readjustment.

Nor must we forget that in some trades—and especially in such as the coal and iron mining industries, where the selling price is the sole or paramount consideration—variations in prices may be taken as a tolerably adequate index of the demand, and correct price, for labour in those particular trades. This is likely to be the case in a still higher degree, on account of the fact that the combinations present material hindrances to the entrance of outside competitors into the market, and thus the supply side of

[1] *Sliding Scales in the Coal Industry*, p. 19.

the question is, in a large measure, robbed of importance, and the supply becomes stereotyped.

Where, indeed, the cost of the raw material is an appreciable and fluctuating element, the index afforded by variations in prices is more deficient. But the inclusion of changes in the cost of the raw material among the various factors entering into the determination of a scale may introduce an added complexity, but is not incompatible with its essential characteristics. We are liable to forget, on the one hand, that sliding scales possess elasticity, and that their reconciliation with economic theory, *if we allow for the presence of the combinations on which they rest*, is, at least, conceivable; and, on the other, that they are in their infancy, and may develop in a manner and degree that it would be folly to attempt to anticipate. They may possibly be reconciled with more completeness to economic theory, and they may help to modify that theory. There is no doubt that they present the spectacle of two combinations expressly recognising, and endeavouring to facilitate in its operation, a fundamental principle of competitive economics—the concurrent variation of wages and prices—and there is also no doubt that, where a sliding scale regulates wages, two combinations may influence the conditions of the competitive market in such a way that no theory of pure competition will enable us to determine the exact point at which they will agree on a price. The starting-point, then, of a scale (the most advanced form of industrial conciliation) is arbitrary: its general working is the exemplification of an economic principle.

X.

SOME ASPECTS OF THE THEORY OF RENT.[1]

FEW economic theories have been more often introduced of late into the discussion of practical affairs than the theory of rent; and, among the causes which have contributed to this result, two are perhaps especially prominent. On the one hand, the attention of Parliament has been largely directed to agrarian matters. The questions, indeed, raised by the Agricultural Holdings Acts and the condition of the Highland crofters have differed in detail and degree from those connected with Irish land legislation; but these differences have been compatible with a broad similarity in the theoretical issues involved. It is true that such differences may be an important consideration for the practical legislator, and that he may refuse to concern himself very seriously with similarities of theoretical principle, if, after the most comprehensive survey that he has been able to make of the conditions of the immediate problem before him, he has reached the conviction that the solution he favours satisfies the demands of practical exigency. But his action is generally regarded by himself, or by others, to be founded on the application, or misapplication, of a theory; and it can scarcely fail to attract attention to the theoretical principles, with which it is

[1] Published in the *Economic Journal* for March, 1891 (vol. i. No. 1).

supposed to conflict, or to be in fundamental agreement, in spite of an appearance of discord. Nor would the theorist, who had formed his theories most carefully, be unwilling to admit the advantage of allowing due weight to the limiting conditions of practice in their application. Although, then, the question has presented itself to Parliament in a different shape, with different antecedents and surroundings, on different occasions, yet certain similar theoretical issues connected with the theory of rent have been brought into recent discussions on the practical relations of landlord and tenant; and, where the support of the theory has not been enlisted, its dismissal as erroneous or inapplicable has been persistently urged.

But there is another cause, which seems also to have been specially responsible for the appearance of the theory of rent in recent discussions. It can scarcely be questioned that the only part of the propaganda of modern socialism, which has as yet obtained any wide currency in England, is that known as the "nationalisation of land." At any rate, it will not be disputed that this side of the socialistic agitation has been brought into greater prominence than the other, which is more comprehensive in its aims, and proposes the "nationalisation" of capital (including land), or the means of production. Different explanations might be furnished to account for the phenomenon that this more limited form of socialism has hitherto found greater favour in England, while enthusiastic support has been given on the Continent to the larger scheme. The "illogical" character of the English temper might be urged by those unwilling to recognise that quality of "animated moderation," which Mr. Bagehot once described as the typical characteristic of a "great practical Englishman."[1]

[1] Cf. Essay i.

The comparative difficulty and expense of the transfer of English landed property might be advanced by those, who maintain that in the past, and, in spite of recent legislation, in the present also, these causes, pressing with greater weight on the small than on the large purchaser, have tended to strengthen those influences of legal tradition, or social prestige, or political power, or economic advantage, which, it is argued, have promoted the concentration of the ownership of land in the hands of a smaller number of persons than in Continental countries. The lingering effects of the struggle between the old privileged landed gentry and nobility and the new manufacturing and mercantile classes might be held responsible by a third set of persons. But, whatever the true reason may be, of the fact there can be little doubt. Whether it be due especially to one or more of the causes which have been noticed, or perhaps in part also to the influence of Mr. George's *Progress and Poverty*, which was written in the English language, and addressed in the first instance to English-speaking peoples, the proposal for the "nationalisation" of land has unquestionably met with the more considerable support. The more recent popularity of Mr. Bellamy's *Looking Backward*, which promised to rival that of Mr. George's book, may possibly have resulted in the withdrawal of part of that support in favour of the larger scheme of socialism described in its pages; but it remains true that the "nationalisation of land" is the more popular part of the socialist programme.

Of the intimate connection of this proposal with the theory of rent there can be no question. Just as the more comprehensive form of socialism, which aims at the "nationalisation" of capital, purports to be based on Ricardo's theory of value, so the proposal for the "nationalisation of land" is avowedly put forward as a practical deduction from Ricardo's theory of rent. In the one case, as in the other, the theory may be unduly strained or perversely misinterpreted, and the details of the practical schemes founded upon it may differ in particular cases. But these different schemes are characterised by the common element of the conception of an "unearned increment" attaching to the ownership of land, and that conception is regarded as a corollary of the theory of rent.

Perhaps, however, the chief form of landed property, against which the criticisms and proposals of writers and speakers have been more recently directed, is that found in urban districts. Although, by a coincidence, which might be quoted as a fresh illustration of the "irony of fate," the popularity of Mr. George's book was simultaneous with the occurrence of a serious and prolonged depression in the agriculture of the old world, which has rendered the landed classes, generally so-called, a specially distressed rather than a prosperous section of the community, yet the increasing tendency of the inhabitants of old and new countries alike to gather together in towns has resulted in a marked rise of urban rent. Such questions as "leasehold enfranchisement," the "taxation of ground rents," and the application of the principle of "betterment," show that the attention of the Legislature, like the criticisms of socialistic and other writers, may be directed more persistently in the future to the consideration of urban than agricultural land.

But, while the action of legislators and the proposals of reformers have been thus busy on matters connected with the theory of rent, economic students have been actively engaged in the examination of that theory, and it has certainly participated as largely as any other theory in recent extensions and improvements of economic knowledge.

It will be the aim of this Essay to consider some aspects of the relations borne by this theoretical criticism to discussions on matters of practice, without venturing further than may prove to be inevitable on controversial ground.

The economic theory of rent is generally known as the Ricardian theory. It is true that Ricardo himself stated in the preface to his *Principles of Political Economy and Taxation* that the theory might be found in the pages of other writers. "In 1815," he wrote, "Mr. Malthus, in his *Inquiry into the Nature and Progress of Rent*, and a Fellow of University College, Oxford, presented to the world, nearly at the same moment, the true doctrine of rent." Later research has added to the names of Malthus and Sir Edward West, who was the anonymous "Fellow of University College,"[1] that of an earlier writer, Dr. Anderson, who stated the theory in 1777 in his *Enquiry into the Nature of Corn Laws ;* and it has also shown that in some respects Malthus' exposition may be considered superior to that of Ricardo, as in others it is inferior. Dr. Bonar, in his *Malthus and his Work*,[2] has urged that here, as on other points of general economics, Malthus anticipated some of the conclusions of later writers and their criticisms on Ricardo's doctrines. Both in his definition of rent, and his enumeration of the causes of its increase, he seems to have been more comprehensive, and later inquiry has tended to justify this largeness of view. But the connection of the theory with the name of Ricardo does not require any formal or laboured justification. His treatment of it has exercised a predominant influence, and his whole scheme of economic doctrine was founded upon it. He gave it the

[1] Cf. an article by Mr. E. Cannan in the *Economic Journal* for March, 1893, on the "Origin of the Law of Diminishing Returns."
[2] Book ii. chap. 1.

most prominent place in his preface; he discussed it in his second chapter, immediately after the question of value; and he connected with it his theories of wages and profits, and of the incidence of various forms of taxation.

This connection of Ricardo's name with the theory suggests of itself some important considerations respecting its application to practice. Ricardo's writing has been generally regarded as the type of an abstract, deductive method of inquiry;[1] and the criticisms of economists of the historical and inductive school have been chiefly directed against his doctrines. If the theories of any one economist were to be selected as an illustration of divergence from fact, the choice of many persons would at once fall on Ricardo, and the opinion of Malthus that the "main part of his structure would not stand" would be considered as being at least as successful as any prediction in hitting the mark. This criticism may be erroneous, or it may be unduly severe; and the publication of Ricardo's *Letters to Malthus* may perhaps tend to moderate the rigorous treatment, which he has sometimes received. But these letters also furnish an instructive commentary on the application of his theories to practice. We have in them a statement from his own lips of the purpose, which he had in view in writing his *Principles*, and a frank confession of deficiencies of composition.

We might have known, before Dr. Bonar edited these letters, that Ricardo's Jewish nationality, and his occupation on the London Stock Exchange, were likely to have nourished a fondness and capacity for abstractions. We might have made ourselves aware that the actual phenomena of industry, when he wrote, presented a scene of

---

[1] Cf. the author's *History of Political Economy in England*, chap. iii.

confusing stir and bustling change, which almost seemed anarchical; and that, in arranging these phenomena in an intelligible order, and interpreting them by the assumption of the pervading presence of competition, he formed a conception of society, which did not appear to differ widely from actual fact. We might have informed ourselves that the subject on which he first wrote—that of money in its connection with the foreign exchanges—had since been recognised as so perplexing in its intricacy that it would be futile to attempt to unravel its tangled web without the aid of an abstract, deductive method.[1] Nor were we without the opportunity of learning that the publication of a systematic treatise by Ricardo was due to the pressure of friends belonging to the school of thought, which centred round the name of Bentham, and believed in the exclusive advantage of rigid analysis and deduction from a few simple principles. So much as this might have been known; and Senior, who was an acute observer, had uttered[2] the pregnant remark that Ricardo's own " sagacity prevented his making sufficient allowance for the stupidity or carelessness of his readers, and he was too earnest a lover of truth to anticipate wilful misconstruction."

But the publication of Ricardo's *Letters to Malthus* has made important additions to this available knowledge. They disclose in a vivid and unmistakable fashion the real intention of his work and the true character of his mind. They show at once in what lay his peculiar strength and his special weakness. " Our differences," he writes to Malthus in one of these letters, "may in some respects, I think, be ascribed to your considering my book as more practical than I intended it to be. My object was to elucidate

[1] Cf. the following Essay.
[2] *Political Economy*, p. 118.

principles, and to do this I imagined strong cases, that I might show the operation of those principles." And on another occasion he remarked : " You have always in your mind the immediate and temporary effects of particular changes, whereas I put these immediate and temporary effects quite aside, and fix my whole attention on the permanent state of things which will result from them. Perhaps you estimate these temporary effects too highly, while I am too much disposed to undervalue them." It would be difficult for a writer to explain more clearly the object, which he had in view; but these passages are contained in Ricardo's *Letters* and not in his *Principles*, and they form part of the contribution made by recent economic research to the correct appreciation of the bearings of his theories on practice.[1]

Nor, again, would it be easy to discover in any writer a more candid avowal of faults of composition than that furnished in some other extracts from this same correspondence. "My speaking," he states, "is, like my writing too much compressed. I am too apt to crowd a great deal of difficult matter into so short a space as to be incomprehensible to the generality of readers." "I am but a poor master of language, and therefore I shall fail to express what I mean." "I am fully aware of the deficiency in the style and arrangement; those are faults which I shall never conquer." In the light shed by such passages as these it becomes easier to understand why his *Principles* have the appearance of a collection of detached notes rather than a formal treatise, and why he is often

---

[1] Cf. Mr. Cannan's articles on "Ricardo in Parliament," in vol. iv. of the *Economic Journal*. Dr. Hollander has recently edited some letters of Ricardo to McCulloch, for the American Economic Association.

content with an isolated statement, unexplained and unrepeated, of the conditions which he assumes. But it also becomes more improbable that the characteristic theory of such a writer can with advantage or success be immediately applied to practice. It is even more likely than the theories of the other writers to stand in need of limiting qualifications. It is more certain to be marked by a nicety of distinction, to which only a rough parallel can be found, or established, in fact. It subjects the student, who would understand its delicate refinements, to a stern intellectual discipline, which might naturally beget an extreme caution in practice.

Professor Sidgwick has remarked,[1] that in what is "commonly known" as "the Ricardian theory of rent" three different theories are combined, based on "different kinds of evidence, and relating to different" inquiries. The first is a "historical theory as to the origin of rent," the second a "statical theory of the economic forces tending to determine rent at the present time," and the third a "dynamical theory of the causes continually tending to increase rent, as wealth and population increases." Although these three theories, as Professor Sidgwick shows, are distinct from one another, there is a bond of connection between them; and, at any rate, the considerations, which bear on their respective relations to practice, are similar in general character. It will, however, be convenient to examine the assumptions involved in Ricardo's reasoning from the standpoint, in the first instance, of the "statical theory." That seems to follow as a corollary from the market-price of the produce of land, which is determined by the expenses of producing and placing on the market that portion of the supply, for which there is a

[1] *Principles of Political Economy*, book ii. chap. vii. sect. 1.

demand, which is produced and placed on the market at the greatest expense.

On the hypothesis of free competition this result will follow. Producers cannot continue to produce at a loss; and, therefore, if the demand for the produce of land is to ensure a supply sufficient to meet it, a price must be offered, which will recoup the expenses incurred by those producers, who are situated in the most disadvantageous position. They cannot afford to produce at a loss; and, if they asked for more, fresh competitors would, on the hypothesis of free competition, leave some other industry and enter theirs. But the market-price thus determined will be the price for the whole of the supply of the same quality which is forthcoming. There is no reason, on the hypothesis of free competition, why the producers, who enjoy greater advantages of production, should be content with a lower when they can obtain the higher price, which the buyers must offer, if all the supply they demand is to be forthcoming. And so the producers, who are more favourably placed, obtaining the same price as those, who are less advantageously situated, for commodities which have cost less to produce and to place on the market, have a surplus in hand, which competition for the enjoyment of their advantages compels them to hand over to those who have their control and disposal.

It is this surplus, which is termed "rent": it is, broadly defined, a payment for differential advantages. Regarded thus broadly, it seems to involve certain conclusions. In the first place, a similar surplus may arise in the case of other kinds of wealth but land. In the second place the differential advantages, of which it is a measure, may conceivably vary in different degrees and opposing directions, according to the special form of advantage which is under

SOME ASPECTS OF THE THEORY OF RENT

consideration; and, thirdly, the theory postulates the action of free competition. We may conveniently confine our attention for the present to the second and third of these conclusions, and, in the first instance, to the circumstances of agricultural land used for farming purposes.

Some of that land is more fertile than other land, and, therefore, the expenses of raising farm produce are less from some than they are from other land. The farmers of the least fertile land must secure for the sale of its produce in the market a price sufficient to cover their expenses of production; and the farmers of the more fertile land, obtaining the same price and incurring less expense, have a surplus in hand, which competition for the enjoyment of their position compels them to transfer to the landlords as rent. This surplus will vary according to the extent to which the fertility of their land exceeds in each case that of the least fertile land, the produce of which must be forthcoming to meet the demand.

But not only has farm produce to be raised: it has also to be placed on the market. The term "production" is sometimes so interpreted as to cover the production of any utility, and to embrace the effort of labour and expenditure of capital undertaken by retail distributors. But, in any event, it comprises the effort and expenditure needed to place commodities on wholesale markets. The expenses of production, then, in the case of farm produce, include its carriage to the market as well as the cultivation of the land from which it is raised. Some land is situated nearer, and some at a greater distance from, the market where the produce is sold. The farmers of the most distant land, if their produce is needed to meet the demand, must secure such a price as to cover their expenses of production, including the cost of carriage. The farmers of the nearer land, obtaining the same price for what costs less to convey to the market, have a surplus in hand, which competition for the enjoyment of their advantages compels them to transfer to the landlords as rent.

To these two reasons for differential advantage in the cultivation of agricultural land, Ricardo, who recognised the second, but laid greater stress on the first, added a third, connected with the law of diminishing returns. After a certain point has been reached in the cultivation of land, the returns of produce yielded to each fresh application of capital and labour will tend, *cæteris paribus*, to diminish and not to increase proportionally. Were this not the case, the whole of the food required might conceivably be raised from a single field, and there would be no necessity to cultivate poorer land. As it is, the returns to different applications of capital and labour tend, *cæteris paribus*, to vary. Some are made under more, and some under less, favourable conditions. A farmer will not knowingly engage in the least advantageous of such applications, unless the price realised will cover the expenses of production; and from the more advantageous, obtaining the same price for what has cost less to produce, he will have a surplus in hand, which competition will compel him to transfer to the landlord as rent.

In a broad sense, then, rent is a payment for differential advantages, which may thus proceed from different sources. It is only by taking all sources of advantage into account that it can be determined whether one piece of land or another is a more productive instrument of wealth; and to this point we shall have to return. What we have now to notice is that the whole of the reasoning rests on the assumption of competition. The expenses of production, which the sale of the farm produce must cover, are the wages and profits paid to all who have co-operated in placing the produce on the market. Sometimes it is convenient to regard the farmer as incurring the expenses of cultivation and carriage, and receiving, in addition to those expenses, ordinary farming profits; sometimes it is more convenient, and it is perhaps more accurate, to look at the whole process from the outside, and to include in the expenses of production the profits of the farmer himself. But, in either case, the price, at which the produce is sold in the market, must be sufficient to afford "normal" wages to all who have contributed their labour, and "normal" profits to all who have given capital and management to the entire process of production, including the carriage to the market. It must form an adequate reward for all the effort and expenditure which have been devoted to the undertaking. It must furnish sufficient earnings of labour and management and interest of capital. So much as this it must yield in the case of those producers, who are placed under the greatest disadvantages, and furnish the last, or, as it may be called, the "marginal," part of the supply for which there is a demand; and it is the surplus above this amount, which competition transfers to the landlords as rent.

All this reasoning, then, rests on the assumption of competition. It is assumed that, if wages or profits fell below the points, which, on a comparison of the advantages and drawbacks, pecuniary and other, of farming and other occupations, are considered to be normal in the farming industry, some labourers and farmers would seek some more advantageous employment; and that, if they rose above, some fresh competitors would enter the ranks of agriculture. It is assumed that landlord and tenant are actuated by competitive considerations alone, the one trying to obtain the highest and the other the lowest rent. The landlord is not supposed to be influenced by kindly feeling, traditional claims, long connection, or political obligation. The tenant is not supposed to be affected by a sense of attachment to a particular farm. But it has generally been recognised that such an assumption may be at variance with fact, and that other but competitive considerations may enter into the determination of the bargain. Land, in England at least, is a species of property, which is considered to be more subject than manufacturing or mercantile wealth to obligations of a customary and non-competitive character, and to the influence of kindly, personal considerations. And hence, it is generally admitted that, taking a broad view of agricultural land, English rents have not reached an extreme competitive limit. But these considerations, however instructive, are not perhaps of such importance in the relations of the theory to practice as others, which are more easily overlooked.

The assumption of competition implies that landlords and tenants are independent, intelligent agents, able to carry their services and commodities to the best market. It implies, therefore, that farmers are able and willing to move to any county, or trade, where they will secure more favourable conditions; that they know, and can compare, the different advantages of different soils and districts and trades. But it is not always the case that tenants are thus independent, intelligent agents; and, even if they are, they may yet be unable to take their wares and services to the best market. They may have given hostages to the land which they cultivate, by investing capital in its improvement; and this is one theoretical justification of the Agricultural Holdings Acts of 1875 and 1883. Those

Acts have recognised the inability of a tenant to remove his improvements, and provided for compensation for such part as may be "unexhausted" at the close of a tenancy. It would not be difficult to show that they are not in conflict, but rather in harmony, with the theory of rent in making such a provision; for the tenants have sunk capital in the cultivation of land, which they cannot withdraw and offer for sale in the best market.

Again, the theory of rent assumes that tenants cultivate with a single eye to the sale of the produce in the market; for it is only by starting with the conditions determining the selling-price that we arrive at the establishment of differential advantages enjoyed by different producers, and the consequent existence of rent. It has sometimes been argued that it is difficult to bring the case of peasant proprietors within the scope of the theory, because they combine in their own person the functions of landlords, tenants, and labourers. But, for the purposes of theoretical inquiry, we may separate what are sometimes conjoined in fact; and one of the most important of recent advances in economic theory has been due to the distinction established between the functions of the employer and those of the capitalist, although these functions are sometimes, and indeed to some extent usually, exercised by different persons, but are also, sometimes entirely, and generally in some degree, combined in the same individual. The existence of a peasant proprietary is not incompatible with differential advantages in the cultivation of land, although the peasant may pay a rent to himself and not to another man. The chief difficulty of applying the theory to the case of peasant proprietors seems rather to arise from another source. They do not always cultivate with a single eye to the sale of the produce in the market. They may intend to consume part of that produce themselves, and they may then be content to cultivate at a cost, which they would not incur, if they regarded only the realisation of a profit in the market. They are, so far, uninfluenced by the competition with rival producers, which stimulates to improvement and checks misdirected energy; and often they are not entirely dependent for their income on the sale of their farm produce. They, or their wives and their children, may be partly engaged in some other employment. They may even regard the cultivation of their land, in some cases, as secondary in importance to the main occupation of their lives, and they may then be content to produce at a loss.

The importance of a second occupation has been lately illustrated by the Highland crofters, who have sometimes added the business of fishing to that of farming. In such cases it is theoretically possible that rents fixed by competitive bargaining may yet vary from a true measure of differential advantage. Higher rents may conceivably be offered than would arise from a single regard to the productive powers of the land and the income accruing from the sale of its produce. The second occupation may be of primary importance; and, even if it is subsidiary, as in the case of the crofters, a sudden failure or unexpected disaster in their fishing ventures may render them not merely unwilling, but unable, to pay a rent, which was fixed with the prospect of securing some part of their income from this subsidiary source. Such cases of by-industries are undoubtedly complex and difficult when viewed from a theoretical standpoint.

There is another aspect from which the assumption of competition may be considered in the case of small cultivators. We have already seen that this assumption implies that tenants can carry their wares and services to the best market, and that the Agricultural Holdings Acts may be treated as a recognition of their inability to remove their unexhausted improvements. We have now to add the consideration that in some cases they may not be able to remove their own persons. The conditions, indeed, of mobility of capital and labour, which are necessary to justify the assumption of a correspondence between the effort and expenditure of different employments and their rewards, require to be carefully interpreted; and it is not necessary that every individual labourer and employer, and every particular portion of capital, should exhibit the capacity to move from the less to the more advantageous occupation. It is only necessary that a sufficient number of workers, which may be found in the rising generations successively entering on industrial and business life, and an adequate amount of capital, which may be discovered in fresh accumulations or floating funds, should move, or be expected to move; and these quantities may vary at different times and in different employments. But it is possible to find cases where the influences of such an amount of mobility as this are inoperative, because the necessary conditions do not exist; and here the assumption of competition implied in the theory of rent does not seem to be realised in a way that the theory contemplates.

It has, for example, been contended that in Ireland, broadly speaking, there has been no alternative occupation to agriculture for a large part of the population. There have been only such other industries as were to be found in a few exceptional districts, and therefore the cultivator of land could not compare his earnings with those to be gained in other employments. So far as this was the case, the assumption of competition implied in the theory of rent did not appear to have been fulfilled. There might be competition; but its only limit would be the necessities of subsistence, and it would not be restrained, as the theory is generally understood to assume, by the alternative of leaving farming and passing into some other occupation. In the case, indeed, of such small cultivators, the comparison would seem generally to lie between the wages to be obtained in other occupations and the earnings of farming, rather than between those earnings and profits; and this consideration may be of more than theoretical importance. But even this lower limit of wages may be conceived as ineffectual, if other occupations are insignificant in extent, or are practically non-existent. Rent is sometimes described as the "leavings" of profits and wages, but in such cases it may rather be what is left when the necessities of a bare subsistence have been met. The cultivator, having no alternative occupation, may conceivably be forced by competition to offer such a rent as will only permit him to live, and he may offer it with a full knowledge of the conditions of his present position and of the future consequences of his act.

But again, even where the possibility of passing from one place or trade to another may not be beyond the limits of conceivable attainment, it may, from the ignorance or incapacity of the cultivators themselves, be outside the bounds of practical realisation. The alternative employments may exist, and yet want of ability or intelligence may debar the cultivators from availing themselves of the opportunities thus presented. This, also, has been asserted to be the case with regard to large districts in Ireland; and the position of some classes of small urban tenants has been represented as similar. Mr. Sidney Webb, in his evidence before the Town Holdings Committee, described[1] "certain localities" of London as "economically equivalent to Connaughts," because the tenants were compelled by an "inability to move," and the "absolute necessity of being near their occupation," "to pay much more than anything which could reasonably be called the economic rent." So far as these tenants are forced to live in certain districts in order to prosecute their special industry, they may be said to resemble those Irish tenants, who are represented as having no alternative employment to agriculture; and, so far as they are compelled by their want of industrial capacity to follow certain trades, they resemble the Irish tenants, to whom the alternative employments, which exist, are said to be practically closed. In any event they appear to share with them this common characteristic, that they are not independent, intelligent agents, able to make the best bargain in the best market.

The failure of competitive influences to be present in their fulness has of late been prominently urged both in connection with the taxation of ground-rents in urban districts, and the payment of tithe on agricultural land; and the public discussion of these questions has brought into notice some nice theoretical points. It has been argued, on the one hand, that the real incidence of local rates, like that of tithe,[2] has fallen on the landlord, although it may nominally have been borne by the tenant, because they are considerations, which entered into the calculation of the tenant, when he made his bargain with the landlord for the occupancy of his farm, or house. They

---

[1] *Report*, 1890, Q. 59.

[2] Before the passing of the Act of 1891, which definitely imposed the liability on the landlord. Much of the reasoning, however, would apply equally to the case of *rates* on agricultural land.

are part of the expenses connected with the occupancy, and rent is the surplus remaining when these expenses, including the profits of the tenant, have been defrayed. But, on the other hand, it is obvious that, so far as competition fails to be operative, this theory of incidence has not been fulfilled either in the case of tithe or that of urban rates. It may, however, be laid down as a more general rule that the farmer was sufficiently alive to competitive considerations to have regard to the amount of the tithe when he concluded his bargain for rent; and there are certainly instructive differences between his case and that of the urban ratepayer.

In the first place, the real incidence of the burden is determined only in the long run. The tenant of agricultural land may indeed enter into a lease, like the tenant of urban land; and, like him, he may have been unable to modify the terms of his lease so as to throw on the landlord the weight of any fresh burden, which may, contrary to his reasonable expectations, have been levied. But leases of agricultural land are generally drawn for shorter terms. They are indeed, in England as a usual rule, of no longer duration than a year; and, in any case, nineteen or twenty-one years are an outside limit. The opportunities for readjustment are thus of frequent recurrence; and it is easy to anticipate the nature and amount of taxation, which will be imposed on the land during the continuance of the contract. In the case of the tithe, indeed, the commuted apportionment had for some time been fixed; but the question of urban rates is different. The leases run for longer periods—in some cases for seventy or ninety-nine years, in others in perpetuity, as in the "chief rents" of Manchester.[1] The burden of

[1] *Reports of Town Holdings Committee* (especially that of 1890).

SOME ASPECTS OF THE THEORY OF RENT

local rates has, it is contended, been mainly imposed, or largely increased, since the conclusion of many of the contracts. It could not have been anticipated by the tenants, when they entered upon their leases; and, while some of the expenditure, for which the taxation is levied, is devoted to objects of present, and temporary, or general convenience, some is incurred for works of permanent improvement, the cost of which will be defrayed before the leases expire, while the benefit will remain to enhance the reversionary value of the interests of the ground landlords. Many, if not all, of these points are controverted; but, taken together, they constitute a wide difference between the position of urban and agricultural land, and, taken singly, they indicate a greater difficulty in determining the real incidence of the rates. There are also, in many cases of urban tenancies, several intermediaries between the actual occupier and the ground landlord; and the effort needed to shift the incidence of the rates may be successfully attempted in some of these successive stages, and may fail, or not be attempted at all, in others.

But not only has the discussion raised by the question of taxing ground rents served, in this way, to induce the careful scrutiny of the assumption of competition, which is implied in the theory of rent, but it has also brought into notice some nice points of another kind. Mr. Sidney Webb maintained, in his evidence[1] before the Town Holdings Committee, that the economic theory of the incidence on the occupier or consumer of that part of local taxation, which is proportioned to the value of the house, as distinct from the ground on which it is built, "assumes that there is no other shoulder on whom the builder can shift it, that he must get his normal interest, that he is between the

[1] *Report*, 1890, Q. 42.

fixed point of the ground landlord and the shifting price of the consumer, and that one of them must give way." "But," he argues, "the ground landlord is not a fixed point; and, in the passage of agricultural land into building land," there is "always a large jump in value." "The freeholder getting, in any case, a much larger than the agricultural value," has "no fixed point of resistance," and "the better economic opinion would now be that, in the same sense that the rate on land falls upon the owner, the rate upon buildings falls equally so." Professor Munro urged,[1] before the same committee, that the "circumstances are so different, that you cannot apply" the "theory of agricultural rent to the rent of building land," "without great qualifications." "The landowner of agricultural land requires to let his land in order to obtain a return," and has to be "content with the surplus that remains over" the "remuneration," which the "farmer has received for himself" and his "outgoings." But "in the case of agricultural land that may be turned into building land there is no necessity for the owner to let it for building purposes. As agricultural land he is obtaining a fair ordinary return for it, and anything that he obtains over and above the agricultural rent is a pure and absolute gain in itself." "He can control the market" "to a very much greater degree than a landowner can control the market for agricultural land." And again, at the time when "the builder purchases the land from the landowner, the only rates that the land is liable to are rates for agricultural purposes, and the future increased rates that may fall upon that land in case it is built upon, and in case a house is erected and occupied," do not enter at all into consideration.

In these different ways both Mr. Webb and Professor

[1] *Report*, 1890, Q. 1804-1812.

SOME ASPECTS OF THE THEORY OF RENT

Munro have laid stress on the distinction between agricultural and urban land. We are not now so much concerned with the practical conclusions, which they deduce respecting the real incidence of taxation, as with the fact that the distinction involves a point of fundamental importance in the theory of rent. Rent, broadly defined as a payment for differential advantages, is measured upwards from a minimum level, where, it is assumed, no rent is paid. The producers on the "margin" of production clear their expenses, but have no surplus in hand to transfer to the landlords. This assumption of a "no-rent" minimum has been often criticised, and many of the objections have been successfully answered. But one criticism seems to be of fundamental importance, and is of the nature of a commentary rather than an objection. This criticism states that the differential advantages, of which rent is the measure, are of various kinds, and do not always vary in the same direction or degree. It is a consideration of this character, which seems to be implied in the arguments of Mr. Webb and Professor Munro before the Town Holdings Committee, and from it the consequence follows that what is a "no-rent" or inferior land, regarded from the standpoint of one particular kind of advantage, may not be so with respect to another.

Ricardo, as his habit was, simplified the problem. He considered, as Professor Marshall has shown,[1] the different crops, which might be raised from the land, as convertible into terms of corn; and, although he recognised the element of situation, he introduced it by a qualifying clause, and traced the rise of rent by differences of natural fertility. It was only at the end of his exposition that he became more comprehensive, and said that the "exchange-

[1] *Principles of Economics*, book v. chap. viii. 3.

able value" of the "produce" of the "most fertile and favourably situated land" would "be adjusted by the total quantity of labour necessary in various forms, from first to last, to produce it and bring it to market." And again, in spite of passages, in which he qualifies his statements, he seems, on the whole, to have regarded wages and profits as more rigidly determined than we should now hold; and, in his exposition of the theory of rent, he appears to have postulated them as practically fixed. Nor, lastly, had he apparently more than a single market in view at any particular moment for the sale of the farm produce. These assumptions were legitimate for the purpose in hand, and they were not at variance with the broad characteristics of the times. But it is necessary to bear them continually in mind in any practical application of the theory to the circumstances of the present day.

Ricardo, then, in expounding the theory, may be considered to have regarded rent as a payment for differential advantages, arising from the different fertility of different soils, for the production of corn for a single market by producers, who paid wages, which were assumed to be fixed, and expected profits, which were assumed to be fixed also.

Thus regarded, the problem was comparatively simple; and such simplicity is an useful, if not a necessary, preliminary, to the successful handling of the complexity of actual fact. But perhaps the most fruitful and important result of economic study since Ricardo's time has consisted in the emphasis laid on the great number, and the variable character, of the elements involved in the determination of an economic problem, and on the way in which they may mutually determine, and be determined by, one another.

SOME ASPECTS OF THE THEORY OF RENT

The differential advantages, for which rent is a payment, may be measured upwards from land which is least fertile, or most unfavourably situated. It is by no means certain that the differences, measured according to these two standards, will coincide. They may conceivably vary in opposite directions in the case of the same soils, and they may also vary in the degree of variation in the same direction. This supposition has, in fact, been recently used by Professor Sidgwick[1] to support the assumption of "continuous variations" in the total advantages of different soils.

Again, a soil, which is suitable for one crop, may be more or less suited for another, and the differential advantages of different soils, as respects their fertility, may conceivably vary in opposite directions, or different degrees, in the case of different crops; while their advantages, as respects their situation and the cost of conveying their produce to the market, may be subject to variations of a similar character, if one crop is more bulky or perishable than another, and more likely to be injured by delay or rough handling in transit. Once more, the cost of conveyance to the market may differ according to the market in view; and lands favourably situated for one market may be disadvantageously placed for another, and *vice versâ*. And, lastly, as rent is the surplus above the expenses of production—or, as it is sometimes termed, the "leavings" of wages and profits—the differential advantages of different lands as instruments of production may vary as the rates of wages and profits themselves vary. All these considerations tend to the general conclusion that what is a "no-rent" or inferior land, regarded from one point of view, may conceivably be a superior land from another;

[1] *Principles of Political Economy*, p. 284, note 1.

and they illustrate the theoretical importance of the distinctions established between urban and agricultural land by Professor Munro and Mr. Webb.

Perhaps, however, they are of especial importance in their bearing on the most conspicuous of the recent applitations of the theory of rent to practical affairs. The popular conception of an "unearned increment" is avowedly based on Ricardo's theory.[1] Rent is considered to be a payment, which is constantly increasing, made to a class, which has not earned it. That Ricardo entertained the idea of a continuous growth of rent as a characteristic feature of progressive civilisation cannot be questioned, and he generalised from the conspicuous circumstances of his times. The law of diminishing returns seemed to be applying rigorously to English agriculture, and the margin of cultivation to be extending to poorer and yet poorer soils. Population was rapidly increasing; and the importation of food from abroad on any large scale appeared to be as far removed from the sphere of practical possibilities as the introduction of any notable improvements in agricultural science or practice. There seemed to be no doubt that the natural tendency of rent was to rise at the expense of wages and profits, as the pressure of population on the resources of land became more urgent.

Later experience has, however, shown that what Ricardo himself regarded as improbable, although he recognised its possibility, has actually occurred. The law of diminishing returns may be postponed or counteracted in various ways. A denser population may conceivably permit of greater organisation and division of labour, and its effective application to the cultivation of land, so as to result in an increasing rather than a diminishing return. Some special

[1] Cf. Essay i.

SOME ASPECTS OF THE THEORY OF RENT

employment of capital on an extensive scale may so alter the character of land, or the circumstances and conditions of production, as to cause for some time more, and not less, abundant returns. Intensive cultivation may be substituted for extensive methods, or improved machinery or fresh manures be used. Or, lastly, an alteration in the means of conveying the produce to the market may diminish the cost of transportation; and in these various ways the practical consequences of the law of diminishing returns may be postponed or counteracted.

Again, changes in transportation may open the resources of more lands than before to certain markets, or bring within the range of certain lands more markets than before. They may alter the relative situation of different soils with reference to the market, and, while producing perhaps a fresh increment of rent in some cases, they may occasion a decrement in others. The serious fall in English agricultural rents of recent years has, for example, been largely due to the immense improvement in the means, and decrease in the cost, of transporting grain from the rich virgin soils of America and from India.[1] These changes also tend to equalise the advantages of different lands in situation with respect to the market; and, therefore, their broad result is to postpone the consequences of the operation of the law of diminishing returns on the one hand, and on the other to reduce the amount of the differential advantages of situation of different soils. In both these ways they tend to arrest the rise of rent.

They may exercise a further influence. As a consequence of changes in the markets, to which the produce of the land is sent, and of fresh demands in those new markets, they may lead to the raising of crops different

[1] Cf. Essay viii.

from those produced before. These crops may, of course, be less suited to the character and conditions of the land in question; but the balance of probability inclines to the conclusion that, with the extension of the number of available markets, and of the area from which the supplies for one particular market are drawn, crops will tend more and more to be raised from the soils, which are best fitted to produce them, and to take their place in the most suitable and productive order of rotation. In this way, again, the practical consequences of the law of diminishing returns are postponed, and the differential advantages of different soils confined within a smaller range. The increase of rent is arrested, and what was in one place an increment becomes a decrement, and in another a decrement is converted into an increment.

All such changes allow of the advance of wages and profits; and in these several ways the problem, so simple in Ricardo's hands, grows very complex. It might be argued that the broad result is to point to a fall rather than a rise of rent, so far, at any rate, as the agricultural rent of the old countries of the world is concerned; and it is at least certain that the measurement of differential advantages from different standpoints renders the existence in particular instances, or continuance, of an increment, or decrement, as the case may be, very doubtful and difficult to determine. Nor is this latter conclusion untrue of the circumstances of urban land; for changes in fashion, or the methods of business or transport, assuredly affect the relative values of different sites, lowering some while raising others. It is even conceivable that improvements in the means of conveyance may, taking a general view, diminish as well as increase the advantages of central sites; and that some industrial or inventive change of the future may arrest the

SOME ASPECTS OF THE THEORY OF RENT 239

tendency to concentration in the towns, and re-awaken the industries of the country villages.

But, even if an increment be regarded as probable, the difficulty remains of determining how much of it is unearned, and how much is earned.[1] Ricardo himself defined rent as "that portion of the produce of the earth which is paid to the landlord for the use of the original and indestructible powers of the soil"; and he drew a distinction between this "strict sense" of the term and the "popular sense," which confounded the "interest and profit of capital" with it by applying the name to "whatever is annually paid by a farmer to his landlord." The unearned character of a payment for the "original and indestructible powers of the soil" can hardly be denied; but the difficulty turns on the identification of rent in this "strict sense," and the distinction established by Ricardo appears to be rather one of those niceties, which are allowable and useful in theory, and may be expected in the characteristic theory of so abstract a writer, but are nevertheless by no means easy to discover or determine in practice.[2] Ricardo himself traced the rise of rent chiefly by differences in "natural" fertility, but the difficulty of distinguishing the earned from the unearned increment is not diminished by introducing the element of situation; and, in a later chapter, he admitted that "part" of the capital applied to the "improvement" of land, "when once expended," "is inseparably amalgamated with the land, and tends to increase its productive powers," and that "the remuneration paid to the landlord for its use is strictly of the nature of rent, and is subject to all the laws of rent." This may indeed be the case, regarded from the standpoint of the existing differential advantages of land; but, viewed

[1] Cf. Essay i.   [2] *Ibid.*

from a historical standpoint, such a payment is earned. Some writers have gone so far as to urge that in modern times in old countries "economic rent," or rent in the "strict sense," has, broadly speaking, disappeared; and a succession of economists has recognised the incorporation of the results of expenditure with the "original and indestructible powers of the soil." For this reason it has been recently contended that the order, in which land may be withdrawn from cultivation, may differ from that in which it was first brought into it, because the "non-recurrent expenditure" sunk in improvements will be considered in the first instance, and disregarded in the second.

The conception of rent as a payment for differential advantages has also been extended by a succession of writers to other forms of wealth; and Professor Marshall, while strongly insisting[1] that the "rent of land" has important "peculiarities of its own," argues that, from the point of view of Ricardo's doctrine that "rent does not enter into the cost of production," it is a "leading species of a large genus." The "inherent properties of land," which "include," and often chiefly consist of, "the space relations of the plot in question, and the annuity that nature has given it of sunlight and air and rain," are a "typical instance" of the class; for, like "other gifts from the bounty of nature," they "are incapable of increase by man's efforts in any period of time however long." But the permanent improvements usually made by an English landlord, although incurred in the first instance with the expectation of an adequate return, when once incorporated with the soil, must also "be taken for granted" over shorter

---

[1] *Principles of Economics*, preface to first edition, and book iv. chap. iii., book v. chaps. viii.-x.

SOME ASPECTS OF THE THEORY OF RENT 241

periods of time, and the "income derived" from them "may be regarded as a Quasi-Rent." And thus by a "continuous series" we may pass to "less permanent improvements, to farm and factory buildings, to steam engines, etc., and finally to the less durable and less slowly-made implements. And parallel to the series of the material agents of production there is a similar series of human abilities, those that are the free gifts of nature and those that are the result of a more or less long and specialized process of training."[1]

The continuity of this series does not, it is true, determine the question of the origin of the differential advantages to which it relates; and Professor Marshall is careful to indicate the dangers of pushing the analogy of rent too far,[2] and to emphasise its intimate reference to the periods of time, which we have in view. But it does seem legitimate to argue from these and similar considerations to the improbability of an abrupt distinction, as we pass from rent in the "strict sense" to rent popularly so-called, and to infer from the more apparent difficulty of distinguishing between what is earned and what is unearned in the case of the other differential advantages to a likelihood, at least, of difficulty in the case of land. A farmer, in making his contract for rent, does not concern himself with the past history of the causes of the fertility or situation of the land, but with its present advantages, and he makes no attempt to draw a distinction between the earned and the unearned. And, in the future, he and his landlord may allow the nominal rent to remain unaltered, in spite of increased prosperity or intensified depression in agriculture, in consideration

[1] The quotations are from the first edition.
[2] Cf. Essay xiii.

simply of lessened expenditure, or added liberality in the matter of improvements. Ricardo, again, himself declares that "there is not a manufacture in which nature does not give assistance to man"; and opportunity, and chance, and society, with its changing demands and altering organisation, play no inconsiderable part in the determination of professional incomes and the earnings of employers and workmen. The very conception of value, as Sir Louis Mallet has aptly pointed out,[1] and as Karl Marx was compelled to recognise, implies the action and influence of society.

The distinction between what is earned and what is unearned would, indeed, seem on theoretical grounds to be more easily established in the case of land than other forms of wealth, and in that of urban rather than agricultural land. Yet even here the evidence given by surveyors before the Town Holdings Committee on the possibility of distinguishing between the value of a house and that of the land, on which it is built, was conflicting; and even here landlords may have developed and improved building sites by expenditure and effort of their own. Even here fashion may shift the abode of the rich, and alter the demand for land; and one quarter of a town may grow at the expense of another, or an entire town decay owing to the removal of an industry elsewhere. As a whole, no doubt, urban rent tends to increase in civilised countries, and sometimes by rapid strides; and municipal owners of building property benefit by this growth. But the increment may in particular cases become a decrement; and the difficulty of determining how much of this increase is

---

[1] *Free Exchange*, part ii. On the Unearned Increment.

earned by the municipality as an improving landlord, and how much is due to it as a social factor, remains. Where, indeed, a public authority executes a definite improvement, which seems certain to result in definite benefit to definite property, the argument for charging a proportion of the cost on the owners of such property is strong, and the reason lies in the possibility of defining, with tolerable precision, the "unearned" increment, which will accrue. There may be practical difficulties in determining the exact extent of the property benefited, and the precise degree of benefit. But there are important theoretical respects in which these proposals for applying the principle of "betterment" differ from the case of the unearned increment generally.[1] There is *ex hypothesi* no question as to an increment, and not a decrement, resulting. The improvement is an improvement, which must add to the value of the property. It may injure other property by diverting traffic or in some other way, and it might seem as if compensation were due for an unearned decrement. But, if the alternative lies between charging a proportion of the cost on the "bettered" property, and meeting it entirely from the general rates, the former course is manifestly for the interest of the "worsened" property, and to this extent it receives compensation. The definiteness of the improvement is so far ascertainable that the cost, which it will involve, is known, and it is a totally new and distinct factor introduced into the situation. If, then, the proportion of the cost to be borne by the bettered property is duly limited, and the area of the property selected is adequately extended, the theoretical case seems to be very

[1] Cf. Essay i.

strong. The nicety of the distinction between what is earned and what is unearned is here a less troublesome factor; and it is the nice refinements of Ricardo's theory, which render its application to practical affairs so full of difficulty, and so open to abuse.

XI.

INTERNATIONAL BI-METALLISM.[1]

I HAVE come here, as an economic student, to address the members of an Economic Society; and I am anxious to emphasise the nature of the relation, which is thus established between us. For the object of such a society is, I imagine, the study of economic matters in the light of scientific knowledge. I do not mean that the members should attempt a task, which appears to me as impossible as it is ill-advised [2]—the preservation of a strict neutrality on debated questions, and the refusal to push scientific reasonings to a practical conclusion. On the contrary, I hold that they may claim the rights and duties of experts, and, as exigency may require, admonish or exhort the practical man in the conduct of affairs. Nor is the sphere of monetary practice least suited to the exercise of this prerogative. It is a sphere, in which abstract reasoning has already won practical triumphs that have extorted general assent; and it is a region of inquiry, where the paths are so tortuous and indistinct that he, who tries to thread them in a darkness unillumined by expert guidance, runs imminent risk of confusion, if not of disaster. But, in order to claim the privileges of an expert, a needful

[1] An address to the Economic Society of Newcastle-upon-Tyne. (November, 1895.)
[2] Cf. Essay viii. above.

preliminary training must be undergone; and the advantage of addressing an economic society is, that the lecturer may assume, as the result of such training, an acquaintance on the part of his audience with the elements of economic science, an honest endeavour, which will not shrink from taking pains, to reach the truth, and an openness of mind, which is ready to allow the possibility of improvement on traditional practice as the outcome of fresh experience, and of displacement of ingrained opinion by more comprehensive and rational belief. The economic student is not likely to dismiss a view simply on account of its apparent conflict with a popular creed, or to rest content with existing institutions merely because they are in possession. He may require the new opinion to justify itself, and urge that the burden of proof lies with disturbers of established routine; but he will judge on their merits alone both the opinion and the reform which it suggests.

On the advantage of the first of the qualities, the possession of which I have ventured to assume—that of an acquaintance with the elements of economics—it is needless to dwell. The question of monetary reform, with which we are dealing, is so large, and the issues raised are so numerous, that in an address, limited by considerations of time, it is impossible to do more than touch the fringe of the subject. I shall, therefore, take for granted some knowledge of the contents of the ordinary text-books, in which the functions generally assigned to money in the economy of business are those of a medium of exchange on the one hand, and, on the other, of a measure or standard of value.

For the first of these functions the most necessary quality is general acceptability; and, by dint of successive improvement, we may claim to have established in this country tolerably convenient media of exchange, which are "generally acceptable," with bronze and silver, in the form of token currencies, for small transactions, with gold for larger dealings, and with notes and cheques, and bills of exchange, and various other credit-instruments, resting, it must be remembered, on a metallic basis, for still greater payments. It is possible that in the future we may devise further improvements—that we may economise the wear and tear of coin by a larger substitution of paper money, such as those one-pound notes so popular across the border, and by an even greater development of credit than has yet been attained. But such questions stand outside the main topic that we are considering. They have a relation to it, which we may endeavour to indicate; but it is necessary to emphasise the distinction.

For, besides its use as a medium of exchange, money is employed as a measure or standard of value for short or for longer bargains; and, when used for more extended periods, it is generally distinguished in the text-books as a "standard of deferred payments." The quality especially needed for this function is that of stability; for it requires little reflection to see that instability in a standard must generate disturbance and confusion, and that, the greater the want of stability, the more serious will be the disturbance, and the more extensive and noxious the confusion. Indeed, so accustomed are men in the affairs of ordinary life to regard that by which they commonly measure the variations of other things as itself invariable, that it requires an effort of reasoning—of which, perhaps, the economist alone is easily capable—to discover, or even to conceive of, imperfections in the monetary standard.[1]

That such imperfections exist is known to economic

[1] Cf. the author's *Money, and its Relations to Prices*, chap. ii.

students. That money has at one time a larger, at another a smaller, purchasing-power is an economic truism. That at one time you can procure a greater quantity of commodities in exchange for the English pound, and at another you will have to be content with less, is proved by recorded facts of history, and by the testimony, sometimes unconscious, of daily experience; and the other side of the truth is expressed in the fall and rise of general prices.

It is true that the same experience, which has led to the use of the precious metals as convenient media of exchange, because not only are they portable, and easily divisible into suitable quantities, which can be readily recognised, but they are also durable in an eminent degree, has prompted their employment as a measure or standard of value. Their durability renders them comparatively independent of changes in supply; for at any moment the stock in existence is so large that the effect of a small change is not appreciable. The previous supply is so considerable that the variation in the annual addition is, in ordinary circumstances, unimportant. And, therefore, when short periods alone are taken into account, the precious metals are peculiarly adapted for use as a common measure of the value of other things, because their own value is comparatively stable.

But, if an increased or diminished production from the mines continues for some period, its influence will be felt. The suitability of the metals as a standard of long or deferred payments is less evident; and economists, from Adam Smith onwards, have recognised, and, in not a few cases, endeavoured to remedy, their imperfections. For in a civilised society there are a number of payments deferred. There are contracts extending over intervals of time; and there are payments, which it is not convenient to be constantly changing, as the salaries of officials, the fees of professional men, the fares and rates on railways. These contracts and payments are expressed in terms of money; and, if the money itself alters in value in relation to other things, justice dictates a corresponding change in the monetary expression, though considerations of convenience may result in allowing one or the other party to remain under a disadvantage. Of the reality of such disadvantage economic science leaves as little room for doubt as of the trouble of making continual changes to meet it; and, therefore, it accords a *primâ facie* approval to proposals, which will satisfy more fully the demands of justice for the standard, and of convenience for the media, than those monetary arrangements, which may be in possession.

In England, at the present time, gold is the standard of value. The currencies of silver and bronze are token-currencies, which do not contain as much metal as their face-value represents, are regulated in their issue, and are limited, as legal tender in the discharge of debt, to payments of small amounts. The notes of the Bank of England, and of the country banks, are issued on a gold basis, are convertible into gold on demand, and special provision has been made for their convertibility by the Bank Act of 1844. The various credit-instruments, in their turn, rest on the foundation of cash in the Bank of England, which, by the peculiarities of our banking system, has acquired an exclusively predominant position, and is the custodian of the central cash-reserve of the nation. These credit-instruments are promises to pay legal tender of the realm; and, in the last resort, payment can only be discharged in gold, or in paper convertible into gold on demand. They therefore rest, ultimately, on the basis of the reserve of cash—of notes and coin—in the Bank of England; and, in seasons of panic, when paper-promises to pay are suspect, and legal tender is urgently needed, the intimate connection of the credit-instruments with the cash-reserve is painfully manifest. In the Baring crisis, for example, of a few years ago, the object lesson presented by the Bank of England importing in haste actual gold from the Bank of France, and receiving leave from the Chancellor of the Exchequer to suspend the Bank Charter Act, if need arose, and to issue a larger supply of legal tender in the form of paper money convertible into gold on demand, could hardly fail to carry its meaning home to the plainest intelligence; and proposals for increasing the reserve of cash have since been the subject of much discussion. In England, then, gold is the standard, and our monetary system is mono-metallic. The coinage of gold alone is unrestricted, in the sense that the Bank, as the agent of the Mint, is always ready to receive gold bullion, and to give legal tender in exchange, while the coinage of silver and of bronze is regulated, and the Mint is not open to their unlimited receipt.

In contrast to such mono-metallism would be a bi-metallic system as it is now conceived by many of the most prominent of its advocates. The essential principle is that the two metals, gold and silver, should jointly form the standard. The mints are to be open to the unlimited receipt of either metal at a fixed ratio, and on this dual basis the monetary system is to be constructed. The two metals are to take the place occupied in the English system by the one metal—gold—as alone legal tender, or the basis of legal tender to any amount, and alone receivable to any amount at the Mint. I lay stress on these conditions, as of the essence of the system, and on the parallel nature of the position, which the two metals would jointly occupy, to that at present taken as a standard by gold alone in our mono-metallic system. And I lay this stress for more than one reason. It is as a standard, as I shall presently endeavour to show, that a single metal is liable to deficiencies, which are counteracted, to a great extent, under a bi-metallic system. And it was with regard to the media of exchange that certain inconveniences were apparent in the older forms of local and national bi-metallism. But the standard may conceivably be improved without interference with the media of exchange current in the internal transactions of a country; and modern bi-metallism is essentially international.

At the present time, under our own monetary system, gold is used as an actual medium of exchange to a comparatively small extent. To that extent it might continue to be used under bi-metallism in the internal business of the country. Coinages of silver and bronze might, as heretofore, be employed in such business for small denominations, be regulated, as now, in their issue, and be limited in their capacity as legal tender in the payment of debt. The requirements of convenient media of exchange, such as bronze for small, silver for larger, and gold, and, to a far more considerable extent, paper substitutes and credit-instruments, for still larger payments, might be satisfied in the way, which experience seems to dictate. For that experience has, in civilised countries, led to the employment of metal, apart from its use as small change, chiefly as a reserve against the issue of paper, and as a basis for the superstructure of credit.

The functions thus discharged possess an importance, which is sometimes forgotten, but is not easily overrated. For the use of a metal as a reserve against paper constitutes a real demand for that metal to the extent that the paper issue is not "fiduciary"—to the extent, that is, that actual coin or bullion is kept as a security for convertibility on demand—and stores of coin or bullion thus preserved in the cellars of a bank are no more "idle" than the actual sovereigns, shillings, and pence, which are passing from hand to hand as small change in the conduct of business. It is an arguable point whether the fiduciary issue allowed in England by the Act of 1844 might not now be safely extended; but experience has certainly shown the necessity of some such restriction. It has also shown abundantly that, though credit may ebb and flow, and prices on this account may fall and rise, yet its movements are controlled ultimately by the changing dimensions in the basis of legal tender on which it rests—of gold, or of paper convertible into gold on demand. In this way gold is chiefly employed in modern times in an advanced nation like our own; and, although the Mint is open to its unlimited receipt, and the Bank, as the agent of the Mint, is prepared to give legal tender of the realm in exchange for bullion, yet the legal tender, which is most generally acceptable, seems to be paper money, and the bullion may never be transformed into coin at all.

In place of the gold thus used in a mono-metallic system the two metals, gold and silver, would be substituted under bi-metallism; and the reform might be effected without any considerable interference with the media of exchange current in internal transactions, or the habits of the people in this respect. For it is not necessary that the standard and the ordinary internal media should be identical; and as, in the course of centuries, improvements have been successively effected in the latter, from the unstamped bars of primitive ages to the finished coins of to-day, with their milled edges and their clear-cut impress, so the economist would be prepared to recognise the possibility of improvement in the standard, and would give an anxious consideration to schemes, which promised it, especially if they involved little, or no, interference with the media of exchange current in the internal economy of a nation. This is one of the points with reference to which it is needful to emphasise the significance of the epithet distinguishing modern bi-metallism from the older forms of the system; for it is with money in its *international* relations that bi-metallism purposes to deal, and it does not contemplate as necessary a disturbance of the ordinary domestic media of exchange.

It need hardly be pointed out how this conception removes the ground from under many objections commonly, and not unnaturally, advanced; but I would merely draw attention to two points in particular. The difficulties, which undoubtedly attend the selection of a suitable ratio for international bi-metallism, are generally conceived to be largely due to the existence of a quantity of silver coin, which has been minted, not at the present market ratio, but at the old ratio, which obtained between the metals, of $15\frac{1}{2}$ to 1, and is still current, with the character of legal tender, in France and in other countries. But the continued internal circulation of these coins seems not incompatible with the adoption of a different ratio for the unlimited sale of bullion at the bi-metallic mints. Even at the present time they pass current, although the mints of the countries, in which they are found, are no longer open to the free coinage of silver, and the ratio has fallen far below the legal ratio, at which they circulate. The question, then, of re-coinage on a wholesale scale of various domestic currencies, with the consequent loss and disturbance of habit involved, does not require anxious and protracted consideration; and the difficulties of the choice of the ratio may be confined to the determination of that figure, which, with the least disturbance of existing contracts, will be best adapted, as Professor Foxwell has urged,[1] to provide a supply of money adequate to the needs of extending trade and of growing population.

The other point, which seems to require emphasis, is this. It may be admitted that a serious disadvantage of the older national forms of bi-metallism, where one country observed one ratio, and a second country another, and a third and a fourth yet another, and where countries were striving, by change of ratio, to attract the metals to themselves at the expense of their neighbours, consisted in the risk of depletion. It may be allowed that some such inconvenience was experienced in England in the last century, and that the difficulty was successfully met by the provisions connected with the introduction of the gold standard. But the device adopted—that of a token currency for small denominations—is not incompatible with a bi-metallic standard as it is now conceived; and the monetary reformers, who introduced the change with happy results as far as the objects in view were concerned, seem to have been so intent on improvement of the media of exchange that they neglected—not unnaturally—the question of the standard. Their action, like the experience of early bi-metallism, offers no barrier to the consideration of schemes for improving the standard, which do not involve any serious disturbance of the aims on which they set their attention.

The ground, then, is clear for a candid solution of the problem whether as a standard bi-metallism is preferable to

[1] Cf. *Transactions of the Political Economy Circle of the National Liberal Club*, vol. ii. pp. 171, etc.

mono-metallism; and it may be considered without reference to the requirements of convenient media of exchange for the transaction of the ordinary business of the plain citizen, or to arguments based on the lightness of the sovereign and the comparative bulkiness of the five-franc-piece. The gold and silver bullion—to the free sale of which the bi-metallic mints would be open, and to the payment of which, with an option of giving either metal, the banks would be liable—would be employed mainly in the form of bars, and not of coin, as a basis on which different domestic currencies would continue to be built, and be actually used for the settlement of international transactions in a form, which for such a purpose is not inconvenient. As now silver coin is obtained by inquiry at the Bank, so under bi-metallism, as Professor Foxwell has urged, the supply of gold coin would depend on the option of the Bank; but there is no more reason for supposing that an amount would be furnished, insufficient for the needs of small change in the domestic business of the country, than there has been for anticipating a deficiency of silver for such purposes in England, or of gold in France. The ordinary media of exchange might thus be left unaffected, while the standard of value would be altered; and the point to be settled is whether bi-metallism or mono-metallism is the more fitted for a standard.

The quality desired here above all else, is stability of value; and the plain man may argue plausibly that the fluctuations of one metal will be less in number than those of two, and that a mono-metallic standard, dependent on a single metal, is likely to be more stable than a standard exposed—as under bi-metallism—to the fluctuations in the value of two. Such an argument has an appearance of cogency, but overlooks the circumstance that the fluctuations in the two metals may not, and probably will not, be always in the same direction, but will counteract one another. The possibility of such counteraction will be admitted by the economist, if the supply of the metals be alone regarded; but the strength of the bi-metallic position turns on considerations of demand. The stock of the metals in existence at any particular moment is so considerable that great and continued changes in supply are needed to produce an appreciable effect on their value; and the conditions of demand are of greater importance than they are in the case of other commodities. The superiority of bi-metallism consists in the circumstance that by an action, which may be called automatic, changes in the supply of one or the other metal are met by alterations in demand, which tend to compensate.

The compensatory influence, thus manifested, is familiar to students of economics, and extends to other articles besides gold and silver. The condition of its operation is that the articles are regarded as alternatives, and that the one will be substituted for the other when self-interest dictates the change. The opening of the bi-metallic mints to the unlimited sale at a fixed ratio of both gold and silver bullion, which are indifferently to form the basis of legal tender, fulfils this condition. For, if through some change in supply, the one metal tends to become less in value compared with the other than the ratio, at which it is received at the mints, it will be advantageous for the bullion dealers, to offer there for sale more of the more abundant metal, obtaining in exchange legal tender at the fixed ratio, and to use for other purposes the scarcer metal. In other words, the demand for the more abundant metal will increase, and that for the metal, which is relatively scarcer, will diminish:

and thus by alterations in demand compensation will tend to be furnished to changes in supply.

It may be conceded that the efficacy of this compensatory action turns on the relative extent of the changes in supply and on the comparative strength of the demand; and here again it is necessary to insist on the international character of modern as opposed to older bi-metallism. But the co-operation of nations of such importance as England, France, Germany and the United States, would, so far as human prediction and estimation can go, be amply sufficient to meet such changes in supply as are easily conceivable; and the experience of bi-metallic France, acting singly at the time of the Californian and Australian discoveries, when changes of revolutionary magnitude in the supply of gold produced a divergence of the market ratio between the two metals in London and Hamburg from the legal ratio observed at the Paris Mint, which, according to the pronouncement[1] of the Gold and Silver Commission, was but small in comparison with the changes themselves, supplies an illustrative instance of the compensatory action, which is not easy, or indeed possible, to explain away. We may content ourselves with a brief reference to the deliberate opinion of the mono-metallist section of the Commissioners, who affirmed,[2] declaring that their conclusion had been the result of *à priori* reasoning and of the experience of the last half century, that "in any conditions fairly to be contemplated in the future, so far as" they could "forecast them from the experience of the past, a stable ratio might be maintained, if the nations" they "had alluded to" (namely, the United Kingdom, Germany, the United States and the Latin Union) "were to accept, and strictly adhere to, bi-metallism at the suggested ratio"—a

[1] *Report*, sec. 187.   [2] Cf. *Report*, sec. 107.

ratio that is, which was not to differ widely from the then market ratio. Such was the conclusion of judges, who certainly evinced no friendly inclinations; and it was based on exhaustive examination of facts and arguments. It need not be pressed to any illegitimate use; but it affords powerful testimony to the compensatory action of the bi-metallic system, and is so far an argument for its superiority to mono-metallism in the provision of a stable standard. It should be remembered that the conditions of the case do not require, as is sometimes contended, an exact unbroken coincidence between the legal ratio at the mints and the ratio prevailing in the open market; but it is maintained, and demonstrated beyond contradiction, that the legal ratio exerts a controlling influence over the market ratio, which prevents any considerable or continuous divergence.

It may be admitted that, where the question is that of the reintroduction of bi-metallism after the metals have, as in the last twenty years, been exposed to the ordinary market influences, the choice of the ratio is one of importance and difficulty. But it may nevertheless be emphatically contended that the compensatory action of the bi-metallic system is in accord with economic theory and proved by historical fact, and that for this reason the chances of stability are greater with a bi-metallic than with a mono-metallic standard. If steadiness be the first requisite in a standard, international bi-metallism recommends itself as an improvement on the present monetary system. The progress of time may bring further improvement, in detail, if not in main characteristics, and in the course of recent discussions suggestions have been put forward which may possibly bear fruit; but bi-metallism seems to have earned the preference by its international character, its comparative simplicity, its sound metallic basis, and its broad historic familiarity.

If I have been successful so far, I may claim to have made good the contention that bi-metallism accords with the conclusions of economic science. I am now going to ask whether such a change is not suggested by practical exigency. For the monetary situation of the last twenty years has been admittedly novel, and cannot be said to have justified itself by results. After the quotation given above it is unnecessary to prove, by formal evidence, that the bi-metallic system preserved a par of exchange between the two metals, even when it was confined to a narrow area; and it is matter of notoriety that the rupture of the system by the suspension of the free coinage of silver at the mints of the Latin Union has been followed by dislocation of that par of exchange. That such a dislocation has proved an obstacle to the smooth conduct of trade between gold-standard countries, like England, and the silver-using East, is not seriously contested, although the extent of the hindrance may be variously estimated. Nor is it denied that the restoration of bi-metallism would remove this difficulty and so far facilitate the trade. It is quite true that similar impediments present themselves in the course of business with countries, which, like Argentina, are on a basis of inconvertible paper; but it is poor logic to adduce the continued existence of one evil as a reason for not removing another. It is also true that, until the suspension of the free coinage of silver at the mints of the Latin Union, England, though mono-metallic herself, secured the advantage of the perservation of the par of exchange through the compensatory action of bi-metallism in other countries. But this argument tends to show that only after that suspension did England realise the full possibilities of inconvenience involved in a mono-metallic system, and that previously she was secured, by the action of other countries, from the natural results of her own. In any case the novelty of the situation since 1873 is patent; and it is not unreasonable to argue that a new position of affairs may suggest the reconsideration of a policy adopted and maintained when the circumstances were different.

Bi-metallism, then, offers a means of restoring the par of exchange between gold and silver; and the only alternative is found in universal mono-metallism on a gold or on a silver basis. It can hardly be seriously urged that either form of this alternative is within the sphere of practical probability. It is true that there are reasons for holding that, judged by experience, and especially by that of a recent date, silver might prove a more stable standard than gold; and it is also true that, unless by international action the present tendencies of national policy are changed, the adoption of a gold standard may extend by successive stages to the chief nations of the Western world. But, at any rate for a long time to come, the larger part of the East is likely to remain on a silver basis, and the experience in the last twenty years of the increased adoption of gold by Western nations is scarcely calculated to allay apprehensions of the results of a further development of that practice on a scale of any importance. Nor does advantage, but rather the reverse, seem to attach to a policy, which, when able to rest the standard on the broader basis of the supplies of the two metals, would willingly confine the world to the narrower basis of one. Taking the facts as they are, the conclusion is inevitable that the only practicable means of restoring the par between gold and silver, and of removing the hindrance presented by uncertainty of exchange to the conduct of a large and increasing part of the trade of the world, is to be found in the reintroduction of bi-metallism.

The question then arises of the politic attitude of England in such a position of affairs. That she is largely —more largely than any other single nation—interested in the smooth conduct of trade with the East, can hardly be denied. That the financial situation of her dependency, India, has been seriously affected by the fall in exchange, is generally admitted ; for it has brought an increase in the burden of debt, and an uncertainty of expenditure, peculiarly harassing in a country where revenue is raised from a population very suspicious of change, and poor when judged by an European standard. It has led to such expedients as the recent monetary legislation, which has nowhere been received with approval, but has been regarded as a *pis aller* by the Home and the Indian Governments alike. It is certainly responsible also for the reimposition of the cotton duties, which has given rise to a conflict of interests between the pressing and pre-eminent necessities of the Indian Government and the fortunes of a very important industrial section of our own population. And the critical character of the situation may perhaps be described by saying that no Indian or English statesman ventures, or indeed is able, to forecast the future of Indian finance, but is content, and is forced to be satisfied, with a "hand-to-mouth" policy. Even if the effective introduction of a gold standard into India, which is the logical outcome of recent monetary policy, were regarded by experts as probable, or indeed as possible, the difficulties of exchange would continue to attend our own trade, and, as actual experience has already proved, would present themselves afresh in the trade of India, with countries like China and Japan. In view of these circumstances it might be argued that it would be worth the while of England to incur some sacrifice to restore the par of exchange; and that she might deem it politic to surrender some of the advantages supposed to be reaped from a mono-metallic system, if by doing so she could accomplish the establishment of international bi-metallism.

On broad grounds alone, as possessing the largest share of international trade, she is peculiarly interested in arrangements which would facilitate it. Her participation in such arrangements, if not necessary to their introduction or maintenance, would certainly render material assistance in securing those ends. Even were the situation itself less novel and critical, the growth of international relations in such matters as postal and telegraphic communication would suggest the possibility of some similar improvement in monetary arrangements; and such improvement, so far as questions of coinage are concerned, has already received the attention of not a few monetary conferences. There is every reason why the question of the standard, which in the early conferences was allowed to fall into the background, should be carefully and earnestly considered, and an attempt made to reach a permanent solution. In the light of the proceedings of the most recent conference, international bi-metallism, as before sketched, seems at once the simplest scheme, which has been put forward for such a purpose, the scheme, which pretends to be more than a temporary expedient, and the scheme, which recommends itself by a broad resemblance to systems, the actual working of which is tolerably familiar.

Nor, viewing the matter from a narrower standpoint, is it unreasonable to suppose that, even had the gold standard been deliberately adopted in England, with full knowledge of its possible consequences, and proved satisfactory from its introduction to the present hour, it might still be possible in 1895 to devise improvements on a system established nearly a century ago. It may be admitted that a change in a monetary system should not be lightly undertaken, and that the mere fact of existence gives it the benefit, which attaches proverbially to possession. It may be conceded that no change should be carried into effect unless it meets with approval so general as to remove any serious danger of panic. But the circumstance that the alteration in the standard proposed by bi-metallists could be accomplished without interference with the media of exchange current in domestic transactions, renders far less appreciable the chance of confusion or suspicion among the mass of the people; and the danger of disturbance in the more select and intelligent region of the money market has been greatly, and even absurdly, exaggerated. Nor need we despair of an early acceleration in the conversion of the banking and mercantile world. The ground, then, is clear for the consideration of the question whether the mono-metallic system, which was adopted in England at the resumption of cash payments, has worked satisfactorily.

For that the system was introduced with a full appreciation of its nature and possible effects cannot stand the test of close inquiry. We need not enter now on any historical dissertation[1]; but recent controversy has prompted a rigorous research into the actual circumstances attending the adoption of the gold standard, with the result that received opinions have been carefully scrutinised. There can be little doubt that the provision of convenient media of exchange was prominent in the minds of the authors of the change, and that the question of the standard was

[1] Cf. *Money, and its Relations to Prices*, chap. v.

practically absent. There can be little doubt, again, that the special difficulty, which they were anxious to meet, might have been solved by the introduction of a token coinage, compatibly with international bi-metallism, as now conceived. And there can also be little doubt that the disappearance of the silver from the currency, which the establishment of a token currency for coins of small denominations successfully arrested, was due to the overrating of the gold and the underrating of the silver; and that about the time of the suspension of the free coinage of silver, which was separated by some years from the formal introduction of the gold standard, the circumstances of the production of the metals were altering in such a way that, had there been no such suspension, the currency would probably have become preponderantly silver instead of being, as it undoubtedly was, preponderantly gold. In view of the recognised compensatory action of the bi-metallic system, the argument that the conscious and deliberate preference of the people had led them to use gold in lieu of silver, and that the Legislature merely sanctioned a voluntary practice by the formal adoption of the gold standard, loses its cogency.

Neither in the possible drawbacks of changing an established system, nor in the circumstances of its original adoption and the opinions of its authors, is there any insurmountable obstacle to the candid consideration of the question whether mono-metallism has proved a success.

The crucial period of trial has elapsed since 1873; for until that date, though not bi-metallic ourselves, we reaped, in the steadiness of exchange and the distribution of the demand for the precious metals, the benefit of the bi-metallic system prevailing in other countries. Of the disturbance of the par of exchange since 1873 no more need be said. But that disturbance coincided with extraordinary accessions to the demand for gold. In evidence before the Gold and Silver Commission, Sir Robert Giffen estimated these extraordinary accessions at some two hundred millions; and, in evidence more recently given before the Commission on Agriculture, he stated that a part of the demands, amounting to some sixteen millions, had proved to a large extent unreal, but that fresh demands had since arisen for some hundred millions. These extraordinary demands occurred coincidently with a diminution in the production from the mines, which, until a few years ago, had declined considerably from the level attained at the Californian and Australian discoveries.

What was naturally to be expected as the consequence of such changes in demand and supply, was an increase in the value of gold, and a fall in gold prices. Had the bi-metallic system been in operation, this fall would have been mitigated by the increasing production of silver, which would have taken, in part, the place of gold in the bi-metallic countries, and tended to relieve the strain on that metal. But the suspension of the free coinage of silver at the mints of the Latin Union was perhaps the most important event of the monetary history of the last twenty years. The full effects of the extraordinary demands fell, accordingly, on the one metal; and, as England, at the time of the Californian and Australian discoveries, although mono-metallic, had experienced the benefits of French bi-metallism in arresting the fall in the value of gold, so she could not fail now, while preserving her own monetary system, to be affected by the changes in the systems of other countries. She was doomed to a divergence in the value of gold and silver, and to a fall in gold prices. By joining in international arrangements, she would not incur responsibilities that she now avoids; but she would rather secure, and exercise, a voice in the determination of matters which are bound to affect her. In this sense, at least, isolation in monetary policy is not possible. That from 1873 the trade of England with India began to be disturbed by the dislocation of the par of exchange is generally admitted. That silver prices had not risen until recently in India itself, and that even now they have not risen in Japan, has been proved by authoritative testimony. The conclusion, which naturally emerges, is that gold prices have fallen, and that the change has been due, in part, to alterations in monetary policy.

The doubt felt of this conclusion seems to be due to a failure to appreciate the conditions of the problem. For, in modern society, we find a number of forces acting and reacting on one another.[1] It is impossible to isolate one or two, and to observe them produce their effects undisturbed. We must depend, to some extent, on arguments based on probability, and look for the broad manifestation of effects, which would naturally follow from causes that we know to be present. That an accession to the demand for gold, coinciding with a decline in the annual production, should exert an influence on its value is probable, and, in the absence of counteracting forces, is certain. The existing stock may be large, but, at any particular moment, the relative value of gold and commodities is adjusted to the then conditions of supply and demand. A change takes place in demand, coincident with a change in supply, and these changes must produce an effect, especially on that portion of the stock which is employed as standard money.

[1] Cf. Essay viii. above, and also *Money, and its Relations to Prices*, chap. vi., for a fuller statement of the following argument.

The amount of the effect will, no doubt, depend on the nature of the changes; but the extraordinary demands of the last twenty years, as statistically computed by Sir Robert Giffen, have been certainly considerable, when added to the normal increase in the ordinary demands arising from the large use of gold in the arts, and from the addition to monetary requirements due to growth of population and extension of trade. Nor have the changes in the annual supply been unimportant. Such changes, undoubtedly, have rendered probable a fall in gold prices, but the fall would be evident only on a general view.

For it is largely through the elastic medium of credit that gold has come into contact with the prices of commodities; and credit has its periodic ebb and flow, its times of contraction and depression and its moments of speculative expansion; and, for this, allowance must be made before it is possible to detect the underlying movement in general prices due to changes in the gold basis on which credit rests. Credit is one of the forces which serve to conceal the probable influence of changes in the supply and demand of the precious metal itself. Another is found in circumstances affecting individual commodities, which increase in some cases, and diminish in others, the apparent influence on prices exerted by changes in the available supplies of gold. Just as the credit influence can only be eliminated by extending the observations over an interval of time, so these various particular influences must be discounted by bringing under examination the prices of a number of commodities and deducing the general change. This deduction is effected by the method of statistical averaging known by the name of index-numbers; and that the evidence of these numbers, some three or four varieties of which have won an established fame, points to a fall in gold prices during the last twenty years, cannot be doubted.

But it is urged that, although these numbers, based on the wholesale prices of certain commodities, exhibit a fall, the same fall would not be shown in retail articles or wages. Here again we meet with probable counteracting forces. Statistical evidence points to the occurrence of a change in the distribution of wealth, which would have tended to raise wages, if prices had not fallen, instead of leaving them in the stationary condition in which they have, on the whole, remained. Such a change would also probably tend to prevent retail prices from falling so extensively as wholesale, as there is a larger ingredient of manufacture, and especially of labour, involved in their production and sale. These tendencies would add their influence to the established facts of greater friction in the adjustment of wages, and in the alteration of retail prices.

Lastly, improvements are continually proceeding, which, in the absence of any corresponding increase in the monetary supplies, would tend to make prices fall, as commodities were produced and transported more easily. But this force would increase, and would not nullify, the effects of changes more specially relating to the gold supplies; and it was present in the middle of the century, when prices were rising, and is therefore no adequate explanation of the fall of the last twenty years. In view, then, of the action and reaction of such various forces, we must be content with broad evidence alone; and such broad evidence is open to the observation of anyone, who has followed with closeness the course of the controversy. The probabilities have pointed to a fall of gold prices; and the broad evidence testifies to the presence of effects, which might naturally be expected to follow a cause, which is known to have been present. Beyond this point it is impossible to go.

The same broad judgment must be exercised in determining the consequences of such a fall to the general welfare. When the matter is thus regarded, it is impossible to doubt that a fall is injurious, just as a rise, if it be not sudden, is advantageous. For a fall acts powerfully on the imagination, and discourages enterprise. As business is a continuous process, it destroys those fine margins, on which profits turn. In the end no doubt it is apposite to urge that the number of counters employed may be reduced, and yet the parties playing the game may be in the same real position. But this argument assumes simultaneity in the operation of the change, and the possibility of harm consists precisely in the absence of this simultaneous action. Nor are the effects less mischievous, because the cause works subtly and is not easy to detect. Men feel that there is something wrong, and do not know where it is; and their confidence is undermined, and their alertness sapped. It cannot be doubted that employers are disheartened by falling prices; and that all, who have to meet fixed obligations from varying incomes, are hardly pressed. It is true that, owing to a certain *vis inertiæ*, the wage-earner may feel the effects more slowly, and that appearances may fail to reveal the existence of suffering on his part. But his income depends ultimately on the production of wealth; and, if the directors of production are dispirited, and a drag applied to the wheels of progress, he must participate in the results. It is also possible that the friction inevitably attendant on an improvement in his real position, due to some such change in the distribution of wealth as has been characteristic of recent years, is lessened, if rising wages show him plainly that he is advancing, and falling prices do not increase the apparent burden to the employer. For the effects of a fall of prices will, like the manifestation of that fall itself, be inextricably mingled with the consequences of other forces. General prosperity may advance, despite of the drag on the wheels; but, had the hindrance been removed, it would have progressed still faster. The position of the wage-earner may improve in consequence of some change in distribution; but it might have been better, but for discouragement occasioned by falling prices to business enterprise. Once more we are driven back by the necessities of the case on the probable operation of the cause, and the broad evidence of the effects; and such broad evidence is manifest in the stationary wages, the falling profits, the failure to recover from temporary depression due to credit fluctuations, and the feeling of *malaise*, which has been a characteristic of business in recent years, attested by successive Royal Commissions. In view of such evidence, our gold standard cannot be said to have been stable, or to have worked satisfactorily.

But we are told, on good authority, that a fresh change is probable, and is even in process. As the result of the increased production of gold from Southern Africa and Western Australia, and the cessation of the extraordinary demands, a rise of prices may be anticipated. About the likelihood of great additions—for a time, at least—to the output of gold, little doubt can now be entertained; nor is it improbable that they should produce an effect on prices. That they have not done so unmistakably, at present, is not incompatible with such a belief; for it takes time for the new gold to find its way into the channels of trade, and to influence appreciably the course of general prices. Some prophets have gone so far as to predict a large rise; and, in the absence of bi-metallism, no compensating influence will be furnished, such as that presented to the Californian and Australian discoveries of the middle of the century. If, indeed, a great and rapid rise were probable, the economist might sigh for such an influence; and one merit of bi-metallism is its mitigation of the consequences of sudden change, whether it be due to an increase or decrease in the output from the mines, or to what some observers have held might follow the outbreak of an European war—the rapid expenditure and diffusion of the gold now hoarded in military chests. But, on the other hand, even when allowance has been made· for the compensatory influence, the effect on prices of the Californian and Australian discoveries was so much smaller than had been feared that it seems more probable that the consequences of the present African and Australian additions will not be very great. The existing stock, on which the supplies have to exert their influence, is much larger; the proportion of the trade of the world, conducted on a gold basis, is far greater; and the growth of trade is more extensive. In spite of the temporary cessation in the extraordinary demands, the production of the new gold may conceivably tempt to new demands. India may strive to introduce a gold standard in earnest, and the United States may substitute gold for the silver purchased under the Bland and Sherman Acts. We may possibly see a rise of prices, followed again in a few years by a renewed fall.

In that case the practical man would, if he followed the counsel of the economist, seize the opportunity to place the monetary relations of the countries of the world on a more stable basis; for one important consequence of a temporary rise of prices, and fall in the value of gold, would be a mitigation of the difficulties attending the selection of a suitable ratio. In this circumstance some consolation might be found for the withdrawal of a certain amount of support from a movement, which is likely to appeal more urgently to the practical man when the sky is overcast, and the clouds are threatening, than when, basking at his ease in the sunshine of prosperity, he has carelessly banished thought of depression and misfortune. So long as human nature remains what it is, the reformer must be content to recognise such a natural tendency; and, in the presence of an economic society, I may surely venture on an admission, which might be considered impolitic, and misconstrued elsewhere. In conclusion, I will ask the members to believe that, in the imperfect presentation of a vast subject, which I have submitted to them, I have endeavoured to give a foremost place to the scientific aspects of the question, and to appeal to considerations, which would commend themselves primarily to students. I am bound to add that I myself am confident that, in the department of economic inquiry to which I have been craving attention, the safest and most advantageous practice is likely to follow the lines of the most profound, the most accurate, and the most comprehensive theory.

XII.

ADAM SMITH AND HIS RELATIONS TO RECENT ECONOMICS.[1]

IT is with a feeling of hesitation that I submit to the Economic Section of the British Association the following remarks. To say anything new on Adam Smith is not easy; but to say anything of importance or profit, which has not been said before, is well-nigh impossible. I have indeed heard the rumours, which have been whispered of late in economic circles, and have hinted that he may be more than suspected of the charge so commonly advanced against writers, who seem to have made some new contribution to the development of human knowledge, or to have given some fresh exhibition of the fertility of the human imagination, and that, like so many before and after him, he was guilty of plagiarism. It is certainly true that the references to other authors in the *Wealth of Nations* are comparatively few and far between; that the years, during which the work was in process of composition, were sufficiently numerous to afford time for accumulating a mass of material in commonplace books and the like, which may have been included among the papers destroyed, as we know, before Adam Smith's death; that his notorious excellence of memory would have assisted conscious or

[1] Read before Section F of the British Association at Edinburgh, 1892, and published in the *Economic Journal* for June, 1893.

unconscious appropriation; and that the comparative absence of systematic continuous development through the separate books of his treatise might be held to point to the reproduction of the views of others, rather than the formation and statement of his own independent opinions. It is certain that there were economists before him, and he himself is emphatic in his recognition of the merits of his French predecessors; and it is no less certain that he was influenced by the particular circumstances of his time, and that he breathed in the atmosphere of thought, by which he was surrounded, to an extent, which recent historical inquiry and criticism have enabled us to apprehend more fully. But I have neither the wish nor the knowledge to enter on the interesting discussion, which these considerations suggest. The determination of the line, where plagiarism ends and originality begins, calls for a fine power of discrimination, and the limits of borrowing without acknowledgment constitute a most delicate and difficult question of literary etiquette. If the ideas, which you are accused of plagiarising, form part of the common stock of the discussions of the day, you may perhaps be allowed to use them without an express recognition of their original ownership. If, in passing them through your mind, you have given them the stamp of your own individuality, it becomes doubtful how far you may claim that they are, in part at least, your own, and how far you are bound to exhibit the precise process, by which they have arrived at their present shape. With these nice questions I do not propose to deal, but to attempt the more modest and agreeable task of trying to indicate some of the qualities, which have given the *Wealth of Nations* so high and permanent a place in economic literature. For, explain it as we please, it would be difficult to deny that Adam Smith's great treatise has

ADAM SMITH AND RECENT ECONOMICS 275

taken and retained an unique position. It has become a "classic." It has, unlike the mass of economic writing, established itself in the affections of the layman as well as the expert; and, unlike the mass of economic writing also, it has exchanged the fading laurels of ephemeral renown for a crown of abiding glory.

First among its titles to enduring fame we may place the fact that it is a piece of literary workmanship as well as a scientific treatise. It has been stated somewhere that Political Economy in its scientific character has suffered from the literary treatment, which it has often received at the hands of practised writers, who wield the effective instrument of a facile pen. This has, so we are told, led to the sacrifice of accuracy of reasoning to finish of expression, and permitted sciolists to enter the domains of science. That there is truth in this argument, no one, who knows anything of the history of Economics, would be prepared to deny; and it might perhaps be urged that Adam Smith himself offended against the conditions of scientific exactitude no less than the graces of literary style by his diffuseness and repetition. But it remains true that the *Wealth of Nations* has a charm in its composition, which reveals the literary artist, and that the happiness of many of its phrases has aided the recollection of what would otherwise have been speedily forgotten. Literary form is, no doubt, a means to an end, which must not be exalted to an end in Economics more than in any other science; but, despite of all the objections, which have been raised, and of drawbacks, which it is easy to indicate, there can be no doubt that the layman will concern himself more closely and frequently with it than with most other sciences, and that he will be attracted by grace, and deterred by awkwardness, of composition. If he cannot—and it is doubtful whether such a result, if attainable, is to be desired, —be prevented from straying into the preserves of the scientist, it is preferable that he should seek the companionship of the best writers rather than the worst, and it is therefore matter for congratulation that in Adam Smith he will find a stimulus to thought added to a gratification of taste.

But the attraction of the *Wealth of Nations* as a literary performance is largely due to the presence of another characteristic, which is held by some critics, and not unreasonably, to militate against scientific exactitude. The exposition of the theory of Economics, we are told, must be carefully distinguished from its application to practice. The theoretical expositor must sternly preserve himself from the dangerous and deteriorating influence of motive or purpose of a practical nature. He must pursue truth and truth alone, turning neither to the right hand nor to the left. Here, again, it would be difficult to deny the force of these arguments, or to ignore the serious mischief, which has resulted from the intrusion of partiality or prejudice into the region of scientific inquiry. There can be no doubt that the distinction between the theory of Economics and the art of political or social or philanthropic practice, which has, by dint of constant repetition and urgent insistence, been forced home on the mind of the student, has helped to clarify his views and to save him from hasty, unwarranted conclusions. There can be no more doubt that, if the "man in the street" could be brought to recognise this distinction, the process would be wholesome for himself and for the science, which he so often misappropriates to his own ends. But in his case it is almost hopeless to expect to achieve success; and the student, with all his watchfulness, will find the subtle influences of motive and purpose continually trying to reassert their sway, and, not unfrequently, triumphing over resistance. To look for any other result is to listen to "counsels of perfection" rather than the plain lessons of common experience.[1] And, whatever may be urged on this point, it is at least certain that in Adam Smith's time the distinction between the scientific study of the causes, which govern the production and distribution of wealth, and the art of increasing the "wealth of nations," had not passed beyond its rudimentary stage, if it had even emerged from obscurity at all. And it is no less certain that the persuasive fascination of his writing is largely due to the presence and prominence from beginning to end of his book of one dominant motive and one ruling purpose. It has been said[2] that every page of his treatise is "illumined" by the "passion" for freedom; and the most cursory reading of the *Wealth of Nations* could scarcely fail to disclose this ardent feeling, while the most diligent and protracted study would serve but to strengthen the original impression. It is the possession of the whole man by such a passion, which renders writers cogent arguers, and their readers willing listeners; and, though the passion may, if it is not curbed and bridled, sometimes run away with the judgment, it may also lend a wonderful force to accurate reasoning, and carry conviction to minds unwilling otherwise to listen to wholesome and important truths. As a literary instrument it is unsurpassed; as a weapon of science it is by no means to be lightly esteemed, or carelessly dismissed.

This instrument Adam Smith possessed in admirable perfection, and this weapon he wielded with marvellous

[1] Cf. Essay viii. above.
[2] By Toynbee in his *Industrial Revolution*.

effect. But it has been said[1] that his passion for freedom was largely a product of the times, and an outcome of French speculation in the period before the Revolution; and it has been urged that it led him into an excessive eulogy of the "obvious and simple system of natural liberty," which was soon to receive a terrible corrective in the misery and suffering apparently due, to a large extent, to unfettered competition in the early days of the factory system. It has been maintained that, while the removal of the old barriers, which impeded the course of trade, and the shackles, which cramped the movements of industry, was then needed, and was powerfully aided by the strenuous energy and perseverance of Adam Smith, the requirements of later times are different, the extension rather than the limitation of the functions of government, and the enlargement rather than the contraction of the sphere within which the State should regulate or supersede the action of individuals, constitute the pressing need of our day and the most urgent question alike of practical politics and of political theory, and therefore the teaching of Adam Smith is obsolete, and the *Wealth of Nations* has no message for us. But, on the other hand, it has been pointed out[2] that Adam Smith himself was too shrewd an observer of human nature, and too keen a judge of the exigencies of practical affairs, to believe in uncontrolled individualism, or, as it has been happily called,[3] "administrative nihilism"; and he recognised that there was a sphere for State action, and departments of life where its absence would be fraught with social injury and danger of the gravest kind. The question is often stated as if the choice lay between no interference on the part of the State and

[1] By Cliffe Leslie.   [2] By Professor Sidgwick.
[3] By Professor Huxley.

complete arrangement and control; but it is really a question of degree, and in this lies its difficulty.[1] Adam Smith, no doubt, inclined to the less rather than the more; we, perhaps, have latterly been disposed to go some way in the opposite direction. But he would be a bold man, who would deny that the crying need of the days of the *Wealth of Nations* was the limitation of State meddling, and the removal of multitudinous restrictions and narrow exclusive regulations. Nor would it argue less ignorance of human nature, or less unintelligent acquaintance with the movement of affairs, to dispute the pertinence to all time of much that Adam Smith urges in defence of liberty. Attacks upon freedom are the melancholy feature of more than one condition of society, and of more than a single epoch in the world's history. The argument in favour of liberty may be pressed too far, and Adam Smith may have fallen into this error; but it is rarely inopportune, and it is seldom, if ever, superfluous. Liberty is assailed in so many and such subtle forms that the claims of its champions have a perennial application; and, when the advocacy of freedom means, as in Adam Smith's case, the pleading of the cause of the weak oppressed by the strong, and the vindication of the rights of the defenceless it is as premature, as it is ungracious, to say that he has no message for our time. His passion for liberty, which illuminates all his pages, sheds its lustre over the problems of this and every age; and it gives a permanent value as well as imparts a persuasive charm to the *Wealth of Nations*.

Adam Smith's merits do not appeal to the lover of the interesting alone. In fact the number of minds, which have agreed, while differing on other subjects, to unite in praising the *Wealth of Nations*, is not the least remarkable

[1] Cf. Essay i. above.

or conspicuous testimony to its unique character. We have already observed that it appeals, and appeals successfully, to the layman as well as the expert; and statesmen and men of affairs, from Pitt downwards, have derived instruction, and obtained guidance, from its pages no less than academic economists. The causes of this wide popularity are not far to seek. The language of Adam Smith is admirably simple and clear, his reasoning direct and forcible to a degree unsurpassed, and perhaps unapproached, by other writers on a subject, which it is only too easy to make repellent and difficult, and his illustrations are at once abundant and apt. The strong motive, by which his argument is informed, gives an air of unmistakable reality to his writing, and he always seems to be in the closest touch with actual present fact. These are the very qualities to appeal to the plain practical man; but the remarkable characteristic of Adam Smith is that he appeals with equal strength to the trained economist. The position of the *Wealth of Nations* in strictly economic literature is as unique as is the fact that it occupies a recognised place among the classic productions of men of letters of all times.[1] The comparative simplicity of economic theory in Adam Smith's day, as contrasted with the more elaborate and complex development of later periods of thought, might have been expected to render the *Wealth of Nations* attractive to the outsider, deterred by the terms and formulæ of more specialised, but exact, knowledge and inquiry; but for this very reason the professed economist might have been supposed to be likely to regard the book as interesting rather as evidence of what Economics had been in a comparatively unadvanced stage,

[1] Cf. the author's *Short History of Political Economy in England*, chap. i.

and as an example of the early form which doctrines, developed since, had then assumed. But he might not improbably have thought that its antiquarian interest was its strongest point, and that later reasoning had superseded it as an engine for inquiry and speculation. Such a conclusion would, no doubt, be natural; and chapters in Adam Smith might be cited in its support. The importance, which, in spite of his criticism of the system of the Physiocrats, he assigned to agriculture, in which, he said, "nature laboured along with man," and the order, in which he ranged the employments of capital in the same chapter[1] —very suggestive as it is in the light it throws on his mental environment, but containing also not a little, which would now be stated differently, if it were not regarded as obsolete—are examples of this. But the surprising fact remains how little is really unimportant now, and how much is supplied in germ in the *Wealth of Nations*, which later investigation has done no more than develop into the maturer plant. Few, if any, writers on a subject, which has to deal with the changing phenomena of human society, could stand so well the test of a hundred years of study and criticism, or, after the lapse of so long a time, appear so fresh and apposite.

To this point I propose to return later; what I wish now to emphasise is the way in which, by writers of almost every school, in England at least, Adam Smith has been regarded as the parent of modern Economics. It is true that recent research has called attention to the important contributions of authors before his time, who had been overshadowed by his fame and greatness; and the *Wealth of Nations* was no more the end than it was the beginning of economic study. But throughout the subsequent history

[1] Book ii. chap. v.

of Economics, at any rate in this country, there has been one writer and one treatise to which all others have in turn traced the origin of most of their ideas; and that writer has borne the name of Adam Smith, and that treatise the title of the *Wealth of Nations*. Even in the generation, which immediately followed its issue, it seemed as if, in the persons of Malthus and Ricardo, Political Economy would break up into two opposite schools of thought pursuing two different methods of inquiry. Certain it is that many of the fundamental issues raised in later controversy were started at that time; and the *Letters of Ricardo to Malthus*[1] may from this point of view be read even now with interest, although they refer in many instances to passing practical questions of the day. And yet Malthus and Ricardo, in spite of their fundamental differences, owned Adam Smith to be their common teacher, although, like able pupils, they were not afraid to criticise, and improve on, their master.

The same feature has repeated itself through the course of subsequent discussion. In Germany, no doubt, *Smithianismus* has become a term of reproach, and the ghost, conjured up under this name, has been assailed with all the weapons, which painstaking research, and wide erudition, and enthusiastic zeal for a new creed, could command; and the attack, perhaps we may add, has after all been eluded owing to the unsubstantial and imaginary character of the object of assault. But, if we turn to the representative of the German historical school, who in recent times has led the onslaught in England, we find that, while he criticises Adam Smith with perfect freedom, and shows how he was influenced by the facts and thought peculiar to his time, he places him on quite a different level from

[1] Edited by Dr. Bonar.

Ricardo, and claims the *Wealth of Nations* as a brilliant illustration of the advantages of the inductive as opposed to the deductive method of inquiry. In one of the most interesting of his essays,[1] Cliffe Leslie observes that the followers of the orthodox school now reply to their opponents by a cry "of the greatness of Adam Smith." "And," he adds, "it is well that the cry is now for him instead of Ricardo." But, he proceeds later, "it reminds one of the contest between the spirits of darkness and light for the body of Moses, to find the followers of Ricardo claiming Adam Smith for their prophet." "'Whom ye ignorantly worship, him declare I unto you,' the true disciple of Adam Smith may say to those who raise altars to his name, but to whom he is virtually an unknown being." And he goes on to argue that the method employed by Adam Smith was inductive, and to illustrate this point in particular by the "famous tenth chapter of his first book." "The notion of evolving from his own consciousness the circumstances and motives that diversify the employments of a nation, and the remuneration obtained in them, would be preposterous, even if Adam Smith himself had not expressly stated at the beginning of the chapter that he had gathered them from observation." Cliffe Leslie's opinion is entitled to great respect, for the influence, which his writings have exercised on the conception of method, and the development of theory, has been considerable; but it is curious to turn from his assertions to the conclusions drawn by other writers.

For what does the author of one of the most recent English treatises on economic theory say? Professor Marshall is even more emphatic than Cliffe Leslie in his praise of the *Wealth of Nations*. "The next great step in

[1] *Political Economy and Sociology*.

advance, the greatest step that economics has ever taken, was the work," he declares,[1] " not of a school, but of an individual." "Wherever" Adam Smith "differs from his predecessors, he is more nearly right than they; while there is scarcely any economic truth now known of which he did not get some glimpse." And what are the grounds on which Professsor Marshall bases this ungrudging eulogy? "His chief work," he observes, "was to combine and develop the speculations of his French and English contemporaries and predecessors as to value. His highest claim to have made an epoch in thought is that he was the first to make a careful and scientific inquiry into the manner in which value measures human motive, on the one side measuring the desire of purchasers to obtain wealth, and on the other the efforts and sacrifices undergone by its producers." The work, however, thus described, is largely deductive as well as inductive, and at any rate it places Adam Smith in the direct line of descent to Ricardo and the so-called abstract school. It is opposed to Cliffe Leslie's verdict, as it is more comprehensive; and Professor Marshall proceeds to remark that the *Wealth of Nations*, "though not well arranged, is a model of method; for" Adam Smith "saw that while economic science is based on a study of facts, the facts are so complex, that they generally can teach nothing directly; they must be interpreted by careful reasoning and analysis. And, as Hume said, the *Wealth of Nations* "is so much illustrated with curious facts that it must take the public attention." This is exactly what Adam Smith did; he seldom attempted to prove anything by detailed induction or history. The data of his proofs were chiefly facts that were within every one's knowledge—facts physical, mental,

---

[1] *Principles of Economics*, vol. i. book i. chap. iv. sect. 3.

and moral. But he illustrated his proofs by curious and instructive facts; he thus gave them life and force, and made his readers feel that they were dealing with problems of the real world, and not with abstractions."

Discussions on method are, perhaps, never very profitable, and Economics has had more than its full share of such discussions. I do not propose to enter now on the treatment of the questions, interesting though they may be, whether Adam Smith reasoned, in the main, inductively or deductively, and whether he more generally constructed his theory from observation of collected fact, or used his facts to verify and illustrate his theory. It is hard to draw a rigid line between deduction and induction, and to say where the province of the one ends, and that of the other begins. It is now generally allowed that Economics may, and, if it is to advance, must, avail itself of all the aids to inquiry and speculation, which the wit of man has discovered. It must use in turn, as the circumstances favour, induction, deduction, observation, experiment, hypothesis, and verification. Later investigation has, no doubt, emphasised the importance of facts; but it has not lessened the advantage of employing the instrument of method, in all its varieties and patterns, to handle facts. And so it seems probable that Adam Smith, like other writers, sometimes used what would probably be called an inductive, and sometimes what would be broadly distinguished as a deductive method, that sometimes he constructed his theory from his facts, and sometimes he employed his facts to verify and illustrate his theory. That it should be, as it still is, a disputed question whether the one or the other form of reasoning predominated in his treatise, is a testimony to the catholicity of his work: that he should be labelled now deductive, and now inductive, may not unreasonably be held to point to the conclusion that he was not exclusively either, but embraced elements of both. And, whatever may be said as to the method he employed, it is certainly remarkable that he should be highly esteemed alike by what we may perhaps, without offence, call historical dissenters and by orthodox believers; and that the germs of the "theory of measurable motives," as well as illustrations of the systematic knowledge slowly built on the observation of a mass of facts, should be discovered in the *Wealth of Nations*. In this respect it is surely unique in economic literature.

Nor· does the theorist find, in its pages, merely the rudiments of the central theory of Economics; but, if he examines the different departments of the science, he is astonished to discover how close Adam Smith is to the latest results of economic inquiry. There is, it is true, no formal or regular division in the *Wealth of Nations* into separate departments, dealing with production, distribution, exchange, and consumption; and the arrangement of the treatise is lacking in system. But the early treatment given to exchange, as arising naturally from division of labour, and facilitated by the use of money, the tool of exchange, the prominence assigned to value as the dominant fact in exchange, the distinction drawn between natural and market value, and then the manner in which, after substituting the consideration of price for that of value, and noticing demand, the "natural price" is resolved into the elements of which it usually consists, and the wages of labour, the profits of stock, and their differences from occupation to occupation, whether due to artificial or natural causes, and the rent of land, are successively considered, are in accordance with the general tenour of recent investigation; and the first two books

ADAM SMITH AND RECENT ECONOMICS 287

of the *Wealth of Nations* may be said to contain a theory of production, exchange, and distribution, which presents in essence the fuller development of later criticism and speculation.

If we take, for instance, the laws governing the earnings of the different classes of participators in the distribution of wealth, it is truly surprising to find how successfully Adam Smith seems to have avoided many of the errors of subsequent thinkers, as they now appear, and to have seized hold of the essential elements of the truth. It appears tolerably certain that he did not fall into the characteristic fallacies of the wage-fund theory, although he speaks of the "funds" from which wages might be paid; and he seems to have grasped the notion of a lower limit to wages in the standard of comfort of the labourer, and an upper limit in the wealth of a nation, between which the market forces might operate.[1] On the subject of profits he writes with a domestic system of industry before his eyes, where there was little scope for the work of management, as compared with the huge industrial and commercial undertakings of the present day. And so[2] he uses the term profits to denote the interest of capital, varying, as he says, entirely according to the amount of the stock employed; and he will not allow the element of wages of management to come into prominence. In the case of the "apothecary," and the "village grocer," he expressly brings under the category of wages, and excludes from the class of profits, what we should now term earnings of management. The American economist General Walker has, on the other hand, employed the term profits to denote these wages of management exclusively, and separated the interest of capital from it ; and, in doing

---

[1] Cf. the previous Essay.   [2] Cf. Essay iv above.

so, he has marked the change, which has taken place in the organisation of industry. But the common English use of the term embraces both elements; and Adam Smith is in accord with the most recent tendency of economic speculation to consider, under one and the same general head, the wages of management and the wages of labour, and to regard as similar the general laws governing the earnings of all descriptions of labour—whether that of direction, or that of obeying direction. On the matter of rent there are reasons for doubting whether he fully grasped, or consistently held, the theory known as the Ricardian theory; but he went some way towards doing so, and his statement that the rent of land "not only varies with its fertility, whatever be its produce, but with its situation, whatever be its fertility," has the merit of stating concisely, and yet explicitly, what Ricardo mentioned, but allowed many of his readers to forget.[1]

So far for Adam Smith's treatment of distribution; and, before we pass to the later books of his treatise, it may be asked whether the advantages and dangers of paper money have, ever since, been more pithily expressed than in his remark that "the gold and silver money, which circulates in any country, may, very properly, be compared to a highway, which, while it circulates and carries to market all the grass and corn of the country, produces itself not a single pile of either. The judicious operations of banking, by providing, if I may be allowed so violent a metaphor, a sort of waggon-way through the air, enable the country to convert, as it were, a great part of its highways into good pastures and cornfields, and thereby to increase very considerably the annual produce of its land and labour. The commerce and industry of the country, however, it

[1] Cf. Essay x.

must be acknowledged, though they may be somewhat augmented, cannot be altogether so secure, when they are thus, as it were, suspended upon the Dædalian wings of paper money, as when they travel about upon the solid ground of gold and silver." The temptation to quote from the *Wealth of Nations* is very powerful, and may easily become irresistible; but we have not time to offer, and we might scarcely have patience to hear, more on the present occasion. The quotation, which I have just made, seems to me to afford so perfect an example of the qualities, which have contributed to give Adam Smith's treatise its high position, that I could not forbear to cite it. We see in it that power of direct and lucid statement, that facility of expressing in a sentence a profound and far-reaching truth, that felicity of apt illustration, which render the book at once so pleasant and valuable. Adam Smith is sometimes diffuse, but he can also be remarkably terse; and he has the rare merit of luminous exposition, and of relieving the tedium of dry reasoning by interesting and appropriate illustration. His wide acquaintance with fact, and his strong sense of its importance, combine with his extensive knowledge of the learning, with which the educated minds of his age were furnished, to enable him to employ, within the compass of a paragraph, a homely metaphor, which he may call "violent," but his readers deem as suitable as it well can be, and also a parallel, just as apt, but as classical as the metaphor is drawn from the common knowledge of the average man.

But we are returning to the consideration of the literary side of the *Wealth of Nations;* and, with a repetition of the opinion that it is only too possible to underrate the value, even for scientific ends, of literary excellence, and a mere passing allusion to the admitted belief of economists of different schools that Adam Smith's treatment of the division of labour, of the origin and use of money, of the rules and maxims of taxation, has perhaps been added to and improved, but has not been superseded, by later inquiry, we must press on to the consideration of that part of the book, which has been most generally associated with the name of its author, and has achieved the most remarkable success in the domain of practical affairs.

Adam Smith's examination of the Mercantile System has been critically reviewed by writers of great ability and learning. Historians have shown that the Mercantilist views were more reasonable than the reader of the fourth book of the *Wealth of Nations* might suppose, and that they were actually in keeping with the practical exigencies of the times in which they were advanced. Able Protectionists have opposed to Adam Smith's undoubted cosmopolitanism a National System; and no fair-minded student can read List, for example, without recognising his persuasiveness, and the force of some of the arguments he uses in reply to Adam Smith. Economic theorists, who believe in Free Trade, or at any rate in Free Trade for England, have brought into the light possibilities of which Adam Smith did not take full account; and the encouragement of "infant industries" by protection, to be withdrawn when they are able to stand by themselves and have attained maturity, has been allowed an economic justification by writers of the rank of Mill, who shocked some of his admirers by his candid admission. But those writers have been careful, in most cases, to add that the selection of the "infants" to be specially nurtured requires an extraordinarily impartial and prudent government, and the removal of the protection, when it is no longer needed, calls for a remarkably strong and discreet administration.

The economic basis of the argument is sound, but the political foundation is weak and shifting. Again, the difference between a country, whose commodities obey a law of increasing returns, and one, whose commodities are governed by a law of diminishing returns, as exchanging parties, has by recent writers been applied to the theoretical question of Free Trade and Protection, and some economic defence discovered for opinions and acts of a seemingly heretical character. Nor can it be denied that the tariff policy of so many European States, of the great American Republic, and of our own colonies, although, in the first case, the eminent desirability of raising a large revenue for military purposes by the easy, imperceptible, and indirect means of taxation of imported commodities, in the second, the immense area—perhaps the largest of its kind—of the United States, throughout which complete freedom of trade prevails, and the comparative unimportance of the question, and, in the third, the revenue considerations, which render direct taxation so difficult and expensive in a comparatively new country, might be advanced in explanation—it cannot be denied that this tariff policy has shaken the hopes raised by the more liberal movement of tariffs some little while ago.

But, with all these adverse influences, it is still surprising to find how fresh and forcible is the reasoning of Adam Smith's fourth book, and with how sure an instinct he seized on the most important and enduring arguments. There are two main grounds, on which he may be said explicitly to base his contentions, and a third is implicitly contained in his language. The first of these arguments is the justice and advantage of freedom. Every individual, he maintains, in his own place and station can judge of the proper employment of his capital better than a lawgiver or government can do for him. It would be difficult to deny the force of this argument, though the further conclusion, which he draws, that the consideration of a man's own interests will lead him to promote the interests of the community, might now be received with some qualification. But the general drift of the argument in favour of individual freedom in the employment of capital is admittedly powerful. Connected with this is the argument, implied rather than stated, that there is a division of labour between nations as between individuals; that similar advantages result from its institution in encouraging production and developing capacities; and that, as domestic division of labour implies, and follows on, freedom of exchange, so the necessary condition of "territorial" or international division of labour is Free Trade.

But, after all, neither of these two arguments, though they are forcibly urged and aptly illustrated, seems to be that, to which he is inclined to give the greatest prominence. It is the erroneous conception of money in the Mercantilist doctrine, to which he devotes most continual attention, and it is on the correct idea of its functions and place in industry and commerce that he lays repeated insistance. No doubt this emphasis was naturally suggested by the arguments of the advocates of the Mercantile System, to whom he was specially replying; but it seems also, in a higher degree than the other arguments, which he advances, to give an enduring application to his reasoning. The conception that trade is an exchange of goods for goods in international as well as in domestic transactions is a touchstone, to which Protectionist arguments may often be brought with serious, if not fatal, consequences to their validity. The fact that a nation pays for its imports by its exports is one, which it is hard, if not impossible, to contest, if it is once apprehended; but there are many Protectionist reasonings which cannot successfully confront it. That the process might be circuitous and indirect Adam Smith freely admitted; and the circuit has extended, and the accomplishment of its passage taken a longer time, since he wrote. The "invisible exports," as they have been called, of the capital and labour engaged in our shipping industry in carrying goods from one country to another, and the interest due on our investments abroad, have grown in volume since the publication of the *Wealth of Nations*. That gold and silver might form part of those imports and exports Adam Smith unhesitatingly allowed; but that they formed a small and insignificant part he stoutly maintained, and that the transit of bullion was avoided as far as possible he strenuously affirmed. Nor, in the case of countries like Great Britain, which did not themselves produce the precious metals to any large extent, could they be procured in the first instance except by the exchange of goods. These arguments have not lost their validity or pertinence; and anyone acquainted with the difficult theory, and complex practice, of the foreign exchanges will remember that they turn on the anxiety to avoid the transit of bullion, while the growth of credit, and its use in international trade, have diminished the proportion of that trade effected by the passage of money to an extraordinary extent. And yet it is scarcely possible to read a Protectionist pamphlet, however able and well-informed, without finding the old mistakes about money making their reappearance in some cunning disguise. It is as true now as it was when Adam Smith wrote it that "even they who are convinced" of the "absurdity" "that wealth consists in money, or in gold and silver,' "are very apt to forget their own principles, and, in the course of their reasonings, to take it for granted as a certain and undeniable truth." Nor is it less true that "writers upon commerce set out with observing that the wealth of a country consists, not in its gold and silver only, but in its lands, houses, and consumable goods of all different kinds. In the course of their reasonings, however, the lands, houses, and consumable goods, seem to slip out of their memory; and the strain of their argument frequently supposes that all wealth consists in gold and silver, and that to multiply those metals is the great object of national industry and commerce."

Adam Smith never anticipated the "complete restoration" of freedom of trade in Great Britain; and, had he lived to see this result accomplished, his disappointment as a mistaken prophet might have mingled with his satisfaction as a convincing reasoner. Few triumphs of a higher kind have ever been achieved by a speculative philosopher in the region of practical affairs; for, while it was the stern logic of fact, enforced by the famine in Ireland, which brought about the repeal of the Corn Laws, some of the most persuasive arguments used by Cobden on the platform reflected the spirit, if they did not reproduce the language, of the *Wealth of Nations;* and certainly Cobden himself and the succession of reforming finance ministers from Pitt —who showed that, had he enjoyed the opportunity, he would have anticipated the liberalising measures of later times—to Mr. Gladstone, who put the finishing touches on a purified tariff, would have been proud to own that they were pupils of the Glasgow professor.

I may perhaps add a word in conclusion, to express the pleasure of being permitted as an Oxonian to do honour to the memory of Adam Smith in this famous and beautiful city, where he first lectured and established a reputation,

ADAM SMITH AND RECENT ECONOMICS

where he formed that intimate friendship with David Hume, which endured throughout life, and where he spent the greater part of his closing years and, dying in the ripeness of age and honour, was laid in his last resting-place. If Oxford treated Adam Smith ill as a student in her unregenerate days, she, in common with the World, accords him a high place on the roll of the World's worthies, and she is proud to number him among the most distinguished of her own sons. But it is to Scotland that Adam Smith owed most, and it is to Scotland also that students of Economics are in duty bound to express their gratitude for having given birth to the bearer of the greatest and most honoured name in the annals of this branch of learning.

XIII.

A RECENT ECONOMIC TREATISE.[1]

ONE of the most prominent of our public men, in a speech of which his political opponents declare he must now have cause to repent, once instituted a comparison between eminent statesmen and great mountain peaks. It was, he remarked, impossible to realise the full grandeur of certain mountains until they were separated by some distance from the spectator, who could then, and then only, distinguish them from the less considerable peaks by which they might happen to be surrounded. And so, in the case of great statesmen, their eminent superiority to their contemporaries was more likely to be estimated aright by posterity than by the generation in which they themselves lived.

The parallel, which Mr. Chamberlain thus drew between public men and natural objects, in his eulogy of the great Liberal statesman, who was then his leader, might easily be extended to include remarkable books ; and it is accordingly with some misgiving that the present paper has been written. The writer has enjoyed the privilege of reading Professor Marshall's *Principles of Economics* in proof, and he is

[1] Published in the *Economic Journal* for March, 1892.

conscious that this circumstance might be considered a serious disqualification for the task on which he is venturing; for he can scarcely flatter himself that the book is parted from him by a distance which will guarantee the correctness of his observations. From the outset he must confess that his attitude is one of admiration, which has deepened as he has withdrawn from immediate proximity, and contemplated from a distance in its entirety what he knew first in its separate parts. The impression of the distinctive unity of the mountain, and the grandeur with which it rises above the neighbouring peaks, has certainly not grown fainter in the process; and he is anxious to set down upon paper, while they are still fresh, some of the thoughts, which have crossed his mind.

In describing Professor Marshall's treatise as one, which is likely to mark an epoch in the history of Economics, the present writer is supported by the judgment of competent critics in every country where Economics is actively studied. From the New, as from the Old, World the same verdict has come; and economists, who belong to a different school of thought from that of the author, have frankly acknowledged the importance of his book, and cordially responded to the conciliatory spirit in which it is written. To any one, who possesses even a superficial acquaintance with the economic literature of recent times, such an amount of unanimity must seem as remarkable as it is welcome. To hope that at last we are escaping from a period of bitter, and sometimes idle, controversy into a period when economists of different schools will pursue their own lines of study, and yet recognise that other methods may lead to useful results, and that they are contributing in different ways and degrees to the promotion of a common object, is calculated to inspire the zealous student with fresh energy and new enthusiasm. But, until recently, in spite of scattered indications, which the sanguine and careful observer might, with the help of a vivid imagination, have pieced together into the semblance of reality, such a hope would have seemed impossible of fulfilment. The work of the past generation was so full of acrimonious dispute, and every writer was so busily occupied in demolishing the structure raised by his predecessors or his contemporaries, that the only legacy, which posterity seemed likely to inherit, was a confused mass of broken fragments, and the ruins of what had once appeared to be solid masonry.[1] But now it can scarcely be denied that a change is taking place. The atmosphere, which controversy had raised to an artificial heat, is growing cooler, and the temper of the disputants is giving way to a more friendly disposition. Continued study, and calm reflection, and the sobering influence of time, have produced a sensible diminution of temperature; and, while real differences may remain, they are narrowed to a more reasonable compass, and are not allowed to interfere with the recognition of useful work. The appearance, at this juncture, of Professor Marshall's treatise is an event of the first magnitude; for it is pervaded by the new spirit, which we have tried to describe, and the reception, with which it has met, shows that this spirit is generally prevalent. It is in this sense that it appears to mark an epoch: it closes an old period and opens a new, it ends a period of criticism and controversy, it commences a period of constructive work.

It is a commonplace of histories of philosophy to divide the epochs of thought into critical and constructive ages, which follow one another in turn. Somewhat the same

---

[1] Cf. *A History of Political Economy in England*, chap. v. etc.

conception may be formed of the development of that special department of human thought, which is concerned with economic study. A period of criticism succeeds to a period of construction; and criticism is, in its turn, followed by reconstruction. It would be as foolish to expect finality in such a process, as it would be irrational to undervalue the profitable results, which generally emerge, it may be slowly and painfully, from vigorous and even bitter criticism. Finality, here as elsewhere, would as surely indicate intellectual stagnancy, as criticism and controversy may be signs of progress. What we may perhaps fairly expect is that the separate products of a critical age may be gathered up and combined into a constructive unity, and that economic thought may thus advance from one generation to another, starting on each occasion from a higher level than before. And so the distinctive characteristic of Professor Marshall's treatise, by which it serves to mark an epoch in the history of Economics, seems to consist in the fact that it introduces afresh the conception of unity.

This unity, then, which may be taken as the keynote of the book, makes its presence felt in various ways. English writers on economic subjects have been often reproached for a certain "insularity" of temper. They have, so it has been argued, failed to appreciate the value of the contributions made to their science by writers in other countries. Cliffe Leslie, for example, reviewing in 1879 the American translation of Roscher's *Principles of Political Economy*, spoke of Germany as "entirely overlooked" by "English opponents of the historical method"; and, referring to the French translation of the same work, which had been made twenty-two years previously, he expressed his belief that at that time it was "doubtful if there was an economist in the United Kingdom besides Mr. Mill, who knew so much as the names of the three most eminent German economists then living—Roscher, Knies, and Hildebrand." That this reproach, although perhaps expressed in extravagant language, was justified by the actual state of the case can hardly be denied; and this was, no doubt, partly due, as Cliffe Leslie himself pointed out, to a prevalent ignorance of the German language. Even Jevons, who certainly could not be accused of a wish to neglect or depreciate the researches of Continental writers into the mathematical aspects of Economics, confessed in the preface to the second edition of his *Theory of Political Economy*, when discussing the writings of Gossen, that his own "unfortunate want of linguistic power" had "prevented" him, "in spite of many attempts, from ever becoming familiar enough with German to read a German book." The great importance of the knowledge, from which English students were thus cut off by their fault or misfortune, has become known to a later generation; and for this result the writings of Cliffe Leslie himself are largely responsible. But even he expressly excepted Professor Marshall from the general condemnation, which he was then passing upon English economists, and from the charge of being ignorant of the German language; and, had he lived to read the *Principles of Economics*, his commendation of that book on this particular ground would, we believe, have been as ample and complimentary as the review, which he wrote of the *Economics of Industry*, was remarkably appreciative, coming from so zealous an adherent of the historical school, and so unsparing a critic of the abstract deductive method. Again and again, throughout his treatise, Professor Marshall refers to German authorities, and he is thus enabled to incorporate in his presentation of Economics some, at any rate, of the most approved results of their abundant and varied work.

Nor is it merely with the writings of distinguished German economists, whether of a theoretical cast of mind, or of a temper opposed to theory, whether concerned with an analysis and comparison of human motives and a classification of human wants and desires, or occupied with the laborious investigation of historical fact, that Professor Marshall betrays an acquaintance. The contributions made to the study of theory by that school of Austrian economists, whose writings have been recently rendered more accessible, by means of translation, to English readers, repelled like Jevons, by the difficulties of the German language from an attempt to grapple with the original, are known, appreciated, and critically estimated by the English Professor. To the French mathematical economist, Cournot, he expresses his indebtedness in ample terms, and he often refers to the facts and the theories of the United States of America. Cliff Leslie, indeed, in an article in the *Fortnightly Review* in 1880, described "American political economy" as being "in the main an importation from Europe," and quoted from Professor Dunbar the candid avowal, that "the United States had done nothing towards developing the theory of political economy, notwithstanding their vast and immediate interest in its practical application." But it is probable that Cliffe Leslie's criticism and Mr. Dunbar's confession would be regarded as conveying a misleading idea of the present position, and that it would now be at once and gratefully admitted that positive contributions of value, as well as important negative criticism, had proceeded from recent American writers. With these contributions, as with the criticism, Professor Marshall is thoroughly familiar. He has, we think, succeeded in avoiding the suspicion of being merely "insular," and embraced within the comprehensive range of his treatise the products of the best economic thought of the different countries of the globe. But he has not lost sight in the process of the claims of unity, and these various contributions are combined into an orderly whole, and their respective importance, on which exaggerated emphasis may have been, not unnaturally, laid by the particular writers from whom they proceeded, is duly subordinated to the main conception of the treatise.

It is in a similar spirit that Professor Marshall has dealt with the work of his own countrymen; and, after all, it is no presumptuous or unfounded claim to advance for England that she may fairly be regarded as the classic home of economic science. But the danger, which is especially to be feared from such a period of criticism and controversy as that through which Economics has been recently passing, is that, in the prominence given to points of difference, the points of agreement may be neglected, and the casual observer may conclude that either party has demolished the erection raised by his opponent rather than contributed, together with him, to the construction of a joint building. There is, no doubt, a popular impression that Economics is now in a condition of suspense and uncertainty, that the old doctrines and ideas have proved to be unsatisfactory, but that nothing has yet been produced to take their place. The common misinterpretation given to an *obiter dictum* of Mr. Gladstone, in which he is supposed to have banished economic science to some planet other than our own, and the contemptuous reference, still not unfrequently made in newspaper columns, to discredited "laws of Political Economy," are among the proofs, which might be furnished of the prevalence of such an impression.

For this charge of suspense and uncertainty, as for that of insularity, it is not difficult to discover plausible and even cogent arguments. When Malthus can be quoted as thinking that the "main part" of Ricardo's "structure would not stand," and Senior as declaring that "Ricardo" was "perhaps the most incorrect writer who ever attained philosophical eminence," and Jevons as maintaining that "that able, but wrong-headed man, David Ricardo, shunted the car of economic science on to a wrong line—a line, however, on which it was further urged towards confusion by his equally able and wrong-headed admirer, John Stuart Mill," the humbler student may be excused for entertaining some doubt of the unity and progressive development of the science on which he is occupied. And, when he turns to the pages of Cairnes, and finds so energetic an advocate of the advantages of deductive reasoning, and so forcible and skilful a manipulator of what he himself describes as the "most powerful instrument of discovery ever wielded by human intelligence," arguing that the "conception of cost," which is "suggested" by Mill's exposition of *cost of production*, is "radically unsound, confounding things in their own nature distinct and even antithetical, and setting in an essentially false light the incidents of production and exchange," he may well be inclined to conclude that the external assaults of Cliffe Leslie, and others, on the deductive method have received material assistance from internal disagreements among its supporters and exponents. It is not easy to believe that, in spite of this bitter controversy and discordant criticism, Economics has been making steady progress; and it is still less easy to conceive that the controversy and criticism may have assisted in that advance.

Professor Marshall's treatise, we believe, has been

thoroughly successful in affording the basis for such an encouraging creed; and we have quoted these passages, not with any wish to recall disputes, which are happily fast being forgotten, nor with any desire to emphasise unduly the differences of the past, but in order to furnish the means for gauging the full magnitude of the task attempted and, we think, achieved in the *Principles of Economics*. That book seems to gather up the results of a period, when criticism attained a degree of bitterness, and controversy reached a pitch of contrariety, which must have seemed to the generation then living to preclude so much as the possibility of a final reconciliation, into an orderly systematic unity, where the different work of different writers is assigned its own place, and its merits are duly appreciated, without being allowed to thrust out another from its rightful position, or to appropriate to itself the recognition, which should properly be bestowed in other quarters. Such a task of reconciliation of views, which apparently conflict, and of harmonious combination of parts, which at first do not seem to fit into one another, would be difficult, if not impossible, during a critical age. It is only fully possible when the smoke of controversy has cleared away, and the errors, which have been successfully slain, and the truths, which survive, can be clearly and definitely ascertained. Even then it is by no means easy; and a book, which marks an epoch in the sense of closing an old period of criticism and controversy, and opening a new period of constructive work, is unquestionably a remarkable and uncommon book.

From this point of view, then, Professor Marshall seems to have been singularly successful. It is true that the student, who knew how to look beneath the surface, might have before formed a somewhat different conception of the state of the case than that which would naturally have resulted from a hasty review. He would have found in the *Letters of Ricardo to Malthus* an admirable pattern of the friendly manner, in which controversy could be conducted between economists, who consistently felt, and frankly expressed, important differences of opinion. He would have discovered in Cairnes' essay on *M. Comte and Political Economy* a vigorous plea for the triumphant acquittal of political economy, when tried by the two tests of "continuity" and "fecundity," which the great Positivist regarded as the decisive criteria of a true science. And, if he had consulted the treatise of Professor Sidgwick, who, in his address to the British Association at Aberdeen, carried the battle into the enemy's camp, and pertinently asked whether that general science of sociology, in which Economics was to be merged, itself exhibited the indispensable signs of "continuity" and "prevision," he would have found an attempt to "eliminate unnecessary controversy," and to state "the really sound and valuable results of previous thought" "in a more guarded manner, and with due attention to the criticisms and suggestions of recent writers." To Professor Sidgwick every economic student must entertain a lasting sense of gratitude; and even so biassed a critic as Dr. Ingram allows[1] that it is "impossible not to respect and admire the conscientious and penetrating criticism, which he applies to the *à priori* system of economics in its most mature form." He adds, indeed, that "it is interesting to observe that the part of the work which is, and has been recognised as, the most valuable is that in which, shaking off the fictions of the old school, he examines independently by the light of observation and analysis the question of the industrial action of

[1] In his *History of Political Economy*.

Governments." Many economic students would be inclined to dissent as strongly from Dr. Ingram's implied disapproval of the earlier parts of Professor Sidgwick's treatise, as they would be prepared to endorse his praise of the third book; but the author himself would be the first to recognise that his Cambridge colleague had brought to bear on some of the subjects, which he himself handles in the earlier portions of his treatise, the more extensive stores of a more specialised knowledge. If we may be allowed the comparison, Professor Sidgwick's book seems to present more resemblance—and it is not the less, but rather the more, valuable on that account—to the excursion of a philosopher into Economics, while Professor Marshall's treatise is more like the production of a specialist writing on his own special subject. But, in drawing this contrast, we do not depreciate the minuteness and accuracy of the knowledge of Economics possessed by the Professor of Moral Philosophy, or the extent and variety of the general information, which the Professor of Political Economy has brought to the composition of his treatise. It is one of the most characteristic features of that book that, like the *Wealth of Nations*, it abounds with felicitous illustrations drawn from a wide area, and is marked by a philosophic breadth of view.

This comprehensive spirit is shown, not merely in an abundance and variety of illustration, nor only in the liberal and tolerant conception of the relations of Economics to other branches of study, and of the methods of investigation appropriate to economic phenomena; but it is especially manifest in the author's treatment of his immediate and more distant predecessors. It would, perhaps, be accepted as a fairly adequate account of the more recent tendencies of economic thought in this and other countries of the world, to say that the two special influences, which have exercised the greatest power, and promise to be the most enduring in their future effects, are the mathematical and the historical. To take our own country, it is clear that Jevons on the one hand, and Cliffe Leslie on the other, may claim a prominent position in the very front rank of the influential writers of the last generation; and, in ways—sometimes direct and patent, more often, perhaps, hidden and indirect— the mathematical and the historical treatment of Economics have made their influence felt. The two methods of approaching the subject would, at first, seem to be mutually exclusive; and the one would appear to exalt, as much as the other to abase, the pretensions of theory. And yet they have contributed, in their respective manner and degree, to the common improvement of economic study, and Professor Marshall's treatise exhibits distinct traces of the influence of either.

We will investigate the less obvious of these influences first. A zealous adherent of the historical school might, no doubt, raise the objection that the *Principles of Economics* avowedly proceeds on the traditional lines of abstract reasoning, and that the method of inquiry employed is largely deductive. But, should such an objector, calling to mind the writings of an earlier generation, peruse with care the chapters[1] on the "nature of economic law" and the "methods of study," he would find that the advantage and necessity of inductive inquiry are frankly recognised; and, if he should turn to the Preface to the first edition, he would discover that "English traditions" are interpreted in a broad and liberal spirit. "The functions of the science," Professor Marshall states, "are to

[1] Combined into one chapter in the Third Edition (1895).

collect, arrange, and analyse economic facts, and to apply the knowledge, gained by observation and experience, in determining what are likely to be the immediate and ultimate effects of various groups of causes." Although, therefore, he is beyond question most stoutly opposed to the more extreme views, which have been sometimes advanced, more especially by German economists, nevertheless, as it seems to us, he exhibits distinct traces of the influence of the historical school; and his treatise affords a fresh illustration of the manner in which some, at least, of the results of their teaching have been incorporated into the main body of direct economic tradition.

The fact appears to be that the revolt, which Cliffe Leslie led in this country, was needed to call in question the dogmatic conclusions of some irresponsible disciples of the great masters, and, in some cases, to emphasise the limiting conditions of the reasonings of the great masters themselves; and, as is usually the case with a revolutionary movement, whether in the sphere of thought or of action, the revolt, and its leaders, betrayed an opposite extravagance perhaps as extreme and as faulty as that of the objects of their attack. Now, when the battle is almost over, and the roar of the cannon is less resounding, and the smoke is beginning to roll away, a calmer and more accurate survey is becoming possible, and the most approved achievements of the historical onslaught can be appropriated even by those who do not wish, or intend, to abandon their former allegiance. It has emphasised the importance of facts; and this may be allowed without neglecting the use of theory. It has drawn attention to the relation of economic phenomena to the whole of our social and political life; and this may be admitted without surrendering the benefits of specialised study. It has insisted on the development of economic theory under the influence of the particular environment of the time and place, and perhaps in this insistence has lain its greatest service. But it is difficult to read Professor Marshall's chapter "on the growth of economic science" without being reminded in almost every paragraph of the historical circumstances, amidst which the great economists lived and wrote, formed their opinions, and gave expression to them. It is, in fact, one of the most serious grounds of complaint against some of the more extreme supporters of the historical method, that they sometimes seem to desert the principles of their method, when they pass from limiting the application of the doctrines of a particular author by the special circumstances of his time and place to forming a judgment on his merits and failings. They do not always appear to give him the benefits of the conditions, which they have themselves laid down, or to allow the verdict, which they return, or the sentence, which they pass, to be affected by the consideration of "extenuating circumstances."

If, however, the historical treatment of Economics, though sometimes extravagant and sometimes defective, has contributed its quota of importance to the advancement of the study, its debt to the mathematical treatment is no less considerable; and that, like the historical treatment, appears, while making economic theory more accurate, to have also rendered it more comprehensive. By emphasising its limiting conditions, the historical treatment has checked the misapplication of theory; and the mathematical treatment, proceeding from a different starting-point by a different road, has reached the same goal, and tended to induce greater precision of statement. Its services in this direction cannot easily be exaggerated; and Jevons' name is among the greatest in the history of economic theory in England, as his judgment on matters of economic practice was as wise and suggestive as it was often bold and original. Nor would it be possible to dispute the mathematical attainments or leanings of a second wrangler, like the author of the *Principles of Economics*, and of the influence of the mathematical treatment upon the ideas of that book it is unnecessary to quote any detailed illustrations. It is more noteworthy to observe the sense of proportion, which has prompted the removal of the explicitly mathematical reasoning to the appendices, and of the diagrammatic examples to the foot-notes. Here, once again, the paramount claims of unity seem to be preferred to the subordinate demands of the different contributions made by different kinds of knowledge, and different methods of study, to the common aim of improving and advancing economic science.

Nor, again, are the important contributions of a later age allowed to dwarf into relative insignificance, or to banish from the line, the productions of the old masters any more than any one of their number is permitted to monopolise the whole of the space at disposal to the exclusion of another. Professor Marshall is exceedingly jealous for the reputation of the earlier English economists; and, if here he may seem to some critics to have erred by excess, the error is, at any rate, of a generous and pardonable nature. The older economists have often been so unfairly and indiscriminately attacked, and so grossly misrepresented or misinterpreted, that even an extreme movement in the opposite direction might be welcomed. But we do not believe that Professor Marshall has erred; and, if we may refer to a recent article in the *Economic Journal* on the " Rehabilitation of Ricardo," in which Professor Ashley has criticised Professor Marshall, we should say that he is arguing, to some extent, at any rate, at cross-purposes. What Professor Marshall appears to be concerned to establish is the continuity of economic thought, as it has been successively developed by the great English economists, while Professor Ashley aims rather at pourtraying the influence of Ricardo on his own contemporaries. The two points of view are, it seems to us, different. For the purpose of establishing the continuity of thought, it is not necessary to estimate, or interpret, that thought only by the impression it may have produced at the time, although for other purposes it may be advantageous and requisite to scrutinise closely that impression. As a historical character a man must, no doubt, be content to be judged by his influence on his contemporaries, and by the sense, in which they seem to have understood his remarks; as the transmitter and developer of a philosophy, it is surely more just that the best construction should be put on his language, if it can reasonably be argued that he himself intended this construction, whatever his contemporaries may have supposed. Into the literary question at issue we shall not enter; we are only concerned to maintain that, in tracing the continuity of ideas, a view, at once narrower and wider, is permissible than would be needed, if the general, as opposed to the special, influence, and the practical, as contrasted with the theoretical, position of a thinker were under consideration. The view will be narrower, because it will concentrate attention on the germ and essence of the thought, and it will be wider, because it will interpret the thought in a broad and liberal sense. We believe that there may be a difference between the "especial message" of a great thinker, and the sense, in which "he was understood by his contemporaries," that in "tracing the growth of economic doctrine" we require to know the former rather than the latter, but that we mean by the message that which is delivered not so much, perhaps, to his own contemporaries, but rather, so to speak, to all time, and that we wish to ascertain its germ and essence more than the impression it may have produced.

The history of economic theory may not be the same thing as the chronological record of the contemporary influence of eminent thinkers; and posterity, which can trace the sequence before and after, may form a better judgment of the development of thought, and of the place occupied in that development by some particular thinker, than the generation amongst whom he lived. Objects, which are only distorted when the camera of the photographer is placed too close, appear in their true proportions, if the apparatus is properly focussed.

The strong sense, which Professor Marshall entertains of the continuity of economic thought, and the firm conception, which he holds of the relations of the new ideas to the old, amending and enlarging, and not overthrowing the earlier traditions, lead him to introduce unity into the science in a third, and perhaps more important, sense than any we have previously noticed. He regards Economics as the study of "measurable motives," and he maintains that, from the point of view of the continuity of economic thought, the most important work of Adam Smith[1] was, not to develop the "Physiocratic doctrine of Free Trade," but to "combine and develop the speculations of his French and English contemporaries and predecessors as to value. His highest claim to have made an epoch in thought is that he was the first to make a careful and

[1] Cf. the previous Essay.

A RECENT ECONOMIC TREATISE 313

scientific inquiry into the manner in which value measures human motive, on the one side measuring the desire of purchasers to obtain wealth, and on the other the efforts and sacrifices undergone by its producers." From Adam Smith onwards the conception of value has been broadened and deepened, until in Professor Marshall's treatise the results of the previous development are gathered up into a fresh constructive unity. By definitely establishing the theory of value as the central theory of Economics, and by tracing the fundamental ideas, on which it is based, into their various applications, the *Principles of Economics* seems, like the *Wealth of Nations* a century ago, to mark an epoch in thought, and to do so by introducing afresh the conception of unity.

For what had been the previous history of the theory?[1] The outlines of such a theory are, as Professor Marshall states, to be found in Adam Smith; and here, as elsewhere, he furnishes some remarkable anticipations of the work of those who came after him. Yet, when compared with that later work, the outlines delineated on the immortal pages of the *Wealth of Nations* are, it must be admitted, faintly and indistinctly traced in some places, and broken and blurred in others. Ricardo and his more immediate followers took up the unfinished drawing; and, working with a firm hand and a hard pencil, they left their impression on the whole of the picture, and, most markedly, on one important part. They devoted their main attention to the side of supply, and to the influence of *cost of production*. John Stuart Mill, in his turn, fully recognising the supreme importance of the theory of value, added to the work of his predecessors, here as elsewhere, careful and dexterous touches. He darkened the shading in some places, he

[1] Cf. *A Short History of Political Economy in England*, chap iv.

relieved it in others. But he did not show how the fundamental conceptions of the central theory might be harmoniously applied to the various departments of economic study; and he did not bring his theory of distribution, or, indeed, his theory of production, into close and explicit connection with his theory of exchange. Nor did he give such definite and detailed attention to the side of demand as some of his successors have done. Their work, like that of the earlier economists, seems to have lain chiefly in emphasising the prominence of a particular portion of the picture; and they have chosen for emphasis another part from that selected by Ricardo and his disciples. In the able and powerful hands of Jevons some portions of the drawing, which had hitherto been comparatively overlooked, were elaborated with skilful care, and the mathematical conception of final utility formed a very important and useful instrument in the execution of this needed work. But, in their recoil from the earlier insistence on the side of supply and the influence exercised by *cost of production*, the later writers seem to have been, not unnaturally, led into the opposite extreme, and to have given exaggerated emphasis to the side of demand and the influence of *final utility*. Had the matter rested here, the charge of suspense and uncertainty, of confusion and discord, which has sometimes been brought against Economics, would have seemed impossible of refutation. It is due to the constructive ability of Professor Marshall that so serious a reproach has now been removed.

As the case then stood, it was difficult for the student, however anxiously he might have tried to rid himself of the blindness of ignorance or the obliquity of prejudice, to believe that in the picture as drawn by Ricardo, and in that executed afterwards by Jevons, he had unfinished sketches before him, which could be combined into one grand whole. It was hard to imagine that by relieving the shading here, and deepening it there, it would be possible to produce afresh on the paper a real unity of conception out of such seemingly incongruous parts. And yet, on the other hand, it was no less difficult and irrational to conceive that the part of the picture, which had so long occupied the attention of uncommon artists like Ricardo and his more distinguished followers, was quite insignificant, when compared with the part so skilfully elaborated by the disciples of a later school. Why should there be such a sudden breach in the continuity of thought, such a complete reversal of an earlier tradition?

To these perplexing questions Professor Marshall's work affords an answer. There is no such breach, and no such reversal. The newer work can be combined with the old, and the result is a grander conception, without any infringement of the first principles of artistic drawing; for the unity of the design is unimpaired. It is even rendered more prominent by the process. Here it is that the importance of the influence exercised by the mathematical treatment of Economics is most clearly apparent; for the conception, which Professor Marshall especially emphasises, is the mathematical conception of mutually determining influences. The exigencies of analysis, and the claims of easily intelligible exposition, may dictate the separate consideration of either side of the problem of value; but, in order to reach a full and satisfactory solution, these separate inquiries must be combined together. To lay exclusive stress on one side of the problem, or to endeavour to merge it entirely in the other, is only to attain a false simplicity and an artificial unity. A real unity can be reached in no other way than by courageously facing the greater difficulty of more complex considerations. If the influence of utility is important, the effects of disutility no less deserve attention, and it was really at this side of the problem that the earlier writers were working, unconscious perhaps of the analogies, which it presented to the other side, when they were studying the influences of the efforts and sacrifices undergone by producers. Their conception of the greatest cost of production, when expressed in different language as the *marginal* cost of production, and given a wider range of application than that to which they confined its use, is not dissimilar from the conception of final utility, when described as *marginal* utility. By bringing out these analogies, without allowing them to be pushed too far, Professor Marshall succeeds in restoring unity to the theory of value. He has called attention to the importance of the *marginal* increment on either side—that of supply and that of demand—and he has exhibited the mutual influence exerted by one side on the other. But he has not permitted any particular part of the problem to be brought into such undue prominence as to thrust another undeservedly into the background, or allowed the side of supply or demand to absorb, or be absorbed in, the other.

In restoring unity to the theory of value, Professor Marshall has also imparted unity to the whole of economic science; and the work, which still remains to be executed in his second volume, will, we imagine, be largely an extension of the fundamental ideas established in the first to some difficult and complicated portions of the subject. In the first volume we have, we believe, the main conception of the entire treatise; and the rearrangements, which have been effected in the later editions, serve to render more apparent the manner in which the central theory — the theory of value—is applied, without breach of continuity, to the various departments of economic science. It is in the exposition of the theory of value that, as the author states in his preface, "personally the chief interest of the volume centres. It contains," he adds, "more of my life's work than any other part; and it is there, more than anywhere else, that I have tried to deal with unsettled questions of the science." The place, which this particular section of his work holds in the affections of the author, is, as it seems to us, by no means unmerited. It appears to contain the very pith and kernel of the treatise, regarded from the standpoint of the development of economic theory. It seems to be the pivot on which the reasoning of the other sections really turns. To it the earlier portions of the treatise seem to lead up, and from it the later part leads down; and this arrangement of material is one illustration of the unity pervading the volume.

It is true that previous writers had given a prominent place to the subject of value. The remarks of Adam Smith occur in an early part of the first book of the *Wealth of Nations*, Ricardo discusses the subject in his opening chapter, and Mill acknowledges its vital importance. In Cairnes' *Leading Principles*, and Jevons' *Theory* it occupies no less conspicuous a position. But it has rarely, if ever, before been so definitely and prominently established as the central theory, about which all the rest revolves; and it is seldom, or never, that the fundamental ideas, on which it is based, have been so harmoniously and consistently applied to all classes of economic phenomena. Previous writers had divided the science into departments, which had become traditional; and it was sometimes hard to remember, nor did the writers themselves with sufficient explicitness show, that these were to some extent arbitrary and artificial, though convenient, divisions. With all his sense of the importance of the theory of value, Mill never brought his theory of distribution into harmony with his theory of exchange. And yet, while there are qualifications which should not be forgotten, the same fundamental ideas may be applied to the exchange of services as to that of commodities, and the mere educational worth of the scientific conception of such an underlying similarity can hardly be rated too high. Again, production had been studied apart from distribution; while consumption had received little attention. And yet the processes of production and distribution and consumption are simultaneously operating, although they may be separately considered for the sake of convenience. From a neglect to bear in mind this essential coincidence in point of time not a few serious mistakes seem to have arisen, and to have lurked in the reasonings of even able thinkers. But, taking no higher view of the matter than the educational advantage of the student, how much more scientific is likely to be his conception of the study, when he finds production coupled with supply, and consumption with demand, as subjects, preparatory and subordinate to that theory of the equilibrium of demand and supply, which is afterwards applied to the determination of distribution and exchange? Other writers, again, had shown that supply was but the other side of demand; but they had not attained to the comprehensiveness of the statement that the "National Dividend" is at once the "product" of the agents of production, and the "source of demand" for all those agents. The analysis, once more, of the ideas involved in the old doctrine that "rent does not enter into cost of production," and the suggestive conception of a *quasi-rent*, applicable to other economic phenomena but land, furnish additional illustrations of the fruitful results, which follow from Professor Marshall's insistence on the "principle of continuity"; and they exhibit the just balance, which he endeavours to hold, between the extended recognition and the exaggerated application of an idea.[1] The statement of the connection and the distinction between *normal* and *market* values in their intimate relation to the period of time under view, and the careful tracing of the working of the *law of substitution* with reference to *marginal increments*, together with the notion of a *consumer's rent*, are some of the bold and suggestive consequences of the same principle of continuity. They serve to connect the various departments of the science together in one great whole, and to bring the different classes of economic phenomena under the comprehensive range of a fundamental unity.

In this Essay we have preferred to dwell on broad, characteristic features rather than on more minute and particular points of detail. We have adopted this course because we have wished to show in what sense the *Principles of Economics* appeared to mark an epoch. We believe that this is so because it has introduced afresh the conception of unity. It has embraced the scattered, and sometimes apparently conflicting, results of the work of Continental, American, and English writers, of earlier and more immediately recent times, in an orderly whole, where each particular doctrine is assigned a place, as it serves to illustrate the fundamental theory, which, with a diversity of application, underlies the various classes of economic phenomena. "*Natura non facit saltum*" is the motto, which Professor Marshall has placed on his title-page; and it is an apt expression of the spirit of his book. But, though Nature works by continuous development rather than by leaps and by starts, she does

Cf. Essay x. above.

now and again present conspicuous examples, which stand out from their surroundings; and so, while Professor Marshall's treatise may be the natural outcome of the economic thought of previous generations, it enjoys the distinctive superiority of marking an epoch. It is in this sense that it is an uncommon book.

INDEX

Agriculture, Commission on, 180.
Agricultural Depression and the Currency Question, 181.
— — and Economic Science, 176-181.
— — and Foreign Competition, 178-181.
Agricultural Holdings Acts, 224-5, 227.
Anderson, Dr., and the Theory of Rent, 215.
Arbitration in Industrial Disputes, 16, 156, 174.
— and Economic Science, 190-210.
— and Legislation, 157, 175.
— and Social Reform, 19-37.
Argyll, Duke of, and Economics, 170.
Ashley, Professor, on Ricardo, 320.
Austrian Economists and Professor Marshall, 301.

Bagehot, quoted, 1.
Bank Act of 1844, 252.
Baring Crisis, 250.
Bax, Mr. Belfort, 12.
Belgium, Commission on Labour in, 40, 43.

Bellamy, Mr. E., quoted, 51, 213.
Berlin, International Labour Conference at, 40.
Betterment, Principle of, 5-7, 243-4.
Bi-metallism, Essence of, 250.
— International, 245-272.
Bonar, Dr., quoted, 215.
— and the Letters of Ricardo to Malthus, 216.
Bryce, Mr., quoted, 21.
Burnett, Mr. J., quoted, 43, 49, 50, 51, 56.

Cairnes, on Comte, 305.
— on Co-operation, 69.
— on Law of Diminishing Returns, 195.
— on J. S. Mill, 303.
Cannan, Mr. E., quoted, 215.
Christian Socialists, 103.
— — and Co-operation, 68, 136.
Combinations and Economics, 194.
Commissions, Royal, Functions of, 145.
Compensatory Action of Bi-metallism, 256-258.
Competition and Economics, 194-6.

Conciliation, Industrial, Position of, 38–65.
— — Methods of, 156.
— — and Economics, 173–5, 190–210.
— — and the Labour Commission, 152.
— — and Legislation, 131, 156, 172.
— — and Social Reform, 19–37.
Conseils de prud'hommes, 40–2, 157.
Co-operation and Thrift, 137.
— Socialism, 97–117.
— Trade Unionism, 97–117, 121–142.
Co-operative Distribution, 14.
— Production, 13.
— — Different Senses of, 113.
— — and Distribution, 111–12, 136.
— — and Industrial Disputes, 114.
— — and Profit-sharing, 66–96.
Credit and Prices, 183, 267.
— and the Gold Supplies, 249–52.
Currency Question, The, and Economic Science, 181–9.

Demarcation Disputes, 88, 129, 153.
Diminishing Returns, Law of, 195, 202, 291.
Dismal Science, Meaning of, 165.
Dock Strike in London, 39, 42, 51–3.
Dunbar, Professor, quoted, 301.
Durham Coal Trade, Joint Committee in, 130.
— — Strike in, 130.

Economics, Controversy in, 297.
— Old and New, 167–8.
Economic Science and Practical Affairs, 161–189.
Eight Hours Day, the Agitation for, 105, 144, 148.

Farrer, Lord, and the Theory of Rent, 176.
Final Utility, 195, 316.
Fox, Mr. Wilson, on Agriculture in Suffolk, 176.
Foxwell, Professor, quoted, 254, 255.
France, Strikes in, 41.
Free Trade, 290–5.

George, Mr. Henry, 213.
Gilman, Mr. N. P., on Profit-sharing, 15.
Gladstone, Mr., and Political Economy, 302.
Graphic Method, The, and Economics, 196.
— — of Statistics, 183.
Greg, Mr. W. R., quoted, 122.
Gold, Sir R. Giffen on Demands for, 189, 265.
— Supplies of, 188.
— — Future Prospects of, 270–1.

Harcourt, Sir William, quoted, 9.
Hartlepool, Shipbuilding Dispute at, 132.
Highland Crofters and Rent, 226.
Historical Method of Economics, 307.
Hobhouse, Mr. L. T., quoted, 97.
Holyoake, Mr. G., and Co-operative Production, 71.
Hyndman, Mr., 12.

INDEX 323

Ibsen, Mr. Henrik, quoted, 20.
Index Numbers, 184, 185, 367.
Indian Finance and Bi-metallism, 261.
Industrial Disputes and Economics, 171-3.
— — and the Labour Commission, 150.
Industrial Reform, Methods of, 118-142.
Ingram, Dr., on Professor Sidgwick, 305.
Irish Farmers and the Theory of Rent, 227.

Jevons and Final Utility, 195.
— — German, 300.
— quoted on Combinations and Economics, 192.
— — on Fall in Value of Gold, 182.
— — and Ricardo, 303.
— as Type of Mathematical Economist, 309.
— on Value, 314.

Knight, Mr. R., quoted, 132, 134.

Labour Commission, The, and Trade Unions, 128-136.
— — Report of the, 143-160.
Legislation and Industrial Conciliation, 131, 157, 172.
Leroy-Beaulieu, M., quoted, 26, 202.
Leslie, Cliffe, and Adam Smith, 283.
— — American Economists, 301.
— — German Economists, 299.
— — Professor Marshall, 300.

List and Adam Smith, 290.
London Conciliation Board, 42.

Mallet, Sir Louis, quoted, 242.
Malthus and Ricardo, 303.
— — The Theory of Rent, 215.
Manufactured Iron Trade of the North of England, Board of Arbitration in, 44-7, 130.
Marginal Increments, Importance of, 316.
Marshall's, Professor, Principles of Economics, 296-319.
Marshall, Professor, quoted, 7, 26, 196, 233, 240, 283.
Marx, Karl, 12, 103, 204, 242.
Mathematical Treatment of Economics, 309.
McCulloch and Socialism, 11.
Media of Exchange, 247.
Mercantile System, The, 290.
Method in Economics, 285.
Mill, James, and Doses of Capital, 195.
— — as a Type of Strict Economist, 168.
Mill, J. S., quoted, 7, 66.
— — on Co-operative Production, 109.
— — on Protection to Infant Industries, 290.
— — Socialism, 12.
— — Value, 313.
Money, The Functions of, 246.
Munro, Professor, quoted on Incidence of Rates, 232.
— — Sliding Scales, 209.
Mutually Determining Causes in Economics, 315.

National Dividend, The, 318.
Neale, Mr. Vansittart, 103.
Neutrality of Economists Impossible, 164-7.
New Unionism, The, 153.
No-rent Land, Meaning of, 233.
Northumberland Coal Trade, Joint Committee in, 56.
— — Sliding Scale in, 56, 63.
— — Strike in, 28, 57-64, 130.

Paper Money Defined by Adam Smith, 288.
— — and the Gold Supplies, 251.
Par of Exchange, 260.
Plurality of Causes, 186.
Prices, Curves of, 183.
— Effects of Fall of, 269-70.
Profits, Definition of, 72-5, 287-8.
Profit-sharing, 14, 111-2, 139.
— — and Co-operative Production, 66-96.

Quasi-rent, 241.

Rae, Mr. John, quoted, 11.
Rates, Incidence of, 229-33.
Ratio, Selection of, in Bimetallism, 253.
Representation and Industrial Conciliation, 47.
Rent, Defined, 220.
— The Theory of, and Agricultural Depression, 176-9.
— — and Practical Politics, 211-244.
Ricardo, His Letters to Malthus, 216, 282, 304.
— His Place in Economics, 310-2.

Ricardo, and the Theory of Rent, 215.
— on Value, 313.
— and Wages, 191, 201-3.
Roscher, on Wages, 201.

Schloss, Mr. David, on Profit-sharing, 77, 92, 138.
Senior, quoted, on Ricardo, 217, 303.
Shaw, Mr. G. B., quoted, 9.
Sidgwick, Professor, on Combinations, 197.
— — Sociology, 305.
— — State Interference, 12.
— — the Theory of Rent, 219, 235.
Sliding Scales, 15.
— — and Economic Theory, 207-210.
— — in Northumberland Coal Trade, 56, 59-62.
— — and Social Reform, 18-37.
Smith, Adam, and Charges of Plagiarism, 273-4.
— — the Distribution of Wealth, 287.
— — Free Trade, 290-5.
— — Method, 285.
— — Natural Liberty, 10, 278.
— — Profits, 72, 287.
— — Recent Economics, 273-295.
— — the Standard of Value, 248.
— — Value, 312.
Smithianismus, 284.
Socialism, 9-13.
— and Co-operation, 97-109.
— in England, 212.
Social Reformers, Correct Attitude of, 37.

INDEX

Social Reformers, Fallacies of, 1-17.
Spencer, Mr. Herbert, 12.
Standard of Value, Desirable Qualities in, 247.
Statistics, Graphic Method of, 183.

Theory and Practice, Differences between, 4-9, 164 170, 179, 245, 276.
Thunen, Von, and Profit-sharing, 16.
Times, The, quoted, 41.
Tithe, Incidence of, 229.
— Septennial Average of, 61.
Token Currencies, 254.
Town Holdings Committee, 229-235
Trade Unions and Co-operation, 97-117, 121-142.
— — Economic Theory, 26, 124.
— — Industrial Conciliation, 48, 115, 123-136, 154-8.
— — Public Opinion, 25 7, 50.
— of Unskilled Labourers, 129.

Trow, Mr. Edward, quoted, 135.
Turquan, M. Victor, quoted, 41.

Unearned Increment, The Conception of, 4-9, 179, 236-244.

Value, Place of the Theory of, 312-7.

Wages, Economic Theory of, 191, 201-210.
— and the Fall in Prices, 187.
Wages System, Elasticity of, 85.
— — Strength of, 83.
Walker, General, quoted, 74, 177, 287.
Webb, Mr. Sidney, quoted, 10, 229, 231.
— Mrs., quoted, 68, 78-96, 124, 137-8.
West, Sir Edward, and the Theory of Rent, 215.
Wood, Mr. Lindsay, quoted, 134.

Young, Mr. Ralph, quoted, 59-61.

PLYMOUTH:
WILLIAM BRENDON AND SON,
PRINTERS.

www.ingramcontent.com/pod-product-compliance
Lightning Source LLC
Chambersburg PA
CBHW021201230426
43667CB00006B/508